Nomadic Food

ROWMAN & LITTLEFIELD STUDIES IN FOOD AND GASTRONOMY

General Editor: Ken Albala, Professor of History, University of the Pacific (kalbala@pacific.edu)
Rowman & Littlefield Executive Editor: Suzanne Staszak-Silva (sstaszak-silva@rowman.com)

Food studies is a vibrant and thriving field encompassing not only cooking and eating habits but also issues such as health, sustainability, food safety, and animal rights. Scholars in disciplines as diverse as history, anthropology, sociology, literature, and the arts focus on food. The mission of **Rowman & Littlefield Studies in Food and Gastronomy** is to publish the best in food scholarship, harnessing the energy, ideas, and creativity of a wide array of food writers today. This broad line of food-related titles will range from food history, interdisciplinary food studies monographs, general interest series, and popular trade titles to textbooks for students and budding chefs, scholarly cookbooks, and reference works.

Appetites and Aspirations in Vietnam: Food and Drink in the Long Nineteenth Century, by Erica J. Peters
Three World Cuisines: Italian, Mexican, Chinese, by Ken Albala
Food and Social Media: You Are What You Tweet, by Signe Rousseau
Food and the Novel in Nineteenth-Century America, by Mark McWilliams
Man Bites Dog: Hot Dog Culture in America, by Bruce Kraig and Patty Carroll
A Year in Food and Beer: Recipes and Beer Pairings for Every Season, by Emily Baime and Darin Michaels
Celebraciones Mexicanas: History, Traditions, and Recipes, by Andrea Lawson Gray and Adriana Almazán Lahl
The Food Section: Newspaper Women and the Culinary Community, by Kimberly Wilmot Voss
Small Batch: Pickles, Cheese, Chocolate, Spirits, and the Return of Artisanal Foods, by Suzanne Cope
Food History Almanac: Over 1,300 Years of World Culinary History, Culture, and Social Influence, by Janet Clarkson
Cooking and Eating in Renaissance Italy: From Kitchen to Table, by Katherine A. McIver
Eating Together: Food, Space, and Identity in Malaysia and Singapore, by Jean Duruz and Gaik Cheng Khoo
Nazi Hunger Politics: A History of Food in the Third Reich, by Gesine Gerhard
The Carrot Purple and Other Curious Stories of the Food We Eat, by Joel S. Denker
Food in the Gilded Age: What Ordinary Americans Ate, by Robert Dirks
Urban Foodways and Communication: Ethnographic Studies in Intangible Cultural Food Heritages around the World, by Casey Man Kong Lum and Marc de Ferrière le Vayer
Food, Health, and Culture in Latino Los Angeles, by Sarah Portnoy
Food Cults: How Fads, Dogma, and Doctrine Influence Diet, by Kima Cargill
Prison Food in America, by Erika Camplin
K'Oben: 3,000 Years of the Maya Hearth, by Amber M. O'Connor and Eugene N. Anderson
As Long As We Both Shall Eat: A History of Wedding Food and Feasts, by Claire Stewart
American Home Cooking: A Popular History, by Tim Miller
A Taste of Broadway: Food in Musical Theater, by Jennifer Packard
Pigs, Pork, and Heartland Hogs: From Wild Boar to Baconfest, by Cynthia Clampitt
Sauces Reconsidered: Après Escoffier, by Gary Allen
Pot in Pans: A History of Eating Weed, Robyn Griggs Lawrence
Screen Cuisine: Food and Film from Prohibition to James Bond, by Linda Civitello
To Eat or Not to Eat Meat: How Vegetarian Dietary Choices Influence Our Social Lives, edited by Charlotte De Backer, Julie Dare, and Leesa Costello
Nomadic Food: Anthropological and Historical Studies around the World, edited by Isabelle Bianquis and Jean-Pierre Williot

Nomadic Food

Anthropological and Historical Studies around the World

Edited by Isabelle Bianquis and Jean-Pierre Williot

ROWMAN & LITTLEFIELD
Lanham • Boulder • New York • London

Published by Rowman & Littlefield
An imprint of The Rowman & Littlefield Publishing Group, Inc.
4501 Forbes Boulevard, Suite 200, Lanham, Maryland 20706
www.rowman.com

6 Tinworth Street, London SE11 5AL, United Kingdom

British Library Cataloguing in Publication Information Available

Library of Congress Cataloging-in-Publication Data

Library of Congress Control Number: 2019948984
ISBN 978-1-5381-1598-5 (cloth)
ISBN 978-1-5381-5964-4 (pbk)
ISBN 978-1-5381-1599-2 (electronic)

Dedicated to all the nomads of the world . . .

Contents

1 From Noun (the Food of the Nomads) to Adjective (Nomadic Eating)   1
  Isabelle Bianquis

2 Mongolian Nomadic Herders Are Sedentary Eaters   13
  Sandrine Ruhlmann

3 McDonald's in the Desert: Bedouins, Fast-Food, and Modernity
  in Southern Israel   35
  Nir Avieli

4 Nomadism in the Food Culture of the Yakuts and the Indigenous
  Peoples of Yakutia   51
  Izabella Borisova and Antonina Vinokurova

5 Circulating Food Practices and Food Representations of Senegalese
  Inhabitants of Bordeaux and Dakar   65
  Chantal Crenn

6 Space-Food: Food in Mobile Technological Environments of Late
  High-Modernity   77
  Alwin Cubasch

7 Eating on Corsica's GR Footpaths and Trails: Choosing between
  Hi-Tech and Tradition   93
  Philippe Pesteil

8 Italian-Sounding: A World Carrier of a Traveling *Cuisine*   107
  Giovanni Ceccarelli and Stefano Magagnoli

 9 Imagining Culinary Nomadism: Food Exchanges Shaped by Global
    Mixed Race, Diasporic Belongings, and Cosmopolitan Sensibilites   125
    Jean Duruz

10 The Traveling Priest: Food for the Spirit and Food for the Body   147
    Luciano Maffi

11 From Anthropology to History   169
    Jean-Pierre Williot

Notes   177

Index   199

About the Editors and Contributors   209

1

From Noun (the Food of the Nomads) to Adjective (Nomadic Eating)

Isabelle Bianquis

Food is certainly a total social fact and it "must now be thought of as a social fact that characterizes new planetary lifestyles."[1] The structural organization of the market and eating behaviors are completely changing. This is not a recent development. Each century, every important break in the history of humanity could illustrate a process of interventions, adaptations, or innovations that have transformed eating habits. However, the contemporary era differs in terms of the extent of the changes and the general character of certain transformations. Thereby, industrialists, the retail trade, and transport companies each exercise their inventiveness to offer individuals food services adapted to their new lifestyles. They are based on, or at least affected by, the growth in mobility and continual relocation. Certainly, travelers who have journeyed across lands and routes throughout history have always looked for ways to feed themselves away from home. Whether it involves long-haul trips, random pilgrimages, or tourist routes, mobility has been an important factor in putting into place complex food supply capability. Today, this increased mobility encourages us to talk about attitudes toward a practice described as nomadic, which is applied not only to taking food randomly according to what is available. But is there a link between the nomadism of populations that move to ensure food for their herds or their own food supplies and the forms of nomadic eating of our mobile societies; which would make the latter the legacy of the former in an equation associating eating and mobility?

NOMADS

The term "nomadism" generally applies to societies that move to obtain resources and that live in space characterized by the absence of permanently established points. The definition was expanded by Edmond Bernus, for whom nomadism generally reflects the customs of populations "which exploit regions of supplementary resources in time and space."[2] These populations are herders, hunter-gatherers, or maritime nomads, but the term has also been used to describe Gypsies or Romany, translated in French to "*gens du voyage*" (travelers) since the July 3, 1969, law that designates, under the name of travelers, the people without fixed residence circulating in France and carrying out itinerant activities. Although mobility is a common denominator of these different groups, it is also true that the designation refers to lifestyles practiced by social groups with specific identities, ways of perceiving the world, beliefs, knowledge, and codes that go together to form a culture.

The concept of nomadism has undergone profound changes in recent decades, taking on a semantic scope that entrusts it with the capacity to encompass not only work practices and communication processes but also unprecedented social behaviors. The twenty-first century demonstrates a new configuration in which, despite the rapid decline of nomadic customs throughout the world, never before have sedentary people so often been described as nomads. Has the sedentary person become the new nomad, deterritorialized, a being connected to others through one or more networks?

The polysemy of the term "nomad" will be investigated with regard to eating habits. Indeed, eating has become one of these "nomad objects" in the same way as the telephone and computer. In an essay on the future, already in 1990, Jacques Attali writes: "the world economy will be led by the demand for new objects which will change our lifestyles and which I call 'nomad objects' because they will be portable and will allow us to fulfil the essential functions of life without ties."[3] The ideology of Western modernity rhymes with the ideology of movement, it is deeply intertwined with a perception of time. Within this configuration space is not only territory, but it is replaced by a space-time dimension. For sedentary people to be modern they have to live, think, and eat "nomad."

The marketing world has taken possession of this nomad eating object to make it into the trademark of contemporary consumption outside the home, which is ever more rapid and practical: the just-in-time meal. Eat as you like, when you like, where you like; opt for snacking, finger food, or street food, trends with an Anglo-Saxon connotation since that is where they originated.

And yet food of the nomads has nothing nomadic about it. Within the context of "traditional" nomadism, despite changing place, populations still eat in their home. In that case have we changed from a collective and territorialized consumption style, nomads' food, to solitary, mobile nomadic eating? How did this transition from the noun form to the adjectival form come about? To understand the process we must return to the specificities of nomad societies as they have been studied in different contexts. Anthropologists have highlighted the knowledge, representations, cognitive structures, customs, techniques, and the types of structural and political organization that define what they have called "nomadic civilizations." They are based on a mobile lifestyle followed by social groups sharing common culture and beliefs. In contrast to roaming, nomadism thus represents a system based on knowledge of spaces, on a representation and symbolic organization of these spaces and their subsequent control and management within the framework of economic and social activities. Although a comparative study of different types of nomadism has revealed variations in social structures, knowledge, as well as size and periods of movement, they nevertheless demonstrate the reality of nomad identities. They are built on a certain number of values and customs shared by nomadic peoples, in contrast, for example, to those of sedentary people. The authors agree particularly on the practice of mobility, a specific relationship with space and its use.

MOBILITY: THE PARADOX OF THE NOMAD

Mobility, use of space, and specific capacities reflect representations that can be linked to what can be observed when we address the current eating habits described as nomadic. It is obvious that mobility, a cornerstone of nomadism, plays a leading role in the imagination of contemporary sedentary people, but it is useful to remember that to be mobile is not nomadic and that nomads cannot be defined solely by their mobility. Indeed, it is important to highlight that populations exist that could be described as nomadic and that are in fact defined as sedentary, as is the case of the semi-nomad Nuer people, described by Evans Pritchard. Furthermore, nomads can often appear much less mobile than they are in the imagination of sedentary people, as is testified by Hélène Claudot-Hawad, a specialist of the Tuareg people: "No one is more home-loving than the nomads of Aïr,"[4] or Bernard Charlier, who talks about a real paradox in the relationship between the nomad and the environment. Regarding the notion of attachment to "homeland" (*nutag*) in Mongolia, he shows that the Mongolian herders are rooted in their homeland (while also underlining that this notion is variable). In the Uvs region of Western Mongolia, herders are generally attached to their birth district during overwintering, which represents the most settled encampment of the year. "The attachment to the winter encampment is strengthened through rituals conducted each year at the family *ovoo*, a small mound of stones installed on a hill overlooking the encampment."[5] Thus, movement and fixity form two complementary dimensions of attachment.

Mobility and Flexibility

Mobility in nomadic pastoral life is generally associated with a production technique, linked as much to the necessity to move as to the characteristic of flexibility. For André Bourgeot, it represents a system of moving that implements "a series of production techniques which it incorporates and which are generated by an economic system; in this way, it can be considered that mobility, a specific feature of human and animal activities, is itself a production technique."[6] For this author mobility would represent the system of moving, while flexibility would be an adaptation to climate or environmental constraints. This flexibility enables herders to move on to different production activities successively or to simultaneously carry out a variety of activities. "Agro-pastoral people (e.g., Peuls, and Tuaregs in Mali or Niger) who initially possess various resources can switch from pastoral to farming or commercial tasks without difficulty."[7]

When looking at mobility it is necessary to focus on the forms of gatherings. Anthropologists have highlighted two characteristics of nomad societies—dispersion and concentration—that can represent responses to climate hazards or environmental conditions and can also be production techniques enabling the renewal of resources.

Neither these movements nor the composition of residential units are ever fixed; examples demonstrate that there can be groups that remain stable for a time and that then change and split up. Since mobility is never a fixed decision, we can find societies that become sedentary for a period and then nomadic again as a result of favorable economic conditions (this is the case in Mongolia, for example, after certain serious climate catastrophes [*zud*]). This flexibility, which depends on the short-term conditions, reflects as much the idea of internal dynamics as the capacity to adapt.

SPECIFIC ENVIRONMENTAL REPRESENTATIONS AND CLASSIFICATIONS

The philosophers Deleuze and Guattari, in their well-known treaty of nomadology, talk about the idea of an open space of the nomad journey: "although the nomad journey follows traditional tracks and routes, it does not have the role of a sedentary way which is to allocate people a closed space, by designating everyone their part and by regulating the communication between the parts. The nomad journey does the opposite, it distributes people (or animals) in an open space, undefined, non-communicating."[8] The concept of deterritorialization is also used by these authors to describe nomads for whom "earth ceases to be earth, and tends to become simply ground or support."[9] André Leroi-Gourhan in *Le geste et la parole* opposes what he calls the "concentric" concept of space, which predominates in sedentary populations with the "radiating" concept of nomads. Sedentary societies would thus have developed a concentric vision that is demonstrated by the organization of village space (and also urban space) in many societies, while the radiating space of nomads is organized cognitively on other bases. Memory and perception of the surrounding style are thus mobilized: "While in a sedentary life style, the relationship with space is often founded on memorizing everyday places and itineraries, nomads must mobilize finely-tuned perceptive and interpretive abilities to analyze multiple signs and places, sometimes unknown and constantly metamorphosing."[10]

Processes to categorize must therefore be implemented. For example, Hélène Claudot-Hawad shows that Tuaregs organize their space according to a plan based on interior/exterior, fixed point/empty complementarity. In this way, she describes the main function of the tent, an inside, female, reassuring space, the core and center of the society, and of the well, the other fixed point, linking up itineraries and enabling encounters. The tent and the well thus represent anchor points essential in the reality of Tuareg daily life. These fixed points are simultaneously in opposition and complementary to the outside, to the world of humans and spirits, to emptiness, solitude, the desert, uncertainty, "In this way nomadism is far from being limited to a way of life conditioned by natural resources which rapidly run out. It is also a way to perceive the world, a philosophy of movement. The path from the tent to the well and from the well to the tent that each night brings the nomad back to their starting point, all beings follow a cycle which when completed marks the beginning of another cycle."[11] The Nenets of Siberia oppose a male sphere (the open tundra) to a female sphere (the home), and this representation corresponds to male and female activities where "women are as active in the tent as men are on the open tundra guarding the reindeer."[12] The case of the Mongolian yurt is also very useful to think through these cognitive processes, in that the inside space is oriented and organized to reflect not only the representation of the human body, but also that of age, sex, and social position. In this family and social center of life, each space is linked to attitudes and their specific customs.[13]

The nomad's space thus includes the accommodation, encampment, grazing land, surrounding area, and the sacred places, and as Golovnev so rightly writes the life of nomads puts down roots between periods of moving. These representations and classifications generate social and symbolic customs of space, which here again seem characteristic of nomadic societies.

SPECIFIC CUSTOMS OF SPACE

Pierre Bonte's work reminds us that collective appropriation of natural plant and water resources is customary in basically all nomadic pastoral societies. This necessity goes hand in hand with customs and rituals aimed at renewing resources. Other elements should also be considered, such as relocation, which is linked to the technics of moving and orientation, and the rhythm of relocation. Golovnev writes that "for a long time, explorers have been struck by the amazing capacity of Nenets to draw a plan of the locality in the sand or snow, or on paper. Their cartographic perception of the Tundra is such that sometimes they are asked to guide helicopter pilots looking for encampments."[14]

The active use of space and movement are acquired by nomads when they are very young. "Very early on Tuareg children learn to recite by heart the names of the valleys of their country and the names of the wells and who dug them,"[15] memorizing places, orientation, and tracking clues on the ground make up important knowledge for an active use of space. Taking Marcel Mauss's notion of training children, Golovnev refers to how in bringing up their children Nenets pass on attitudes and knowledge according to the child's sex. "From birth the child is faced with difficulties of moving around and bears different traces. Firstly, the infant receives a descriptive nickname: the baby born on the road is called *Mùsèna*, from the term *mùd* 'caravan';

the one born in a snow storm is called *Hadko*, from *had* 'snow storm.'"[16] Throughout childhood what the child learns is intended to prepare it for nomad life and for the place it will take in the social group. "Children's games such as 'catch the reindeer,' 'nomadization,' 'guests,' or 'the wedding' imitate adult activities in such a way that the transition from childhood to adulthood takes place imperceptibly."[17]

Regarding food more specifically, studies mention techniques for preparing, preserving, consuming, and sharing specific foods in the nomad environment.

The emphasis is always placed on the social and symbolic function of sharing food according to rules linked to social status, gender, age, and relationships between groups. S. Boulay writes about the Maurs in Mauritania: "In the absence of visitors, the wife and children eat with the father of the family. Otherwise, the wife, young children, and pubertal daughters go and sit on the *sâhel* (north or west side depending on the region) of the tent, the head of the family, his sons and the guests sit in the *sharg* part (south or east side). Lunch is always taken in the tent because at this time of day the sun is at its zenith. Dinner can be taken on a mat placed in front of the entrance to the tent."[18]

Boulay continues about meal guests:

> In this society of Bedouin culture, eating with guests is a golden rule and it is frowned upon for a person to take a meal alone. Consequently, a man traveling alone, for example looking for stray animals, will endeavor to find a "tent" on his route which will provide him with a meal and accommodation. In the absence of a "tent: he will generally go without a meal or wait to encounter another traveler to share his meal with. Indeed, over long distances men arrange to travel together and in this way organize their own supplies. The desert is seen as a sterile and dangerous place, inhabited by *djinns* (empty people), where it is not good to spend a night alone."[19]

The rules of eating together hold an important function in the context of nomadic populations for whom the obligation of hospitality is essential. Eating together enables them to forge alliances and maintain social ties. The food should be shared with the family, the guests, and also invisible entities within the context of domestic rituals or more widely collective rituals because the spirits watch over and supervise the renewal of goods. Only sharing can ensure health, happiness, and prosperity. Codes regulate how portions are shared according to each person's place and the guest always has pride of place. In Bedouin society the calendar also enjoys particular attention, and consumption is structured according to the seasons as is also seen in Mongolian culture in which the calendar is divided into a black winter season and a white summer season linked to an abundance of milk products.

The specificity of nomadic life, the importance of networks, and the question of hospitality is found even in the form of certain dishes as demonstrated by the *ul boov* (shoe-sole cakes),[20] exchanged during a new-year ritual in Mongolia. These cakes, cooked by men (remembering that their role lies in constructing links with the outside), symbolize footprints in the snow of those that are hoped to come and visit the family in the coming year.

Extensive data exists about managing resources or ways of preserving, such as the Bushmen of the Kalahari who suck the moisture from the sand with a straw and then leave this water to settle in an ostrich egg before drinking it.[21]

In addition to eating in the family setting, there are many customs and rituals aimed at providing renewal of resources. Finally, we should mention sharing between groups. We know, for example, that in hunter-gatherer societies appropriation of game is collective and is expressed by sharing the meat within the community. This should be considered as much a means of managing resources as social relations.

These multiple examples lead us to understand to what extent nomad societies are based on principles of occupying space, using resources, social organization, rituals, specific knowledge, and know-how, very far from "the nomad" as perceived in our urban societies. In that case, what motives or constraints have led to the term "nomad" undergoing such a shift in meaning in the contemporary world? The reader could rightly wonder why the title *Nomadic Food* has been chosen for this work. Regarding what has been developed above, the provocative resonance of the title is simply seeking to deconstruct precisely a transformed, denatured, and instrumentalized concept, but which in the end provides social sciences with the opportunity to investigate customs and practices in terms of their meaning, history, development, and logic.

A CONCEPT OF HETEROTOPIA

Regarding what has been developed above as the specificity of the nomad world, how can we broach the notion of nomadism as driven home in modern Western sedentary societies? Within a context of globalization of goods and models, the image of the nomad so reviled by sedentary people becomes a flagship product of sedentation, a product of urbanization. The concept of heterotopia meant as "others spaces" according to the formula of Foucault, it takes on a new meaning and thus reflects its own identity space, a sham (Baudrillard), a metaphor, an illusionary space, or else a poetic image (Bachelard).

The mistrust and devaluation of nomad life is transformed into an anthem to the glory of the "nomadized" sedentary person. It means forgetting the opposition that has always existed between nomads and sedentary people (even though there are many exchanges and complementarities between them): "Are all nomads not mutating beings, destined one day to settle and leave an unstable state? For that matter, sedentary people think that nomads find themselves in a temporary situation and that they are going to rally behind their condition."[22] This vision is expressed in the representation of the state, which sees the nomad as a threat. Is it a quirk of fate? Has globalization boosted the image, being freed of borders? Is it easier to accept the crossing of virtual rather than physical borders? The sudden fascination for a world that moves, a free life, for a mind that is able to adapt, "tinker," and invent seems limitless hereafter. In an article in *Le Monde* in 2011, Jean-Loup Amselle writes:

The representation that we in the West have of nomad societies, under the form of essential mobility, was established as a model by contemporary ideology, in particular regarding the future of the individual. So that there has been a shift in meaning, tangible modes of how certain human communities function, at a certain stage in their history and in a defined geographical environment, becoming the optimal way for the individual to behave in the postmodern society.[23]

The nomad previously perceived as a threat has become a model of civilization. The metaphoric use of the term has reached all sectors, including relationships, work, thought, religion, the economy, and eating. Media and marketing firms relentlessly convey positive stereotypes of a "nomadic sedentary person" fitting in with an ideology of modern, free, individualist adventurer, capable of adapting to all situations, and juggling with the most incongruous models. This construction is obviously based on a fantasy of nomadism that conserves only certain stereotypes (liberty, flexibility, and adaptation). The reference to a social organization with its codes, beliefs, ways of working, and its relationship with the environment has disappeared, as has the notion of territory, replaced by an indissociable idea of space-time. Much more, the organized mobility of the nomad has made way to a form of vagrancy, roaming to the antipodes of the nomadic tradition. Don't we talk of food zapping, which is the attitude of moving from one food model to another, to allude to combinatorial arrangements? By developing the notion of eating space, Jean-Pierre Poulain draws our attention to the different spaces where meals can be taken and to the changes resulting from eating outside the home or even outside meal times. He highlights two important factors regarding our object: food industrialization and the shift from eating at the same table to food roaming.[24] He says that industrialization is increasingly distancing the individual from the socialization role of cooking and food. Food roaming, on the other hand, reflects eating divided-up food in individual portions. We often eat alone and quickly while walking in the street or doing something else, and in this sense nomadic food is not only a type of food but is also an attitude, a way of life, even a philosophy. Its consumption is linked to "customs" and "protocols" that are no longer just eating, as Barthes highlights regarding sugar in the United States and which he says has become a "world category."[25] In the same logic, when focusing on the function of the symbol of eating, Barthes also writes about snacking, which not only meets a new need but to which he gives a "certain theatrical expression," transforming those who practice it into "modern men, managers having the power and control over extremely rapid contemporary life."[26] Indeed, nomadic eating constantly echoes a representation of mobility, individualism, and pleasure, much more than one of nomadism. Obviously, it should also be understood as a world category. Going beyond the simple act of eating, and in the same way as any other food, "it tends to change continuously in situation."[27] This change appears at the same level as behaviors, but it also subscribes to many technological innovations and new forms of packaging. For that matter, it is interesting to note that for marketing specialists, it is not the product that is at the heart of innovation but the packaging. Today, it is the product design and often its packaging that changes. However, although nomad products aim to satisfy a need at any given moment, freeing themselves from the classical supports of plates, cutlery, and glasses, they are not only reserved for outside consumption, quite the opposite. The idea here is to develop a concept called "cocooning nomadism." This term reflects for the authors a paradoxical behavior that describes nomadic consumers even inside their house: "indeed today, the consumer has a nomadic attitude even inside the home more often than not with the goal to do several things at a time: having breakfast while preparing the morning, a TV tray, or simply snacking throughout the day by opening the fridge or cupboard."[28] These new behaviors require appropriate products that position themselves as new niches for the industrial world.

Nomadic products, nomadic attitudes, cocooning nomadism—how in the end can we define what is presented as eating nomadism by those who prescribe it? The fact of eating outside the home? Eating while moving? Eating while doing other things? Eating on the go? Eating alone? Associating heterogeneous types of food? Definitions abound and seem to be limitless. However, they have a common feature in that none of them correspond to the eating habits of nomads. In mathematical terms we could say that it is a question of two different sets whose only point of intersection is formed by the element of mobility.

We have moved from nomadism with collective structures to individual zapping but which brings together singular identities under the banner of "modernity." In a collective work by Garabuau-Moussaoui and colleagues published in 2002 under the title *Alimentations contemporaines*, the authors draw a distinction between two forms of mobility: moving carried out to do the shopping and moving to take a meal outside the home. They saw in the former the specificity of a sedentary person, and in the latter a "nomad," an expression placed in quotation marks, and linked to a world said to be "semi-nomadic." Included in this second category are emigrants who meet in public places such as Sahelian cafés in Paris, described by one of the contributors. By comparing different situations some of the main common features of this eating mobility were identified: the idea of saving time, the limited degree of social control, experimenting, for young people, or strategies of eating opposition. The authors also highlight that eating outside the domestic space should not be seen as an exclusively solitary experience. It aspires to a social meaning depending on whether we want to eat in pairs, avoid family pressure, take advantage of an opportunity to build up a network, etc. What some have called the "gastro-anomy" should thus be qualified.

In a context of mobility, consuming leads to specific ways and means of supplying, transporting, preserving, and preparing food. These practical elements double as specific forms of consumption (sitting, standing, together, alone, walking, with your fingers, etc.). The meeting of new models, integrating processes through the exchange of recipes and techniques, discovering new products, and also transforming representations of the body and health are all parameters that influence implementing eating systems that reflect at some point or another the concept of nomadism. They are issues addressed in this work and developed from three different perspectives by history, anthropology, and sociology researchers: the food of nomads, eating and mobility, and imaginary worlds.

In chapters 2, 3, and 4, we present three types of nomadic societies. Sandrine Ruhlmann, a specialist of Mongolia, searches to understand why nomadic societies are actually less nomadic than sedentary. Her chapter, therefore, focuses on how nomadic herders eat. Nir Avieli studies the population of Bedouins in Israel and this focuses on ethnographic research conducted in several McDonald's branches in Beer-sheba. The third case is developed by Izabella Borisova and Antonina Vinokurova. They suggest an insight into the phenomenon of northern nutrition from the point of view of nomadism philosophy.

Chapters 5, 6, 7, and 8 deal with the question of practices, techniques, and products. Chantal Crenn's interests lie in the circulation of food practices and representations among Senegalese retirees in Bordeaux and Dakar. She studies the effects of migration and reverse migration. Alwin Cubasch looks at how food played an essential role during ever longer missions in space after World War II. NASA's spacecraft became a laboratory for mobilizing food in mobile technological environments. Philippe Pesteil describes how hikers in Corsica expect to have an adequate diet to help them respond to the predictably intense and continuous physical effort they expend. Giovanni Ceccarelli and Stefano Magagnoli explore how Italian food traditions (and their imaginary) spread to and changed in North America.

Chapters 9 and 10 are dedicated to imaginary. Jean Duruz, in a text called "Imagining Culinary Nomadism: Food Exchanges Shaped by Global Mixed Race, Diasporic Belongings, and Cosmopolitan Sensibilities," deals with the notion of "ingested nomadism." Its specific focus is on the everyday food exchanges of the second-generation owners of an Ethiopian restaurant in Adelaide, Australia. Luciano Maffi tells the story of Don Marchelli, a young priest from Pavia who started to travel around Northern Italy once a year. The priest's journeys explain the growing interest in Italian society for tourism, traveling, and gourmet traveling, and he describes Italy after its unification, between 1865 and 1876. In the conclusion, Jean-Pierre Williot underlines that there is a history of economic and behavioral shifts from mobile cooking to mobile ways of eating. The practices of traditional nomads have not been fully assimilated by sedentary people simply because they are increasingly mobile. Habits that have been changed by travel are the real and most effective promotional support of other culinary cultures, and in that is created food nomadism.

BIBLIOGRAPHY

Amselle, Jean-Loup. "Méfions-nous de l'idéologie du nomadisme." *Le Monde*, 24 June 2011.
Attali, Jacques. *Lignes d'horizon*. Paris: Fayard, 1990.
Barthes, Roland. "Pour une psycho-sociologie de l'alimentation contemporaine." *Annales. Economies, Sociétés, Civilisations*. 16ᵉ année, no. 5 (1961): 977–86.
Bernus, Edmond. "Le nomadisme pastoral en question." *Etudes rurales*. 120 (1990): 41–52.

Bernus, Edmond. "Mobilité et flexibilité pastorales face à la sécheresse." *Bulletin de liaison de l'ORSTOM* (1986): 137–45.

Bianquis, Isabelle. "Le mois blanc en Mongolie, traditions et mutations." *Anda* (2000): 9–18.

Bonte, Pierre. *Les derniers nomades.* Paris: Solar, 2004.

Boulay, Sébastien. "Alimentation, diététique et relations sociales au Sahara: l'exemple des pasteurs nomades maures de Mauritanie." www.lemangeur-ocha.com—Texte exclusif de Sébastien Boulay—mise en ligne: 17 June 2008.

Bourgeot, André. "A propos du pastoralisme nomade." *Esprit d'Avant*, 20 October 2009. http://www.espritdavant.com/DetailElement.aspx?numStructure =79255&nu.

Charlier, Bernard. "Ritual actions, mobility and attachment to the "homeland" among nomadic herders in Mongolia." *Études mongoles et sibériennes, centrasiatiques et tibétaines* [En ligne], 47 | 2016, mis en ligne le 21 December 2016, consulté le 24 September 2018. http://journals.openedition.org/emscat/2779; DOI: 10.4000/emscat.2779.

Claudot-Hawad, Hélène. *Touaregs. Apprivoiser le désert.* Paris: Découvertes Gallimard, Culture et Société, 2002.

Deleuze, Gilles, and Guattari, Felix. *Mille plateaux.* Paris: Minuit, 1980.

Frey, Philippe. *Kalahari, désert rouge.* Paris: Laffont, 1993.

Garabuau-Moussaoui, Isabelle, Palomares, Elise, and Desjeux, Dominique (Eds). *Alimentations contemporaines.* Paris: L'Harmattan, 2002.

Golovnev, Andreï. "Naviguer dans la toundra." *Nomadismes d'Asie centrale et septentrionale.* (ed. Stepanoff, Charles). Paris: Armand Colin (2013): 68–71.

Golovnev, Andreï. "Les étapes de la vie chez les Nenetses." *Nomadismes d'Asie centrale et septentrionale.* (ed. Stepanoff, Charles) Paris: Armand Colin (2013): 126–29.

Poulain, Jean-Pierre. "Mutations et modes alimentaires." *Le mangeur et l'animal. Mutations de l'élevage et de la consommation* (ed. Paillat, Monique). Autrement, Coll. Mutations/ Mangeurs, no. 172, Paris: 1997.

Rasse, Paul, and Debos, Franck. "L'alimentation, fait total de la société de communication planétaire," *Communication* [En ligne], Vol. 25/1 | 2006, mis en ligne le 06 May 2010, consulté le 24 September 2018. http://journals.openedition.org/communication/1413; DOI: 10.4000/communication.1413.

Ruhlmann, Sandrine. "Une curieuse pâtisserie en forme de semelle / A Mongolian pastry," *Anthropology of Food*, S0, Varia, le numéro permanent, [En ligne], mis en ligne le 15 décembre 2009.

Senépart, Ingrid. "Nomades ou sédentaires mobiles?" *Techniques & Culture* 56 | 2011, 1, Paris, MSH: 30–47.

Stepanoff, Charles. *Nomadismes d'Asie centrale et septentrionale*, (dir. Stepanoff, Charles). Paris, Armand Colin (2013): 7–12.

Terlet, Xavier and Laurent, Philippe. "Quel nomadisme alimentaire?" 1 June 2002. http:// www.e-marketing.fr/Marketing-Magazine/Article/Quel-nomadisme-al.

2

Mongolian Nomadic Herders Are Sedentary Eaters

Sandrine Ruhlmann

Mongolia is a postcommunist country hosting fifty-two million animals and more than three million humans, as of 2014.[1] One-third of its economic production is linked to herding. In the steppe most families carry out an extensive multispecies animal husbandry. This technique, consisting in herding at least two categories, combining "large" (cattle, horses, camels) and "small" (sheep, goats) livestock, is a way to preserve the fragile ecosystems and the scattered and irregular natural re-sources. More precisely, these techniques are optimised according to the ecosystem, fauna, flora, and rainfall specific to the different steppe, woodland, and desert areas. But since the 1990s, the country has been confronted with formidable challenges in the wake of the recent rapid socioeconomic, environmental, and political changes, such as the steep increase in livestock numbers following the transition from a Com-munist to a democratic and capitalistic system. Privatization of livestock, cuts in government aid, and the growth in livelihood needs have affected herding practices and land preservation, as Troy Sternberg noticed when he studied herders' percep-tions of the major challenges facing nomadic pastoralism today.[2] This is the second time that Mongolian pastoralism has been significantly impacted, the first being under the yoke of the Communist regime and ideology. Thus, in some provinces, herders have been capitalizing on the goat herding system for it is the only one that still allows them to ensure both self-consumption and some income in cash by selling cashmere to cover incompressible expenses.[3] Today, some herders alter rangeland by inadequate nomadic pastoralism practices: they reduce their mobility by limiting the number of seasonal nomadizations or moves (*nüüdel*) and by reduc-ing the distance between their camp installation, that is, the use of grassland. Other herders do not preserve nor perpetuate customary land use whatsoever. In addition, the severe climate changes of the past three decades have led to the multiplication and intensification of disasters (*zud*), apparent in extreme frost or drought, which hampers livestock's access to grass or shrubs. This results in pasture degradation and unsustainable land use.

However, many herder families strive to maintain an environmentally friendly livestock. They limit the number of heads in their cattle, breed at least two species, and move their camp two or four times a year to provide their herd with enough pasture in order to fatten them up while preserving soil, vegetation, and water sources. I have conducted ethnographic research in two steppic lands since 2000, that is, Hentii and Töv Provinces. I met thirty nomadic herding families who practice an extensive type of herding characterized by low densities of cattle per hectare. This has implications for their way of life, more specifically the quantity of their material belongings. They must ensure their subsistence, and as a result everything must be transported and thus transportable. The yurt, a circular dwelling with a conical dome-shaped roof, furniture, tools, and cooking utensils are no exception to this rule.

Based on ethnographic observations, the purpose of this chapter is to discuss how nomadic societies are less nomadic than sedentary ones when they eat. Based on data relating to techniques and material culture, I will first discuss mobility and the necessity of being, relatively, in movement. Then, I will show how the necessity of moving induces a specific storage design. Finally, I will highlight ritual and/or ritualized obligation for any family to receive visitors in order to provide hospitality and put food into circulation, which are essential principles that preserve domestic happiness, happiness being assessed by the good health of the household members and the good health and prosperity of the herd—diseases and natural or climatic disasters indicating on the contrary that something bad or wrong has happened and thus has to be fixed.

HERDERS' MOBILITY

Although they move out of necessity only, Mongolian herders have different mobility motivations: shepherding their herd to the pastures and leading it back to the camp; visiting families in other camps, and thus maintaining a daily practice of hospitality; buying manufactured goods in city centers and, at the same time, supplying urban relatives and friends with livestock products; moving their camp in order to preserve the biodiversity and care of their livestock; more rarely, when necessary, consulting with a veterinarian, a doctor, a monk, a shaman and/or a bonesetter; at the opening of the season, going hunting (though in a limited way); more recently, for the wealthiest herders making tourist trips to discover other Mongolian landscapes, etc. Considering these different types of moves, it seems that, in general, nomadic herder families are relatively more often at rest than on the go compared with sedentary families living in urban centers in their everyday lives.

Because of the ecological necessity of relocation, families can dismantle their flexible and portable yurt with ease. They start by removing the metal chimney flue

Figure 2.1.   Sherping herd to the pastures
Copyright: Sandrine Ruhlmann (Gov'sümber province, August 2017)

from the ventilation hole and its base. Then, they take down the different wooden architectural elements of the yurt one by one: the removable folding wall lattices; the roof, which is composed of a compression ring, and its beams placed on the lattice's heads; the two central holding poles of the compression ring; the door and its lintel; the enveloping felt layers and its fabric covering the wall and the roof; and finally, the interior decorative wall fabric.

Covering
roof: a. closing felt for air hole
       b. roof felt
walls: c. wall felt
       d. tensioning rope

Frame
roof: 1. compression ring
       2. beam
       3. center pole
walls: 4. expandable lattice
       5. fixing rope
       6. door frame
       7. fixing rope

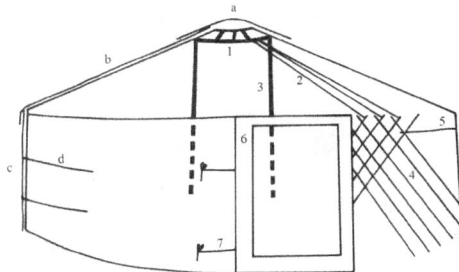

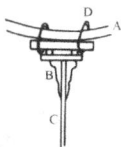

Center pole (front view)
A. compression ring
B. crown
C. pole
D. rope attaching
   the compression ring

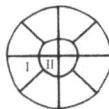

Compression ring (seen from above)
I. concentric ring with 8 spokes
II. concentric ring with 4 spokes

Figure 2.2.   Architecture of the yurt
Copyright: Sandrine Ruhlmann

Figure 2.3. Yurt in the steppe, connected to the grid
Copyright: Sandrine Ruhlmann (Gov'sümber province, August 2017)

When all the furniture and objects are loaded on the pack animals (oxen, yak, or camels) or into Jeeps, the families carry the stove, a closed central stove, on board as well.[4] They carefully transport live embers from the fireplace to rekindle the fire in the stove once the new campsite has been found. The stove is the first to be installed, around which the elements of the yurt are quickly reassembled.

DOMESTIC ECONOMY: MINIMALIST, LIGHT, TRANSPORTABLE

Because they must be mobile, nomadic herders have few material belongings, which we can consider as a minimalist esthetics of some sort. Thus, the domestic economy is limited to light and transportable goods, starting with fire-making equipment that will allow for the heating and lighting of the yurt, and for the cooking of food and the preparation of beverages (Ruhlmann 2019). The stove used to be an open central stove called "open fire" and the fire was built between the four feet of an iron stand (*tulga*) on which was placed the cast-iron pot. Families are today equipped with a closed, central cast-iron stove (*zuuh*) (see the drawing below). Each family generally owns one removable stove, with some having another lighter stove to cook outside with when temperatures soar to unbearably high levels inside the yurt during the summer months. The inside or outside stove is square or rectangular—more rarely round—in shape. The inside stove rests on a substructure, such as the four-legged support of the open stove in the past. Its seams are covered with a mixture of earth and ash to ensure its airtightness. To cook food, the stove has an adjustable opening with nested and removable concentric rings and a small removable circle. Depending on the type of cooking, the bottom of the pot rests on one or the other of the two rings. To supply it with combustible materials, that is, dried dung and/or wood for the inhabitants of the steppe, or charcoal for those of the town, it is built with a lateral opening, called a "stove mouth" facing the south or the east—the socially devalued feminine part of the yurt—slightly inclined upward, with a hook to handle it. When removing ash from the fireplace, a removable iron chimney is sealed with a thin metal slab that is inserted into a half-height slot to obtain different draft qualities. Two tools are used to handle the fire: long tongs called "fire scissors" to insert and remove the combustible materials into the furnace and stoke it to revive the fire, and a poker called a "fire hook" to drop the ashes in the compartment provided to recover them, also used to remove or replace the concentric rings according to the degree and quality of cooking required.[5] Women are in charge of taking care of these tools, the stove, and the fire. Embodying the paternal lineage perpetuation, the household mistress must continuously nurture the fire; she must always be able to revive its embers early in the morning. The spirit master of the fire is the household protector; its extinction would endanger the good health and happiness of the family members and the prosperity of the herd. According to some herder families, during nomadizations, although they take care that the embers do not extinguish, they are in danger when they venture across the steppe, just like men when they go visit

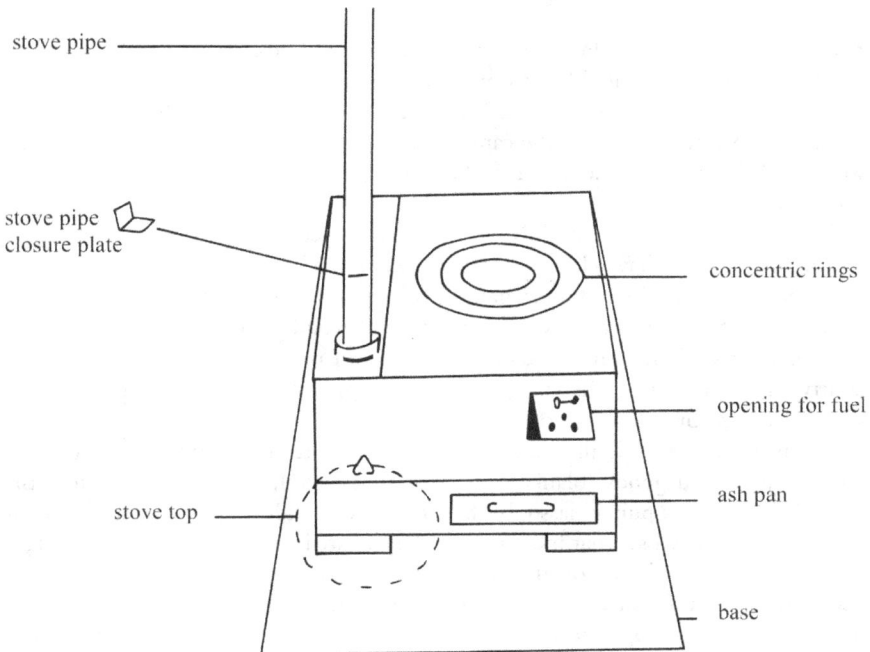

Figure 2.4.   Closed stove
Copyright: Sandrine Ruhlmann

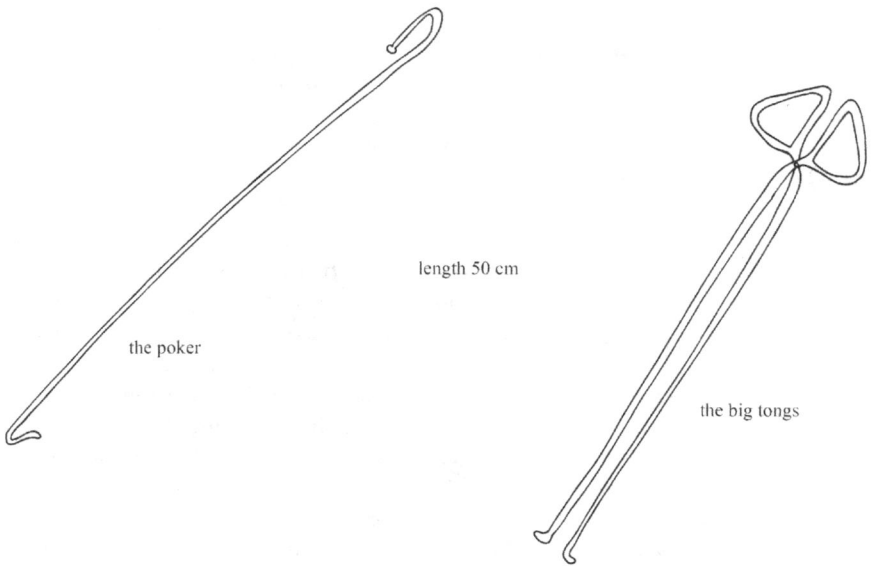

length 50 cm

the poker

the big tongs

Figure 2.5. Fire tools
Copyright: Sandrine Ruhlmann

families in other camps. Nomadic herders should never be disturbed on their way to their new camp; they should not stop unless another family offers them hospitality for a break. To this end, to travel a "white road," which means without encountering any problem, the elder of the camp or a household mistress, possibly the oldest woman of the camp, makes a ritual libation of milk tea, milk or fermented mare's milk, upon departing.[6]

In yurt districts, which are in the urban center periphery and connected to the power grid, families have electric steam cookers in addition to a central stove and a pot. They are not limited in their material belongings and collect many objects in or around their hard-build warehouse (i.e., made of wood, cob, bricks) that is erected in their courtyard. It is not uncommon to see an old refrigerator cast aside in a courtyard, at the edge of the village, or in the steppe, that has been replaced with a state-of-the-art, brand new refrigerator.

In contrast, herder families aspire to store the bare minimum: little furniture, few manufactured goods (blankets, clothes, shoes, etc.), few but important basic tools (hammer, saw, punch, lasso, leather strips, horse saddle, etc.), and a somewhat rudimentary kitchen set that includes just the essentials. Thus, they use several light aluminum, wood, plastic, or animal material storage containers. Only one heavy cast-iron pot to boil water collected from the river, a well, or from snow collected from the mountain top, and to prepare meals, tea, soup, and transform milk into dairy products, etc. They have one cleaver used to mince onion and meat and cut

handle   hook

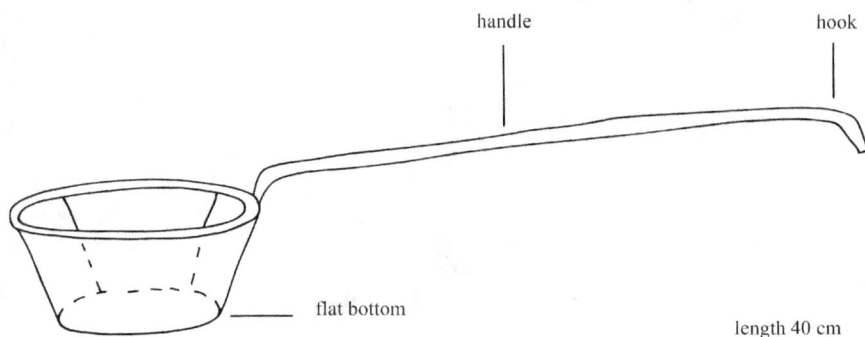

flat bottom

length 40 cm

Figure 2.6.   Ladle
Copyright: Sandrine Ruhlmann

discs from dough, one carving knife to slaughter an animal, butcher its carcass, then cut the meat to cook it, one ladle to aerate milk for skimming and milk tea, one bucket for milking, per household, and one bowl and one tablespoon per person. These are the only objects required for livestock products (meat and milk, according to seasonality diets), storage, cooking, and consumption.

RELATIVE FOOD STORAGE

Generally, storage, and therefore food storage, is to be understood in terms of limiting the number and volume of material belongings to facilitate their transport, particularly during moves, particularly during nomadizations. Alain Testart, who has been interested in the issue of storage in nomadic hunter-gatherer societies, analyzed the forms of societies and economies according to the presence/absence of intensive storage.[7] Concerning Mongolian nomadic herders, I would argue that storage is *relative*. In fact, nomadic herders consider the storage and transport of food products to be decisive, while conservation in the sense of non-alteration is accessory for some products. This is the case for butter, which is rancid by the end of the churning process, and therefore at the maximum possible stage of deterioration. In a previous article, I tackle the "chaîne opératoire" of making butter and one of the most usual and immediate conditioning methods consisting in storing it in a cæcum, a sack made of a mutton's digestive tract dedicated to this use.[8] Herders can use sacks of ruminants as soon as they have slaughtered an animal. These containers are space-saving, strong, hermetic, lightweight, durable, and transportable. Resulting from recycling animal material, either a cæcum or a rumen to preserve butter or cook offal with blood, are environmentally friendly too, while plastic or aluminum containers that have popped up recently are not biodegradable. Most of the latter are also more rapidly perishable, heavier, and bulkier.

Figure 2.7. Cæcum filled with butter
Copyright: Sandrine Ruhlmann (Töv province, August 2017)

Storage is performed according to a categorization of foods and their condition. "White foods" or dairy products, "brown-grey foods" or meat, "food with flour" or homemade pasta or rice, and more recently "vegetables," mainly carrots, potatoes, onions, cabbage, and turnips, are placed everywhere inside the yurt; on or under a bed; on, under, or in the kitchen furniture, or in the outside warehouse, depending on whether it is for immediate or deferred use, depending on whether they are fresh (thawed in winter time), dried, fermented, steam-cooked, or fried, depending on whether the meal is going to be prepared or whether they are leftovers kept for the evening or the next morning. Some foodstuffs change places several times according to whether they are raw or processed. For example, whether it is just milked or transformed and thus considered as milk, the product changes place: the milk that has just been milked is filtered in the southern part of the yurt, that is, its socially devalued part, then stored in a bucket in the feminine southeastern part. Once boiled, some is taken to make the morning milk tea: the kettle then lies in the honorary northern part of the yurt, the masculine part, where visitors are received. The other part of boiled milk is processed into various fresh and fatty, or dried and lean, dairy products: at the end of the fabrication process, they are stored in the external warehouse, some in airtight containers, the others, once dried, tightened in jute cloth bags. In the fall, storing food (meat, milk, yogurt, fresh curd, butter, ravioli, pastries) in the outdoor, freezing-cold warehouse carries out freezing them. For defrosting, they are placed in the yurt near the stove or onto the stove, or cooked directly. During the summer, meat and drained or pressed curd are dried by exposure to the sun and wind, usually on the yurt roof.

Mongolian nomadic herders store, sparingly maybe, but they do store. This issue of storage is deeply connected with that of mobile versus sedentary societies, a question

Figure 2.8.   Curd put to dry on the yurt roof
Copyright: Sandrine Ruhlmann (Gov'sümber province, August 2017)

that was incidentally dear to Alain Testart.[9] The economy of these herders being based on seasonal production, as well as on relative and punctual mobility, storage must be understood here more as a "temporary accumulation," in Tim Ingold's words applied to hunting societies.[10] Among Mongolian herders, the reduction of livestock products (milk, meat), characterized by a reduction in milking for humans and the suspension of slaughter during the long winter period, induces limited storage of food. During the summer months, as people are crowding and gathering, the accumulation of products is regulated by sharing the food or putting it into circulation in order to supply family members or markets in the urban centers and the capital, Ulaanbaatar. Having said that, there has been a remarkable new tendency, in recent years, among some nomadic herder families to accumulate more and more consumer goods and simultaneously reduce the number of nomadizations and reduce the distance between the previous and the new campsites.

At any rate, the principle of food storage is not so much based on the conservation of food, the Mongols not fearing the alteration of taste and texture, smell and color, but rather on their sharing and circulation. Evidence of this is the sedentary families who, equipped with a refrigerator, store everything, not only food, inside—money, identity papers, empty refills of thermoses, makeup, cigarettes, and so forth—and do not systematically plug it into the grid.

FOR WHOM EATING IS EATING MEAT

According to Sidney W. Mintz's theoretical framework, traditional agricultural societies' diet is usually a "starch-centered diet," which means that the "core" element of the meal is some starchy food, served with one or more peripheral side dishes.[11] Among many nomadic societies, the core element of the meal cannot be starchy. For Mongolian people, and not only nomadic herders, the main ingredient is "meat" (*mah*), that is, the flesh taken from the bone, and the typical ordinary dish is meat soup. Meat is the food "that nourishes" and "makes the meal," even if it is eaten in a smaller quantity and even if it is nowadays present in some dishes in smaller quantities than pasta or rice. Each daily meal usually consists of a single dish, soup (*shöl*), and a drink, tea (*tsai*). Soup is by definition a meat soup, generally mutton, the fattiest of the five animal species raised in Mongolia. It consists of a broth (*shüüs*) (liquid element), precisely a fatty broth, which can be eaten at breakfast the next morning should there be no meat pieces left over from the previous dinner. Under the effect of the boiling process, the meat gives the broth its fatty quality, since the fat dissolves in the water during cooking; boiling allows this essential element of the Mongolian diet to be preserved. In addition to this dissolved fat (*tos*), which gives the soup all its nutritive, caloric, and calorific character, families also introduce small pieces of hard fat (*ööh*). This kind of fat is resistant to cooking: it does not melt but it does crunch under the teeth. Families take it from the large fat tail of the mutton.[12] Meat and hard fat are the two elementary solid elements of the Mongolian soup. Meat has two

Figure 2.9a.   A bowl of ordinary soup (with meat and dissolved and hard fat)
Copyright: Sandrine Ruhlmann (Gov'sümber province, August 2017)

forms: pieces of meat detached from the bone called "meat" (*mah*) or parts of meat on the bone called "bone" (*yas*). To designate the soup, there is no inclusion of the term meat. However, it is specified whether the soup contains vegetables, "soup with vegetables," and/or starchy food, "soup with flour/pasta/rice." The cooking broth can also be tea with milk: milk is fat by nature and milk tea is then used to reheat the leftovers from the previous day's meal. It is called "soup with milk tea."

Figure 2.9b.   A bowl of ordinary soup (with meat and hard fat)
Copyright: Sandrine Ruhlmann (Gov'sümber province, August 2017)

In theory, Mongols have a three-meal-a-day food system: the "morning," "noon," and "evening" meals. Only during the evening meal do all the household members usually gather together because the men shepherd the herd to the pastures in the morning before tea is prepared, and they visit other families who live in other camps or in town, during the day. In ordinary (daily; hospitality) or extraordinary contexts (feast, that is, births, weddings, Mongolian lunar New Year; and "reverse of feast," an expression borrowed from Yvonne Verdier,[13] that is, funerals), the meal structure is almost identical in composition, service, and consumption order: a single dish, soup (of meat), and a drink, tea with or without milk. I will call it the "tea-soup-tea structure."

For the past twenty years the daily diet of many urban families has included rice and fresh or dry pasta, both often in larger quantities than meat. However, urban and rural, pastoralist or not, many of the families I have met do not consider starchy meals or dishes containing starch, literally "dishes with flour," as nutritious. Flour, pasta, or rice provides the dishes with consistency and vegetables with taste, but they "do not nourish." If they are added as solid elements to their soup, they do not replace meat and fat under any circumstances. A gradual change in a society's diet does not necessarily or completely alter the ideal eating pattern and the food categories classification. Thus, in Mongolia, food is generally based on seasonal consumption of livestock products: they are always the only foods that "nourish." The food that gives the feeling of being "full, satiated" is and remains meat. Only livestock products satisfy alimentary tastes and responds to the caloric and calorific needs of many Mongols. Thus, every meal contains meat, even in small quantities, and can consist of a single dish on the condition that this dish is meat. Consequently, Mongols define themselves as meat eaters, and meat consumption integrates the young child into the domestic group and society.[14]

Eating Techniques and Gestures

Eating relies on tacit rules incorporated from early childhood: techniques, gestures, and ritual or ritualized practices such as table manners that include service, etiquette, and consumption. The hostess is responsible for the service and etiquette. She must, therefore, respect two primary rules: primacy to the elder and the "rule of three."

The household mistress successively serves tea and soup from hand to hand, in the same individual bowl: a large bowl for the household master, other men or elderly men or women visitors who form the "elders" group, a smaller bowl for the household mistress, the other women, and the children who together compose the "cadets" group. The elders sit in the honorific northwestern part of the yurt, while the cadets take their place in the socially devalued southeastern part. For all meals, the mistress customarily serves the elders first, then everyone else, but in priority the elders, at least three times. Served once, the cadets can then help themselves. Three times means three bowls of soup; thus, the consumption is one bowl of tea,

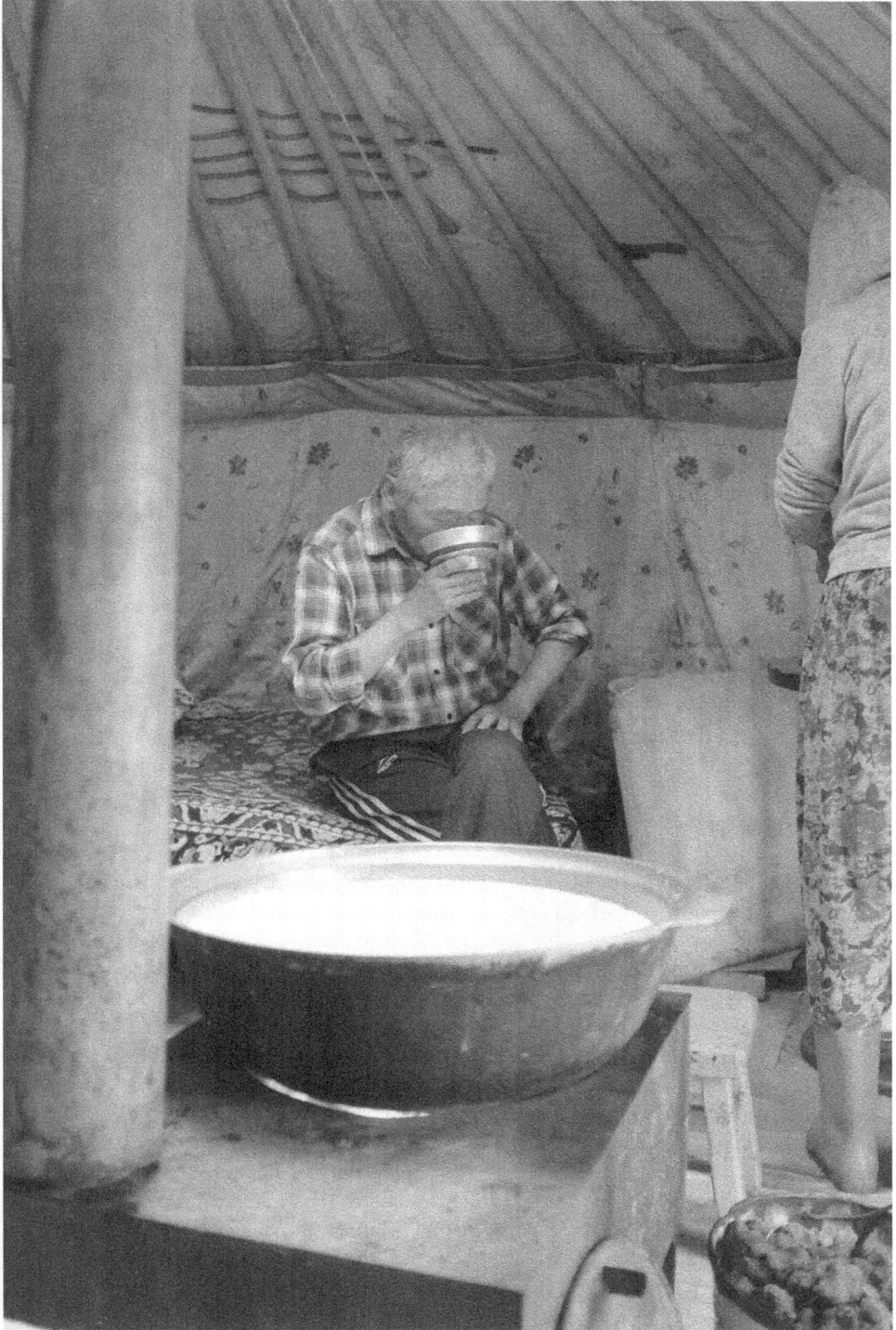

Figure 2.10.   Eating
Copyright: Sandrine Ruhlmann (Gov'sümber province, August 2017)

Figure 2.11.   Eating
Copyright: Sandrine Ruhlmann (Gov'sümber province, August 2017)

at least three bowls of soup, then one bowl of tea. This rule consists in satisfying the eaters, whether they are visitors or household members. The number of three and multiples of three are favorable numbers required in almost all food practices, including offerings to spiritual entities. The auspicious numbers are also found in the service of other meals and beverages, such as ravioli presented by the mistress and which the visitors eat in multiples of three. In the everyday life among household members, certain rules can be relaxed, but in hospitality situations these two rules are inescapable.

Another basic rule is that Mongols generally do not eat or drink alone. Drinking and eating take place in the presence of other people, whether household members, hosts, or other visitors. Eating alone would be like isolating oneself or not eating, which is unthinkable because the human soul lodges in the skeleton and must be nourished just as much as the body itself, the soul's support. A lonely eater would then be suspected of being ill, of having lost his/her soul, or of being invaded by the wandering soul of a deceased. However, eating in company does not mean eating together—with other people, in groups, or units—and at the same time. In Mongolia, the action of eating differs from the commensality dear to some other cultures. In Jeffery Sobal and Mary K. Nelson's words, who consider commensality as "eating with other people," commensality is structurally "conceptualized in terms of commensal units and commensal circles."[15] As Claude Fischler notices, commensality, that is, eating together or in groups, cannot be systematically equated with conviviality: there is a "gradient from intimate, familiar, informal, convivial to unfamiliar, formal, strictly etiquette-driven occasions."[16] For Mongolian people, there is a clear boundary between intimacy and distance,[17] and hospitality is a way to give the visitor a chance to be recognized as a benevolent person even if carrying, unwittingly, some wandering souls of the dead.[18] I prefer here not to speak in terms of commensality, but of eating *in the presence of*, and in terms of a visiting scenario, where a form of codified conviviality may occur, on certain occasions, and along a whole series of preliminary and progressive sequences.

Another important rule is that Mongols must not eat or drink when they are standing, since it is the position of animals grazing in the steppe, or when they are lying down because it is the position of the dead: they must be sitting. Nomadic herders always eat seated and inside the domestic space, therefore inside the yurt, precisely under the protection of the fire master-spirit. The ways of sitting vary depending on whether you are eating, having a conversation, or performing a manual activity.[19] But the soles of the feet or shoes should never be directed toward the stove, otherwise the fire master-spirit will be offended. Families must not threaten the master-spirit in any way by inappropriate, clumsy gestures, such as pointing the knife tip at the stove, or step on or over it. In order not to jeopardize the family's happiness, the soles of the feet should never be directed toward the central poles holding the yurt in place or toward the altar. It is necessary to sit with the back toward the altar and the soles of the feet directed toward the entry door to prevent the "bad spirit" (*muu süns*) from penetrating the domestic space when welcoming visitors. The body being well positioned, gestures well made with the hands and forearms to offer and receive food are also expected. The household mistress can put the tea or soup bowl on the low table but usually offers it directly to the eater. The eater, a household member or a visitor, receives it with the right, pure hand that he/she extends, his/her left hand coming to support the gesture at the elbow level of the right forearm. It is the appropriate gesture to offer and receive food; it is obligatory in a hospitality situation. The eater must carry the bowl of food directly to his/her lips before putting it on the low table, even if the content is hot. In this case, the eater must suck the liquid content noisily in order to cool it with the air he/she introduced into his/her palate at the same time as the soup broth or tea. The mistress and the eater tilt slightly their upper body as well as the head. They hold the bowl with the last four fingers of the right hand underneath and the thumb on the edge. To show greater respect, the mistress is expected to hold the bowl with both hands joined at wrist level, fingers open on each side of the bowl, then lift it up to the level of her forehead, tilting the upper part of her body. The eater must receive it with identical body and hands positioning. The most important offerings are also made with both hands, flat palms facing up to the sky.

Nomadic herders eat seated in the yurt, never alone, respecting the requested technical and customary ritual or ritualized gestures. However, there are a few exceptions to these rules when the situation requires that they eat outside, specifically in the steppe, a wild natural space where herders are no longer under the protective shelter of the fire master-spirit. For example, when they go hunting for several days, keep the herds on the fattening summer pastures for a few days or weeks, travel by car or on horseback in the steppe with the purpose of making long-distance visits, or when they nomadize, that is, move from their campsite to find new pastures for their herd. In fact, the food they consume then, while they are moving or making a stopover, is not identical. Herders eat transportable foods: in this case dried curd or meat that they put in the upper inside part of their Mongolian coat, then suck and chew; or which they smash with a hammer or a stone in order to reduce it to powder that they then rehydrate with a small amount of water. For this purpose, they start a campfire in the center of three stones set on the ground that replaces and materializes the former stove, that is, the open stove or quadripod (*tulga*). They thus create a domestic fire outside the yurt. They also place three stones on the ground in a triangle shape in a manner that the stones touch each other, at the exact location of the closed stove for marking the new yurt site at the end of nomadization.[20] With the temporary outside domestic fire they can prepare a tea broth with added powdered, dried, curd and/or meat in a small quantity of water contained in a small transportable aluminum closed vessel. They can also, and especially, cook hunted game such as parts of a marmot roasted on a spit or stew with hot stones introduced into its carcass.[21] Even outside the yurt, all food is usually consumed in a fixed and seated position, for instance when a rider temporarily gets off his/her mount; when the caravan stops on the way to the new camp site; or when a herder takes a break beside the herd or walks away at little distance while keeping an eye on it, usually with the help of a shepherd dog.

Over the past twenty years I have never seen a herder, man or woman, eating standing in or out of the yurt. Even the fruits are consumed when they return to the camp, in a sitting position, in the presence of the other camp members. Only young children seem to be allowed to eat standing, in between meals, while doing another activity and especially when they move from one yurt to another, from one place to another in the camp.

A ritual practice precedes the act of eating: offerings to spiritual entities. Every morning outside the yurt the household mistress sprinkles one half of the upper part of the daily milk tea as an offering dedicated to the nature master-spirits. She then makes an offering to a deceased relative's soul of the other half of the upper part of the milk tea onto the altar where a photograph of the deceased is placed. Similarly, anyone who is getting ready to eat offers the upper part of his/her bowl in the form of a flick (*nyasalgaa/nyaslagaa*): he/she flicks milk tea or fermented or distilled mare's milk droplets onto the stove to the fire master-spirit. The sprayed liquid emits a crackling sound when it comes in contact with the burning walls of the stove, which proves to be auspicious. Then, he/she projects the liquid into the air, generally at the level of his/her right then left shoulder, toward the altar, to the ancestors' souls, and to Buddhist divinities. A man or a woman sitting, head covered, coat closed, flicks the milk drops in the honorary part of the yurt. This gesture consists of dipping the annular of the right "pure hand" in the liquid, pressing the nail on the right thumb pad, and releasing the pressure in order to project drops of liquid. This propitiatory gesture is generally performed in a series of three.

Figure 2.12.   Morning libation to the nature master-spirits
Copyright: Sandrine Ruhlmann (Gov'sümber province, August 2017)

HOSPITALITY, FOOD SHARING, AND HAPPINESS

The observance of rules when eating and drinking is required in a situation of hospitality, even in the minutest of details. The reason is that a vital principle stands behind food sharing and consumption: the family's happiness and lineages' perpetuation, but also the society's reproduction and order. This happiness relies strongly on food sharing, food circulation. There are different food sharing modalities. Food sharing is restricted, that is, closed to family members in an ordinary, daily situation. In a hospitality situation it opens to a reduced network of regular visitors that must be maintained and expanded over the years in order to have a large number of visitors on exceptional occasions, when the soul's fate is at stake: at the time of birth, when a soul can be reborn into the skeleton of a descendant, or at the time of death when the soul sets out the process of becoming an ancestor's soul who one day will in turn be reborn.

In other words, the hospitality, that is, the receiving and giving, and its corollary, food sharing, are at the heart of a conception of relations between humans and different spiritual entities, such as ancestors' souls, recently dead souls, wandering souls of the dead, nature's master-spirits, and Buddhist divinities. Food sharing occurs on two levels: the horizontal between humans and the vertical with various invisible spiritual entities. The Mongols, who were my informants (not only nomadic herders), share cooked food—edible food for humans—within the domestic space (yurt, house, apartment) with humans, the souls of the deceased, the ancestors' souls, and Buddhist divinities. Outside the dwelling (in the steppe, in an alley, or a street), they offer cooked food—inedible for humans—to spirits if they wish to please and appease them, and raw food—inedible for humans—if they intend to chase them away and thereby protect themselves from them. Families thus nourish the souls of the deceased condemned to wander with cooked and then raw food, to calm them at first, and then chase them away. Thus, the upper part of all culinary preparation and consumption between humans is inevitably removed for benefit of the spiritual entities, whether they are benevolent or not, whether families seek to obtain their grace or favor, or if they want to keep them at bay.

In nomadic or of nomadic custom Mongolian society, circulation is a fundamental issue: a movement that goes beyond hospitality and food sharing. It follows the cycle of nature (which allows the herds to access new pastures and which induces families to gather together, at the time of nature's renewal, that is, when one enters a new series of seasons), the biological life cycle (birth and death, soul rebirth), the social life cycle (seasonal dispersion and regrouping), the seasonal acquisition and production food cycle (meat, dairy products), and also happiness-support food (white foods, shoe-sole-shaped pastry), and in parallel, the circulation of wild animals and the dead's wandering souls they carry when they cling to their feathers or hairs. Families must necessarily circulate happiness after they have summoned it, that is to say after they have produced and accumulated (or stored) it. Following that order, they avoid the risk of losing everything and attracting misfortune (on their household members and their herd). I here concur with Rebecca Empson's[22] analysis according to which happiness (*hishig*), which is understood as a collective good that can be contained in an object and accumulated, in reasonable proportions, must be shared and dispersed, vertically and horizontally, at the appropriate time and in the suitable manner.

In a context where the family's or society's happiness is at stake, all families share food (*hool*), happiness-support food (*hishigtei hool*), via a hospitality process, in exceptional context requiring the gathering of the greatest number of visitors possible, that is to say the sharing of a great quantity and diversity of food, called "merit" (*buyan*) or "white merit" (*tsagaan buyan*) that families share in "multitude" (*zöndöö*). Thus, during the funeral meal, the grieving family prepares and serves a "multitude, multitude" of "merit foods" that are contained in the soup, such as long and thin spaghetti and small pieces of vegetables. Or during the morning closing meal, the "ten white merits": milk tea, compact milk, rice and raisin porridge, milk tea soup with millet and small boiled ravioli, creamy milk and rice porridge, candies and small dried curd. This meal is dedicated to the children, who by analogy, represent the newborn children into whom the dead's souls are supposed to be reborn.

They are different kinds of visits: fleeting visits, extended visits, and long stays.[23] Fleeting visits punctuate daily life. They involve members of the camp or a nearby camp, but also often relatives or close relatives who live in the vicinity of one another, one hour from the campsite on horseback, or thirteen minutes on foot when in the same village. The principle is to "come and go swiftly." The household mistress ceremoniously hands the visitor a milk tea bowl and, on the low table, puts a plate full of fresh and dried dairy products, sometimes added with small fried doughnuts or industrial biscuits, which I name the "hospitality plate." This is the minimum hospitality offering required for this type of visit. The visitor takes a small piece on the plate only. He merely takes a tiny bite (*amsah*) from the upper part of the plate; he does not eat (*ideh*). Meanwhile, the mistress accompanies her offering gesture with injunctions, such as "Drink the tea!" and "Eat the soup!" On each visit she adds fresh dairy products on top of the plate in order to display abundance, and the visitor must help himself only from the upper part. The mistress must also always have enough hot milk tea available for visitors who come from outside the camp. Extended visits are less regular than fleeting visits. They can last until dinner, include the following night, or turn into a longer or shorter stay. The visitor signals his/her desire to prolong his visit by removing his hat/her headscarf and removing or opening his/her coat. After the minimal hospitality offering, the mistress thus cooks a meal, a dish (with meat), but a specific one: dishes with a festive character, in this case steamed ravioli or steamed pasta and sometimes, and especially in the presence of the household master, three small glasses of Mongolian or Russian vodka or homemade distilled fermented milk alcohol. Whether the visit is swift or prolonged, the visitor is offered a last tea milk bowl when he/she leaves. In the case of a long stay, the mistress will wish the visitor a safe journey by placing a milk tea or fermented mare's milk libation onto his/her horse's back or onto the rear part of the car or the bus.

In a hospitality situation, food sharing includes snuffing tobacco or smoking a pipe, and also greetings exchanges. It structures an identical reception protocol among nomadic and sedentary families, except in the capital Ulaanbaatar, which I will not describe here. The visits follow a scenario with fixed sequences for the visitor: arriving, having the dogs held back, sitting in the honorary part of the yurt, receiving a tea bowl and a hospitality plate or food bowl, exchanging decorum greetings and possibly snuff boxes, then discussing, laughing, and singing, declaring oneself satiated, receiving a last tea bowl, and finally leaving. The mistress wishes the visitor to "go well!" to which the visitor answers "stay well!" The families are thus in a round of visits where the women receive and the men (and women to a lesser extent) visit while the food circulates from one hand to another and while the visitor, on certain occasions such as the lunar New Year, carries home a happiness-support food as a token of hospitality, which guarantees happiness to both the host and the visitor. In this visiting and sharing food paradigm, inscribed in a nomadic minimalist domestic economy, it is common that a man carries his personal bowl and spoon on his journey.

BIBLIOGRAPHY

Accolas, Jean-Pierre, and Jean-Pierre, Deffontaines. "Les activités rurales en République populaire de Mongolie. I. Agriculture et élevage." *Études mongoles* 6 (1975): 9–53.

Blanc, Morgane, Oriol, Christine, and Sophie, Devienne. "Un siècle d'évolution du système pastoral de la steppe désertique de Mongolie: diminution de la mobilité des troupeaux, dérégulation de l'accès aux parcours et crise de surpâturage." *Études mongoles & sibériennes, centrasiatiques & tibétaines* 43–44 (2013). http://journals.openedition.org/emscat/2154. DOI: 10.4000/emscat.2154.

Chabros, Kristina, and Sedenžavyn, Dulam. "La nomadisation mongole: techniques et symbolique." *Paper on Inner Asia* 13. Bloomington: Indiana University, 1990.

Devienne, Sophie. "Régulation de l'accès aux parcours et évolution des systèmes pastoraux en Mongolie." *Études mongoles & sibériennes, centrasiatiques & tibétaines* 43–44 (2013). http://journals.openedition.org/ emscat/2104. DOI: 10.4000/emscat.2104.

Douglas, Mary. "Deciphering a meal." *Daedalus* 100, no. 1 (1972): 61–81.

Fernández-Giménez, María, Batkhishig, Baival, Batbuyan Batjav, and Tungalag Ulmanbayara. "Lessons from the *dzud*: Community-based rangeland management increases the adaptive capacity of Mongolian herders to winter disasters." *World Development* 68, April (2015): 48–65. https://doi.org/10.1016/j.worlddev.2014.11.015.

Fernández-Giménez, María, Batkhishig, Baival, and Batjav, Batbuyan. "Cross-boundary and cross-level dynamics increase vulnerability to severe winter disasters (*dzud*) in Mongolia." *Global Environmental Change* 22, no. 4 (October 2012): 836–51. https://doi.org/10.1016/j.gloenvcha.2012.07.001.

Fischler, Claude. "Commensality, society, and culture." *Social Science Information* 50, nos. 3–4 (2011): 528–48.

Hamayon, Roberte. "Façons de s'asseoir." *Études mongoles* 1 (1970): 145–207.

Ingold, Tim. "The Significance of Storage in Hunting Societies." *Man* 18, no. 3 (1983): 553–71.

Lkhagvadorj, Dorjburgedaa, Hauck, Markus, Dulamsuren, Choimaa, and Jamsran Tsogtbaatar. "Pastoral nomadism in the forest-steppe of the Mongolian Altai under a changing economy and a warming climate." *Journal of Arid Environments* 88, January (2013): 82–89. https://doi.org/10.1016/ j.jaridenv.2012.07.019.

Mintz, Sidney W. "Core and fringe." *Indian International Center Quarterly* 12, no. 2 (1985): 193–204.

Mintz, Sidney W., and Daniela Schlettwein-Gsell. "Food patterns in agrarian societies: the 'core-fringe-legume hypothesis' a dialogue." *Gastronomica* 1, no. 1 (2001): 41–52.

Reading, Richard P., Bedunah, Donald J., and Sukhiin Amgalanbaatar. "Conserving biodiversity on Mongolian rangelands: Implications for protected area development and pastoral uses." USDA Forest Service Proceedings RMRS-P-39 (2006). https://www.fs.fed.us/rm/ pubs /rmrs_p039/ rmrs_p039_001_017.pdf.

Ruhlmann, Sandrine. *Inviting happiness: Food sharing in Mongolia.* Leiden/Boston: Brill, 2019.

Ruhlmann, Sandrine. "La seconde vie du cæcum ou le stockage ingénieux du beurre en Mongolie." *Techniques & Culture* 69 (2018): 74–87. http://journals.openedition.org/tc/8809. DOI: 10.4000/tc.8809.

Ruhlmann, Sandrine. "Usages et fonctions de la marmite en Mongolie. Un outil de cuisson, des techniques culinaires et bien davantage." In *Du feu originel aux nouvelles cuissons: pratiques, techniques, rôles sociaux,* edited by Jean-Pierre Williot, 333–356. Bruxelles: Éditions Peter Lang, 2015.

Sobal, Jeffery, and Mary, K. Nelson. "Commensal eating patterns: A community study." *Appetite* 41 (2003): 181–90.

Sternberg, Troy. "Environmental challenges in Mongolia's dryland pastoral landscape." *Journal of Arid Environments* 72, no. 7 (July 2008): 1294–1304. https://doi.org/10.1016/j.jaridenv.2007.12.016.

Testart, Alain. *Les chasseurs-cueilleurs ou l'origine des inégalités.* Paris: Société d'Ethnologie, 1982a.

Testart, Alain. "The Significance of Food Storage among Hunter-Gatherers: Residence Patterns, Population Densities, and Social Inequalities." *Current Anthropology* 23, no. 5 (1982b): 523–37.

Testart, Alain. "Some Major Problems in the Social Anthropology of Hunter-Gatherers." *Current Anthropology* 29, no. 1 (1988): 1–31.

Verdier, Yvonne. "Repas bas-normand." *L'Homme* VI, no. 3 (1966): 92–111.

3

McDonald's in the Desert

Bedouins, Fast-Food, and Modernity in Southern Israel

Nir Avieli

In Middle Eastern Arab societies, a basic distinction exists between *falahin* (sedentary farmers) and *badawin* (literally "desert dwellers"), with many of the latter practicing a semi-nomadic lifestyle, which includes winter cropping in permanent villages and summer herding, restricted by ever decreasing grasslands and water sources. The Bedouins are looked down upon by Middle Eastern sedentary dwellers, both falahin and urbanites, as is the case with so many contemporary nomad societies living in proximity to farmers and urbanites.

Some two hundred thousand Bedouins live in southern Israel's Negev desert.[1] Roughly half of them were invited, lulled, or forced by the state into seven "Bedouin towns" built during the 1960s and 1970s in the vicinity of Beersheba, "Capital of the Negev (Israel's southern desert)," the largest and most important city in Southern Israel. The rest remain in what the authorities define as "unrecognized villages": clusters of mostly tin houses and sheds where they struggle to maintain semi-nomadic practices such as herding and winter cropping, while clinging to the lands over which they claim ownership. The Israeli authorities do not recognize their claims for land rights, arguably granted during the Ottoman period, and insist on urbanization and sedentarization within a general scheme of modernization.

It is beyond the scope of this chapter to deal with this complex issue, but it should be noted that while the authorities make benevolent claims about education, health, and an improved standard of living, the existing Bedouin towns suffer from institutional neglect and discrimination and are hubs of poverty, crime, and violence. Their residents, who lost access to traditional nomadic occupations, were practically forced into blue-collar jobs, or unemployment, with the ensuing negative consequences.

Meanwhile, and despite the authorities' claims for modernization, the dwellers of the unrecognized villages are denied access to water and electricity, while the government was forced only recently by the high court of justice to provide accessible

35

schooling for their children. They also face constant attempts of forced eviction that often culminate in violence. The state's claims for modernization are accompanied by attempts at grasping the lands over which the Negev Bedouins claim ownership and turning them into Jewish settlements as part of the conflict between Jews and Arabs in contemporary Israel.

There are two prevailing stereotypes in Israel about the Bedouins, similar to those attributed to nomadic minorities elsewhere. The more positive view perceives them as exotic noble savages, masters of the desert, with their camels, sheep, and horses, tracking skills, coffee, mutton, and *mansaf* (mutton pilaf), hospitality, and prowess. The negative view distinguishes them as unreliable, lazy, and dishonest nomadic thieves. Both stereotypes, however, define the Bedouins as "traditional" and therefore old-fashioned, conservative, and nonmodern.[2] Patriarchy, polygamy, reliance on national security remittance, the practice of so-called family honor killing, as well as reckless driving, are also perceived by Israeli Jews as negative features of the Negev Bedouins. The fact that poverty and limited opportunities for education and employment make crime one of the few socioeconomic venues available for the Bedouins further contributes to their negative image in Israel. The tension is exacerbated by the ongoing national conflict between Jews and Arabs in the country.

So, when I decided to take my "Anthropology of Food" students to McDonald's in Beersheba's BIG power center in 2008, none of us expected that roughly half of the customers would be Bedouin, and for that matter, Bedouin women. And since my plan was to teach a class on George Ritzer's McDonaldization theory[3] right at McDonald's, we couldn't but notice the discrepancy between Ritzer's claims regarding McDonald's globalizing universal homogeneousness and our ethnographic observation that something was clearly very local and very unique in this McDonald's branch.

This chapter is based on dozens of visits to this McDonald's in Beersheba from 2009–2018. I went there alone, with Jewish and Bedouin students, and with my children. As a participant observer, I ordered food, observed the dynamics and interactions with diners and staff, and held short conversations with them. I further conducted four open-ended interviews with Bedouin women who frequent McDonald's with different levels of frequency. I also asked some of my Bedouin and Jewish students to visit that location and submit a written report of their visit, so as to make sure that my presence as a Jewish middle-aged man is balanced by observers of different ages, genders, ethnicities, and religions.

My findings suggest that this McDonald's location is popular among Bedouins, and specifically among Bedouin women, members of the most marginalized and disempowered social echelon in contemporary Israel, even though they do not particularly like the food. What makes McDonald's attractive is that it is perceived as a liberating space where many social restrictions these customers face as members of a discriminated-against Arab-Muslim minority, and in the case of women, as members of a patriarchal group, are relaxed and even suspended. I conclude by arguing that the stated egalitarian ideology of McDonald's in Israel, and the resulting inter-ethnic dynamics, overcome Israeli-Jewish, Arab, and Bedouin ethnic and gender hierarchies and prejudices.

It should be noted that there were other unique features at Beersheba's McDonald's— for instance, the large number of young soldiers who tended to describe McDonald's as a liberating space, or the many parents who felt obliged to somehow justify what they described as giving in to their children's demands. Since this volume is dedicated to nomadic foodways, I shall limit my discussion to the Bedouins.

MCDONALDIZATION AND ITS DISCONTENTS

In 1993, sociologist George Ritzer published *The McDonaldization of Society*. Ritzer turned to Max Weber's classic analysis of modern bureaucracies and argued that the secret behind McDonald's unprecedented success (at the time of writing) was the outcome of its unique implementation of the principles of bureaucracy as outlined by Max Weber: a modern rational organization that rigorously applies the principles of efficiency, calculability, predictability, standardization, and control. Ritzer notes that this emphasis on bureaucracy means that irrational and incalculable elements such as taste or pleasure are not, and cannot be, components of the McDonald's experience.

Following Weber, Ritzer also points to "the irrationality of rationality" embedded in the fast-food franchise, and stresses the fact that McDonald's, like all bureaucracies, inevitably creates what Weber terms "the iron cage": a rigid, alienated, and nonhuman environment that makes for a disenchanted world. As Ritzer states, "Most specifically, irrationality means that rational systems are unreasonable systems. By that I mean that they deny the basic humanity, the human reason, of the people who work within or are served by them."[4] At McDonald's, disenchantment lies in the fact that the food itself is heavily processed and totally standardized: there are no culinary surprises at McDonald's.

Ritzer, however, did not stop at the fast-food chain. He goes and argues that society (he was speaking about American society, but the implications were obviously global) was going through a process of "McDonaldization," in which the principles of rationalization and modernization, implemented through efficiency, calculability, predictability, standardization, and control, were gradually taking over all realms of life. This, he argues, would lead to the standardization of everything, and therefore to the disenchantment of life everywhere, as everything would be expected, prefabricated, and predefined. In other words, Ritzer was depicting a social setting in which a set of small volcanos, located at McDonald's branches, were pouring sticky, homogenous lava that was gradually covering the entire cosmos, drowning everything else and creating a standardized and, indeed, disenchanted world. British journalist Polly Toynbee describes this process when discussing globalization: "sometimes it seems as if a tidal wave of the worst of Western culture is sweeping across the globe like a giant strawberry milkshake . . . tasting the same from Samoa to Siberia to Somalia."[5]

Ritzer's work drew a lot of attention and criticism and launched ongoing debates about the nature of globalization. For anthropologists, however, this theory was simply unbearable: as scholars of culture, how could we tolerate the idea that culture was so weak, fragile, and vulnerable, that the mechanism of a fast-food chain, as successful and sophisticated as it may be, could simply level it?

James Watson's *Golden Arches East*[6] is an ethnographic project aimed at challenging the McDonaldization theory right at its core. Watson and his colleagues conducted ethnographic fieldwork in five Asian metropole McDonald's locations: Beijing, Taipei, Seoul, Hong Kong, and Tokyo. In a nutshell, each of these ethnographies shows that the local is not replaced, overwhelmed, or otherwise erased by the global (i.e., submerged by McDonald's milkshake), but just the opposite: local cultural arrangements, values, and practices are clearly evident in each of the locations, making them, at least to a certain extent, local culinary establishments.

Thus, in Beijing, McDonald's is a hub of modernity, Americanization, and personal freedom that specifically attracts young female professionals.[7] In Taipei, customers choose whether to frequent franchises owned by native Taiwanese or by immigrants from the mainland depending on their own political dispositions regarding the relations between Taiwan and China.[8] In Hong Kong, McDonald' is a place where children go as a safe haven as their parents are busy offering them a refuge from urban alienation, and also serving as a practical playground in an otherwise extremely overcrowded space.[9]

New York Times columnist Nicholas Kristof summarizes the main argument of *Golden Arches East* as follows:

> *Golden Arches East* . . . explores issues of globalization by focusing on the role of McDonald's in five Asian economies and [concludes] that in many countries McDonald's has been absorbed by local communities and became assimilated, so that it is no longer thought of as a foreign restaurant and in some ways no longer functions as one.[10]

Golden Arches East prompted a series of ethnographic studies in different parts of the world,[11] which further show how local cultures influence and shape McDonald's.

Israeli social scientists were also keen to engage with the McDonaldization theory. Geographer Maoz Azaryahu analyzes the case of a specific McDonald's location and its strained relations with the next-door commemoration center for Israeli soldiers.[12] For him, this is a clear case of "The Americanization of Israel" and the processes of cultural homogenization it entails. He acknowledges, however, that processes of hybridization are also evident in McDonald's in Israel:

> [t]he chain also developed a new type of hamburger to conform to Israeli preferences and tastes. As advertised, the McRoyal was more of everything: bigger, spicier, and juicier. Accordingly, even if the idiom appeared to be American, both content and accent were unmistakably Israeli.[13]

Sociologist Uri Ram, in an attempt to rescue the McDonaldization theory from the grip of ethnographic critique, suggests that McDonald's in Israel (and probably elsewhere), is a good example for glocalization: the structure is global (i.e., the modus operandi and organizational language are those of McDonald's international/USA), while the content is adjusted to the Israeli/local preferences and tastes.[14]

While articles on the Israeli case challenge and complicate Ritzer's theory, what is still missing from the debate is the local. By "local" I am not referring to the national (Israeli), nor to the regional, which although liberally used in food-related literature and anthropology, is vague and contested (see Ulin's analysis of the precariousness of *terroir*[15]). What I mean by "local" is precisely what anthropology has been praising itself for highlighting throughout its history as an academic discipline: that which is clearly bound in space and time—the village, town, or city that anthropologists study. This chapter is therefore an ethnography of McDonald's in Beersheba and deals with the social relations and complications characteristic of this city, and specifically with the strained relations with the Bedouins who dwell around town.

BEDOUINS AT MCDONALD'S

Whenever I visited the McDonald's at Beersheba's power center during the fieldwork period, many if not most of the customers were Bedouin women. Some could be easily recognized by their hijab (headscarf), while others spoke Arabic. There were several instances when I realized that a customer was Bedouin only during our conversation—when I recognized the accent or when my interlocutor referred to herself as one. I have no doubt that other customers were Bedouin, but I did not recognize that they were.

Most of the Bedouin women were in the company of other Bedouin women or children. There were also young couples and larger groups of young women and men. Many of the employees were Bedouin too. Some of the female employees were wearing headscarves. In some Muslim countries, McDonald's female employees wear "McHijabs" (hijabs with a McDonald's logo on them)—but I never saw them used in Israel. During interviews and conversations I was told that some of the shift managers were Bedouin too, and I did manage to talk to two of them, though only briefly. While the employees were willing to answer my questions, shift managers were obviously uncomfortable, probably because their manuals do not include procedures for talking to paying customers that present themselves as anthropologists doing research in their location.

During these conversations and short interviews, three themes came up regarding my questions about the popularity of McDonald's among Bedouins, and specifically young Bedouin women: a sense of freedom and ease of control; the fact that many of the employees were Bedouins; and issues that related to modernization. In what follows I discuss each of these themes, but before I do that, I briefly discuss the food they consume at McDonald's and how they feel about it.

BEDOUINS AND MC'ROYAL MEALS

> Nir (pointing to the large number of visible Bedouin clients): "Why do Bedouins prefer McDonald's over all other food venues here?"
>
> Jewish Employee: "They come here because it is cheap."
>
> Nir: "What do they order?"
>
> Jewish Employee: "McRoyal meal, always the same, chips and coca cola."
>
> Nir: "It is not cheap at all [42 ISL for a large meal; roughly equivalent to 10 US dollars in 2009]."
>
> Jewish Employee: "It was cheap in the past and they got used to coming here."

One particularly intriguing feature of the McDonald's Bedouin experience in Beer-sheba is the preference for the "McRoyal meal," which includes a charcoal-grilled[16] beef patty, a soft drink, and a portion of fries ("chips" in contemporary Hebrew). In fact, I have never seen a Bedouin customer ordering any other hamburger or meal. When I asked customers and employees to explain this preference, most interlocutors did not know why. In the interview above, the explanation that this particular meal was cheap, was inaccurate at the time of the interview and in previous years[17]—McDonald's in Israel was never cheap. For the price of a McRoyal meal, for example, customers could purchase two or three falafel portions with soft drinks in other venues at the power center, and five or six falafels with drinks in any of the Bedouin towns. For 50 ILS they could order two shawarma portions with drinks, or a family pizza with a large bottle of soda, both much larger and filling than a single McRoyal meal.

Since price was not a factor, perhaps we should consider taste. Here again, one of the most intriguing aspects of the Bedouin penchant for McDonald's fare is the fact that no one I talked to admitted to liking it. To the question whether the food was tasty and whether they liked it, Bedouin customers would respond in terms such as "it's okay" or "yes" with a skeptical expression. When I suggested, for instance, that it wasn't so tasty, or that there were tastier options available at the power center (such as falafel, shawarma, or pizza), and certainly tastier dishes in their hometowns, most would confirm my arguments, sometimes with obvious enthusiasm.

One of the pillars of the anthropology of food is that "taste is culturally constructed." Indeed, it took me more than twenty years of ethnographic research to be able to argue that the definition of food as tasty or not, has very little to do with the material composition of the dish itself or the physiological reaction between the food molecules and our taste and smell buds. We like or dislike different foods and dishes, develop a taste for some, and an aversion to others, through the process of socialization.

It would have been hardly surprising if my Bedouin interlocutors responded that they didn't like it much at first, but later began to like it, but this was not the case: though none of those I talked to expressed a dislike for McDonald's fare, or offered a critique regarding its taste or unhealthy components (as many Jewish customers did), they were hardly enthusiastic about it (as many Jewish customers were), and their attitude was reserved at best. Altogether, both price and taste were not the key factors that drew Bedouin customers to McDonald's in Beersheba. In what follows, I turn to their own explanations regarding their attraction to the fast-food franchise: the large number of Bedouin employees, the sense of modernity, and the toning down of social restrictions.

BEDOUIN EMPLOYEES

A young Bedouin man was eating (a McRoyal meal) alone when I approached his table. He told me that he actually came for a job interview. When I asked whether there was a "help wanted" sign or ad, he explained that the shift manager called him and suggested the job interview.

Nir: "Does he know you?"

Man: "No, he is from Aroer and I am from Kseife" (Bedouin towns).

Nir: "So how did he get your phone number?"

Man: "Maybe my mother gave it to him."

The subtext of this short conversation includes two intriguing notions. The first and more obvious one is that recruitment to this McDonald's did not follow the transparent, universal, and standard recruitment procedures most outsiders would attribute to McDonald's (or other bureaucratic institutions), and which are presented as such at McDonald's in Israel[18] and US[19] recruitment web pages. It is very much in line, however, with the Israeli tendency to rely on informal social networks when dealing with all kinds of bureaucratic institutions. Indeed, scholars of the Israeli "Startup-nation" phenomena point to these networks as instrumental in creating the synergy behind the very high success rate of Israeli startups.[20] Social scientists, too, point to the extreme importance of social and specifically kin networks in Israel[21] and their role in circumventing bureaucratic barriers. The "Bedouin twist," however, had to do with the mentioning of the two Bedouin towns, Aroer and Kseife, built by the government and imposed on the Bedouins as essential to one's social networks and identity. The answer suggests that the sedentarization of the Negev Bedouins altered their self-perception from members of extended families or tribes to the dwellers of towns developed by the state.

The other important feature of McDonald's exposed in this conversation was the fact that there was a Bedouin shift manager, and for that matter, one charged with recruitment and hiring. For a non-Israeli this might seem obvious, but in contemporary Israel, and specifically in the Negev region, Bedouins are looked down upon and are economically limited to blue-collar and menial jobs. The fact that McDonald's treated Bedouins differently in terms of employment opportunities is observed in the following conversation with a Jewish female employee on a cigarette break "at the back" (a privileged spot for talking to employees). Responding to my query regarding the popularity of McDonald's among Bedouins, she points out that Bedouin customers are attracted to this location because "so many employees *and even managers* [her emphasis added] were Bedouins."

Nir: "But Bedouins are employed in each and every food venue in Beersheba."

Employee: "Yes, but can you see them? If you go to Kampai [a very trendy Pan Asian restaurant in the same power center] can you see any of them? They are washing dishes at the back [*me'ahora*]. At McDonald's—you can see . . . [pointing toward the counter to two of the four employees who were Bedouin; one wore a hijab and the other was talking in Arabic with a customer]."

Nir: "How do you feel about working with the Bedouins?"

Employee: "I am not disturbed [*li ze lo maf'riah*]."

Nir: "And what about other Jewish employees?"

Employee: "It is up to them—if they don't like it, they can leave."

The fact that Bedouin customers were drawn to McDonald's because of the relatively large number of Bedouin employees was confirmed by a Bedouin shift manager who said that "young Bedouins like coming to McDonald's because many of the workers are Bedouins, and so they can order and get service in Arabic, which makes them feel comfortable."

The important point here is the suggestion that the attraction does not lie solely in the fact that there are Bedouin employees at McDonald's, but in the position they hold: not as "dishwashers at the back," but as counterworkers that serve Bedouins shoulder to shoulder with Jewish Israeli employees, and for that matter, as shift managers. Bedouin employees themselves are also recruited through social networks by Bedouin shift managers, an avenue that allows circumventing Israeli-Jewish prejudices and also one that presents options for career development that hardly exist when "washing dishes at the back" seems like the only option. I later return to the issue of employment and discuss its political context.

SPEED AND MODERNITY

Returning to the young man anticipating a job interview, later in the conversation he adds: "Did you see how fast the food comes out? At the shawarma you have to wait, but here you order and you get the food before you finish paying." In another conversation, a Bedouin interlocutor points out that he came "for the speed, which is the most important thing for me." I later observe him spending more than thirty minutes with his spouse at the location, in what seemed a leisurely conversation that went on long after the food was consumed. Apparently, speed was important to him not because he was in a rush.

The emphasis on speed and fast service, expressions of the modern "time is money" approach, is incompatible with the stereotypical perception of Bedouins in Israel, and of nomads elsewhere,[22] as laid back and relaxed (the more positive view), or careless and lazy, and generally unreliable and unpredictable when it comes to time management. Israeli Jews and non-Bedouin Arabs often describe Bedouin time as nonlinear, non-systematic, and even bewildering ("you can wait for him all day and he will not even call to say he is not coming").

Johannes Fabian, in his critique of anthropology, terms this view allochronism: "the denial of coevalness"[23] between researcher and researched, and "the assigning of the anthropological other to a time past relative to the ethnographer."[24] While Israeli Jews are generally allochronistic toward Arabs, when it comes to the Bedouins, their (now very much bygone) nomad lifestyle is often associated with their time management. Jokes and comments abound regarding "Bedouin time," described as flexible, unimportant, and incompatible with the mainstream (Jewish-Western-modern) conception of time. In Jakubowska's words: "The plethora of jokes about the Bedouin points to their incompatibility with progress and pictures 'people whom time have left behind.'"[25] Similarly, the popular Hebrew "Bedouin Love Song" reflects and maintains an image of an unstructured, unstable, and even chaotic lifestyle, with the Bedouin protagonists carried away by the desert storms as if they were rag dolls.[26]

Speed was central to the McDonald's experience of the above-quoted interlocutors even though they were not in a hurry: one was waiting for an interview while the other lingered for quite some time. Speed of service was desired in its own right ("Speed . . . is the most important thing for me"), watched with awe, and described in an admiring tone ("You get the food before you finish paying"). I argue that speed was desired because it represents modernity and because it undermines the degrading stereotypes regarding Bedouins as "people whom time has left behind."[27]

Lingering, however, was common among many Bedouin customers I observed. They ate leisurely and remained at in the McDonald's long after the food was eaten. I did not time their stays, but my impression is that Bedouin customers remained significantly longer than Jewish customers (taking into account that families with children, young couples, groups of youngsters, or individuals have different time patterns).

Lingering in a fast-food restaurant is paradoxical, at least to a certain extent. Returning to the McDonaldization theory, Ritzer notes that the franchise wishes to control not only the processes of preparation and service executed by employees, but also the behavior patterns of the customers, inclusive of their length of stay. This is determined by the rate of food preparation and service ("Here you order, and you get the food before you finish paying"), but also by the design of the eating space. Ritzer thus notes: "To prevent this [lingering], McDonald's created . . . uncomfortable seats, and other amenities . . . that make customers feel unwelcome,"[28] so as to ensure that they would eat and leave, vacating the space for the next customers.

In his analysis of McDonald's in Beijing (within the Golden Arches East project), Yan[29] explains: "the transformation of fast food establishments from eating place to social space is the key to understanding the popularity of fast food in Beijing." He further notes that hanging out at a location is an important aspect of the Beijing McDonald's experience. However, managers of Beijing fast-food restaurants he interviewed pointed out that they didn't like lingering clients, while he himself "was indirectly urged to leave by the restaurant employees; they either took away my empty cup or asked if I needed anything else."[30]

In the sixth edition of *The McDonaldization of Society*, however, Ritzer[31] notes that McDonald's has somewhat altered its seats and tables and made them more comfortable and inviting for a longer stay so as to compete with Starbucks (and presumably other successful cafés) that offer more comfortable setting. It seems, then, that McDonald's had to somewhat relax its antilingering policy and practices, as can be observed at the Beersheba location, where I have never seen attempts such as those described by Yan, to encourage customers to leave. One possible reason is that the large number of Bedouin customers and employees affects the way in which the location operates, with Bedouin employees and customers following conventions of Bedouin hospitality, which expect, and even demand, long visits while enjoying the sense of modernity entailed by the speed of operation, which is appreciated for symbolic rather than practical reasons.

Two other components of the McDonald's ambiance mentioned by my interlocutors as appealing are: cleanliness and low sound levels (silence or *sheket*). Since these qualities were mentioned offhandedly in different conversations, it took me some time to realize that they were somehow referred to in many of the conversations I held. Here again, just like with the notion of time, Bedouins (and Arabs in general) are stereotypically described as dirty and noisy. Opting for a place that's efficient and fast, clean and quiet, can be understood as a critical rejection of Bedouin traits—as when my interlocutors compared McDonald's to food venues in their home towns and pointed out that they're clean and quiet, while Bedouin food venues are dirty and noisy. It could also be a critical rejection of the Jewish stereotyping of the Bedouins as slow, dirty, and loud. Most probably, both explanations contribute to McDonald's popularity.

It is important to note that the word "modernity" in any form never came up in my conversations with Bedouin customers. Modernization was referred to indirectly through the appreciation of speed, cleanliness, and silence.

FREEDOM

Yan[32] argues that a sense of *equality* among customers, and between customers and employees, are important elements to the attraction of McDonald's for Beijing customers. This is especially true for those located lower on the People's Republic of China social ladder: that is, youngsters and specifically young female professionals. In a hierarchical society where gender and age define social rights and determine acceptable behavior in public spaces, a new generation of young female professionals find in McDonald's a space where the social intolerance to, and critique of, dining publicly alone, eating in the company of women only, or just being a female and eating alone, are suspended: everyone who comes to McDonald's is treated equally by the employees. And while Chinese restaurants are geared toward food sharing among co-diners, McDonald's and the other fast-food venues Yan studied accommodate, and even promote, personal preferences and offer individual meals and seating arrangements by default.

While a sense of equality (between Jews and Arabs/Bedouins) and modernity entice Bedouin customers to Beersheba's McDonald's, my data suggests the (relative) *freedom* from Bedouin social restrictions and boundaries plays an important role in attracting these customers. Like in Beijing, this is especially true for those at the lower levels of the Bedouin social structure: youngsters, women, and especially young women. The next several dialogues, though short, are quite complex and are therefore discussed in some detail to render their meanings and show how they relate to freedom.

Mother and teenage daughter from the largest Bedouin town of Rahat: "We ordered in 130 shekels [two meals and a salad]."

Nir: "Isn't it very expensive, like a restaurant?"

Mother: "Yes . . . she was at a medical check and I wanted to make her happy."

Nir: "Do you like the food here?"

Mother: "Yes . . . it's okay."

Nir: "In Rahat there is *Mansaf el Amir* [a venue that prepares takeaway trays of rice and meat] and the kebab shops at the market, which are much cheaper and tastier I think."

Mother: "Yes . . . I order on the phone from one of the places, which I know is clean. We pick it up and eat at home."

Nir: "Why don't you eat at the place?"

Mother: "It is dirty . . . and in the middle of the market, everyone is looking . . . here it is quiet."

Mother: ("from the North"—the Arab town Aarabeh—with two young children, commenting on the conversation above): "It is not acceptable (*mekubal*) for young women from the sector (*migzar*) to eat out . . . so in Rahat they can't, but here they can . . . even if some men will see them here, they will not say anything."

Nir: "So, it's a question of control [*pikuah*]?"

Mother: "I think so."

First, let me emphasize again the disproportionate number of Bedouin women at the location. Beersheba's official webpage indicates that the city is the fourth largest metropolis in Israel, with a population of 215,000 residents, "serving a total of seven hundred and fifty thousand citizens of the region."[33] Other sources indicate slightly different numbers, but the data in different sources indicates that the Bedouins make up roughly one-third of the Northern Negev population. If McDonald's Beersheba's branch had attracted customers randomly, one-sixth of its clients would have been Bedouin women. The rate of Bedouin women, however, was more than 50 percent on any of my visits. Moreover, the majority of these women were in the company of other women (older or younger). Some were in the company of young men or in mixed groups of youngsters. Though the Negev population and specifically the Bedouin population are young, the salience of young Bedouins, and of young women (teenagers and those in their twenties) in particular, was clear.

The exceptional popularity of McDonald's among young Bedouin women was also confirmed by another ethnographer. I told an overseas anthropologist conducting fieldwork in a Bedouin town about my McDonald's study and her response was: "Of course, this is where young women want to be taken. When my spouse came to visit me in the *filed* [one of the Bedouin towns], the men invited him to Rahat, were they ate kebabs and smoked *nargile* [a water pipe], and the girls asked me, as they often did, to drive them to McDonald's." When I asked her why she thought the young women preferred McDonald's, she responded: "It's out of town." As we shall see, the fact that McDonald's is located out of (the Bedouin) town is crucial for the sense of freedom from social control experienced by these women.

Returning to the conversation quoted above, the first idea conveyed by the first interlocutor had to do with taste preferences. She said that the food was "okay," but agreed that she could find tastier (and cheaper!) food in her hometown. She explained, however, that she opted for McDonald's for two reasons: hygiene and social control.

Uncleanliness was the reason for avoiding Rahat's food venues, while cleanliness was the reason for purchasing to go food only in one of them (and note the internal contradiction). As noted in the previous section, cleanliness stands for modernity, and describing Rahat's food venues as dirty suggests that the speaker perceives them as old-fashioned or traditional in the negative sense of the term. In a similar vein, she juxtaposes the market to the location and suggests that the latter was quiet. Here again, the dichotomy of noisy versus quiet stands for old-fashioned versus modern.

Hygiene and noise notwithstanding, the first interlocutor explained that she was reluctant to eat at Rahat's market because "everyone is looking." Here she was making a clear statement about social control: in Rahat, and for that matter in any Bedouin public space, she would have been exposed to the Bedouin gaze and its disciplining effect. The second interlocutor, commenting on the first conversation, confirmed this point. As an outsider ("from the North"), she presented the social norms ("it is not acceptable for young women to eat out"), elaborated the consequences ("in Rahat they can't [eat out]"), and explained why both norms and consequences were not relevant to that McDonald's ("even if some men will see them here, they will not say anything"). When I finally suggested that it was about control, she agreed. Indeed, when I asked another female interlocutor whether the Bedouin employees of that McDonald's were not watching over the behavior of Bedouin customers, she responded assertively: "They will not speak." McDonald's, it seems, is perceived by the Bedouins as an ex-territory or a liminal space,[34] where the social norms are suspended and egalitarianism prevails.

This relaxation, perhaps even suspension, of Bedouin social norms and the sense of liminality it entails was also evident in the interaction between young Bedouin men and women. Such interactions are strictly limited and controlled in Bedouin public and private spheres, and breaches may lead to serious conflicts with potential dire consequences, inclusive of severe violence. Young Bedouin men and women thus look for quiet, hidden corners in non-Bedouin spaces in order to interact. Ben Gurion University's deserted staircases seem to be privileged meeting places for Bedouin students who are engaged in intensive conversations that may last hours (and include no physical contact).

But at Beersheba's McDonald's I observed loud, joyous, and assertive conversations, and even some physical contact, such as holding hands or patting shoulders. This point was stressed by a Jewish student who joined me in one of my visits, who pointed out that she has never seen young Bedouin men and women interact so freely before.

DISCUSSION: MCDONALD'S AS A LIBERATING SPACE FOR THE NEGEV BEDOUINS

How is it that the Negev Bedouins, members of a nomadic group forcefully settled by the state, and "the most marginalized and impoverished group in historic Palestine"[35] find freedom in one of the most rigid and coercive global institutions? And more specifically, how is it that young Bedouin women, who are twice and even trice marginalized (as Muslim-Arabs-Bedouins, as women, and as youngsters), find McDonald's, the epitome of modernity and globalization, a contemporary manifestation of Weber's bureaucratic iron cage, notorious for its ruthlessness in business, unhealthy food, and abuse of employees, a liberating space? In what follows I turn to the political context and specifically to the political disposition of the Israeli franchise owner and to its implications.

Omri Padan, McDonald's Israel owner and CEO, was a prominent left-wing political activist during the 1970s and 1980s, founding member of the then influential "Peace Now" movement, and an active player in the Israel-Egypt peace process. As McDonald's CEO, which he brought to Israel in 1993, he challenged hegemonic Israeli business conventions such as operating some of his branches during Sabbath or serving nonkosher food in some of them. In 2013, he refused to open a McDonald's in the Jewish settlement of Ariel in the occupied West Bank.[36] He was also early to condemn the discrimination against Arab employees in the Israeli job market.

In a rare interview with sociologists Eva Illouz and John Nick,[37] he elaborates on this last point: "The adult Arab population makes up 13% of the general population. And yet, if you look at government offices only 3% to 4% of workers are Arabs. . . . In our organization, 20% of the workers, including the managers, are Arabs."[38] Illouz and Nick, developing the term "global habitus," suggest that Padan's personal commitment to liberal ideology enlisted McDonald's Israel "in a local meaningful struggle, most noticeably for political liberalism."[39]

In this chapter I present the consequences of Padan's ideology and managerial policies. His decision to employ Arabs as equals, in regular and managerial positions, made Beersheba's McDonald's an attractive working place for Bedouins. The large number of Bedouin employees made it attractive to Bedouin customers and especially to Bedouin women, who feel more comfortable in the presence of other Bedouins. As everyone is treated equally in McDonald's (in a correct and nonpersonal manner, "by the book"), Bedouins are treated like everyone else in McDonald's and are not looked down upon or mistreated as they are all too often handled in other food venues in town. And finally, as McDonald's locations are "out of town," at least as far as my Bedouin interlocutors were concerned, these locations are perceived as liminal zones, where rigid social norms are replaced by more equal social relations. This "out of time and out of place" liminality is protected by the general agreement that all those present, customers and employees, "will not speak," that is, will not report on breaches of social etiquette that occasionally take place at McDonald's.

In this sense McDonald's, Weber's oppressive bureaucratic iron cage, the site of "the irrationality of rationality" and disenchantment and Ritzer's prime example for oppressive globalization, is a space where members of a nomadic group going through an oppressive process of sedentarization, and specifically the female members of this group, who are further marginalized due to their gender, find freedom.

BIBLIOGRAPHY

Atwood, C. P. Buddhism and popular ritual in Mongolian religion: A reexamination of the fire cult. *History of Religions*, 36(2): 112–39, 1996.

Azaryahu, M. McDonald's or Golani junction? A case of a contested place in Israel. *Professional Geographer*, 51(4): 481–92, 1999.

———. McIsrael. On the "Americanization of Israel." *Israel Studies*, 5(1): 41–64. 2000.

Beng-Huat, C. "Singaporeans ingesting McDonald's." In *Consumption in Asia* (199–217). New York: Routledge, 2002.

Brembeck, H. Home to Mcdonald's. The Domestication of Mcdonald's in Sweden." *ACR European Advances*, 7: 256–61, 2005.

Caldwell, M. L. Domesticating the French fry: McDonald's and consumerism in Moscow. *Journal of Consumer Culture*, 4(1): 5–26, 2004.

Debouzy, M. Working for McDonald's, France: Resistance to the Americanization of work. *International Labor and Working-Class History*, 70(1): 126–42, 2006.

Fabian, J. *Time and the other: How anthropology makes its object.* New York: Columbia University Press, 2014.

Fischer, C. S., and Shavit, Y. National differences in network density: Israel and the United States. *Social Networks*, 17(2): 129–45, 1995.

Illouz, E. and John, N. Global habitus, local stratification, and symbolic struggles over identity: The case of McDonald's Israel. *American Behavioral Scientist*, 47(2): 201–29, 2003.

Jakubowska, L. "Resisting Ethnicity: The Israeli State and Bedouin Identity." In C. Norstrom & J. Martin (eds), *The Paths to Domination, Resistance and Terror*. Berkeley: University of California Press, 85–105, 1992.

Massad, J. A. *Colonial effects: The making of national identity in Jordan*. New York: Columbia University Press, 2001.

McKee, E. Performing rootedness in the Negev/Naqab: Possibilities and perils of competitive planting. *Antipode*, 46(5): 1172–89, 2014.

Ram, U. Glocommodification: How the global consumes the local-McDonald's in Israel. *Current Sociology*, 52(1): 11–31, 2004.

Rarick, C., Falk, G., and Barczyk, C. The Little Bee That Could: Jollibee of the Philippines V. Mcdonald's. *Journal of the International Academy for Case Studies*, 18(3): 83, 2012.

Ritzer, G. *The McDonaldization of society: An investigation into the changing character of contemporary social life*. Thousand Oaks, CA: Pine Forge, 1993.

———. Sociological Beginnings on the Origins of Key Ideas in Sociology. New York: McGraw-Hill Education, 1994.

———. The McDonaldization of Society 6. Thousand Oaks, CA: Pine Forge, 2011.

Rothschild, L., and Darr, A. Technological incubators and the social construction of innovation networks: an Israeli case study. *Technovation*, 25(1): 59–67, 2005.

Samman, K. The temporal template of tourism: a comparative analysis of Epcot Center (Orlando) and Wadi Rum (Jordan). *Journal of Tourism and Cultural Change*, 8(4): 305–15, 2010.

Toninato, P. Romani Nomadism: "From Hetero-Images to Self-Representations." *Nomadic Peoples*, 22(1): 143–61, 2018.

Turner, V. *The Ritual Process: Structure and Anti-Structure*. Chicago: Aldin, 1969.

Toynbee, P. "Who's afraid of global culture?" In W. Hutton and A. Giddens (eds.), *Global capitalism* (pp. 191–212). New York: New Press, 2000.

Ulin, R. Terroir, and Locality: An Anthropological Perspective. In Black, R. and Ulin, R. (eds.), *Wine and culture: Vineyard to glass*, 67–84. London and New York: Bloomsbury, 2013.

Watson, J. L. (ed.) *Golden Arches East: McDonald's in East Asia*. Stanford, CA: Stanford University Press, 1997a.

———. "McDonald's in Hong Kong: Consumerism, dietary change, and the rise of a children's culture." In Watson, J. L. (ed.), *Golden Arches East: McDonald's in East Asia*, 77–109. Palo Alto, CA: Stanford University Press, 1997b.

Wu, D. Y. McDonald's in Taipei: hamburgers, betel nuts, and national identity." In Watson, J. L. (ed.) *Golden Arches East: McDonald's in East Asia*, 110–35. Palo Alto, CA: Stanford University Press, 1997.

Yan, Y. "McDonald's in Beijing: The localization of Americana." In Watson, J. L. (ed.) *Golden Arches East: McDonald's in East Asia*, 39–76. Palo Alto, CA: Stanford University Press, 1997.

———. "Of hamburger and social space: Consuming McDonald's in Beijing." In Davis, D. (ed.), *The Consumer Revolution in Urban China*. Berkeley: University of California Press, 201–25, 2000.

Yiftachel, O. Critical theory and "gray space": Mobilization of the colonized. *City*, 13(2–3): 246–63, 2009.

4

Nomadism in the Food Culture of the Yakuts and the Indigenous Peoples of Yakutia

Izabella Borisova and Antonina Vinokurova

Today, the philosophy and idea behind nomadism in its general sense as a term provokes interest not only among experts from diverse fields of studies but the general public as well. In modern-day circumstances, when people live in a strictly hierarchical society and have many burdens as well as rules to follow. Eventually, they express a desire to escape from all the pressure. Many undergo this process on a mental level, that is, an individual becomes an ideological nomad; for some people, nomadism becomes a way of life. An even more interesting paradox occurs due to the accelerating pace of life, information transmission, and cultural globalization. As strange as it may seem, the nomad philosophy of idea and culture becomes more contemporary in the age of globalization, when the cultural interweaving and interaction processes are enhanced. The aim of our research is an attempt to explain the mechanisms of interweaving and interdependence of nutrition culture of the former nomad peoples of the North, who have retained their philosophical outlook, through the prism of the nomadism philosophy. Therefore, we set a specific goal—an attempt to analyze the nomadism features in the nutrition culture of Yakutia, which is one of the autonomous republics of the Russian Federation and a former colony of the Russian Empire. Apart from the Turkic-speaking Yakuts (the Sakha), who settled these lands in the fourteenth century, and the Russians, who settled in Yakutia in the seventeenth century, there are also indigenous peoples, such as the Tungus-speaking Evens and Evenki; the Yukaghirs, speaking in an isolated language; the Turkic-speaking Dolgans (assimilated Tungus); and the Chukchi, speaking a language of the Chukot-Kamchat language family.

The concept of nomadism takes its complete form in Deleuze and Guattari's joint work *A Thousand Plateaus: Capitalism and Schizophrenia*. A complete scope of the nomadological project idea is presented in the English edition of *Nomadology*.[1] In its general meaning, nomadism is a fundamental postmodernistic attitude aimed at rejecting presumptions, which are typical for classical metaphysics, mainly: (a) presumptions of a strictly organized existence; (b) presumptions on the space being a discreetly differential category with a semantically and axiologically defining point (predominantly, of the center—acentrism and centrism); (c) the understanding of determinism as an involuntary causality, external effects (neodeterminism); (d) the distinction of fundamental oppositions of the external and internal, past and future, etc. (binarism); and (e) presumptions of the sense being an immanent object of the world, which opens up to the subject in cognitive procedures (metaphysics).

MATERIALS AND METHODS

In order to retrieve data on nomadism as a phenomenon existing in the nutrition culture of the northern peoples, it was important to study and analyze the fundamental research materials on nomadism presented by history experts in northern nutrition culture; a general overview of the interview materials gathered from informants as well as the linguistic analysis of several examples. Next, using the method of analyzing and generalizing the contemporary research materials in interdisciplinary studies, we gathered data that will further allow us to popularize them and develop a philosophical basis for studying nomadism in the context of nutrition culture through the prism of the mentality of the indigenous peoples of the North.

RESULTS

In the nomadism theory, there is a concept of nomadic singularity dispersion; these singularities "are characterized by mobility and the immanent ability to reconnect independently," which differ significantly "from the fixed and settled dispersions." The environment is seen as a "non-differential" one: "a world filled with nomadic singularities."[2] In terms of topology, this means that within the nomadic project, the environment is organized radically and nontraditionally. Firstly, this is connected with its representation as a two-dimensional space (cf. surface, two-dimensional space). In accordance with the nomadic point of view, "the genetic axis is seen an objective core unity, which gives an impulse to subsequent stages; the inner structure of similarity"; in contradiction to this, "the rhizome is anti-genealogical": it is "put into force in another dimension, which is transformational and subjective," that is, it is particularly not linear, or axial and "does not follow any structural or constituent model," "it rejects the mere thought of a genetic axis representing the deep structure."[3]

Deleuze and Guattari see the "settled" (Western) culture, as opposed to the nomad one, as one on the understanding of movement along an axis, for which the topologically external factors serve the axiological external force, which can be neglected without any semantic loss. This stands in a contradiction to the nomadic understanding of movement as a dispersed settlement, which immanently integrated the external aspects: "We create history . . . from the settled human being perspective. . . . History never comprehended nomads, books never understood external aspects of life."⁴ The most important presumption of nomadism is the one connected with programmed acentrism: space completely lacks what could have become the center (or the "General" in Deleuze and Guattari's terminology). The understanding of a rhizome as a decentered environment gives grounds for interpreting it as a self-organized system that has creative potential: "A rhizome can be split and curved . . . transfer itself to a new axis."⁵ In this particular case, the immanent nonfinal system, which is neither "stable or unstable, it is rather 'metastable' and 'possesses potential energy,'" and serves as a source of transformation and not the external causes (Deleuze).⁶

Thus, the concept of "metastability" in nomadism typologically coincides with the concept of "instability" in modern natural sciences, which deals with the process of system existence and its creative potential for self-organization and variability of the space configurations. None of the plural variants of defining rhizomes can be axiologically chosen as the favorable one (autochthonic in the ontological and correct in the interpretational sense): "Any point of the rhizome can and must be connected to any other."⁷ The objectivity of these possibilities forms a motion picture of rhizome self-organization by constituting between its temporarily important components ("singularities") of correlation, that is, *a plateau*. Singularities are not only "capable of auto-reuniting" their presence in the "nomadic dispersion" field, but also forces them to "communicate with each other,"⁸ given the obligatory condition that the rhizomes interact with the external environment (a plane serving as an interaction zone). A specific inspiring impulse (justification) for creating a dissipative plateau is the so-called paradox element in nomadism, which in itself is practically an accidental fluctuation; the paradox element also provides a certain point of versification in the process of self-organizing rhizomorphic zones forcing the singularities "to resonate, communicated and disperse."⁹ Consequently, a key moment in rhizome processing is the principal unpredictability of its future conditions: "The paradox element" is a paradox precisely because it surpasses the boundaries of knowledge, which encompasses the projected transformation space under analysis. According to Deleuze and Guattari, "This is a multitude . . . but we do not know yet what it may result in, when . . . it acquires a substantivized form."¹⁰ According to the postmodernist view of the situation, the nomadic interpretation of the world is not an exotic version of a philosophical process modeling; on the contrary, it is multiple world practice of the nomadic peoples, which philosophy is trying to comprehend from the theoretical perspective. Today, however, as strange as it may seem, nomadism helps to explain the transformations that take place in the life of the people when different cultures intervene, communicate with each other, and create new forms of culture. In the Western tradition, nomadism in its general philosophical sense is interpreted as an escape from the gestalt of a structured way of life guided by the modern government structure. Today, the nomadism of ideas is accelerated by the global network and the philosophy of globalization. However, we would like to devote our brief historical, philosophical, and anthropological study to the phenomenon of nomadism in northern nutrition. In the present study, nomadology serves as an area of interdisciplinary humanities studies; nomadism as a philosophical, culturological, and symbolic principle. Taking this into account, our philosophical, anthropological, semiotic, communicative, folklore perspective of the problem is seen as a contemporary and reasonable one.

The ethnographer S. I. Nikolaev (Somogotto) sees the multilayer nature of Yakut cuisine as its distinctive feature. Yakut cuisine comprises of Yakut-, Turkic-, and Tungus-speaking national group representatives with Samoyedic layers and, finally, adapted elements of Russian cuisine.[11] This multilayer feature, which is built following the rhizome principle, is a characteristic feature of northern nutrition.

The mechanisms of transforming and intervening nutrition cultures can be interpreted in theory from the nomadism point of view.

Rich in natural resources, the Arctic and the North provide the peoples of the North with a place for living and developing in extreme climatic and permafrost conditions. Despite their low level of population, the northern peoples have a unique culture and a high level of social and biological adaptation. Properly selected nutrition enhances the human body's adaptation to the extreme environmental conditions. It is a generally known fact that the traditional nutrition structure is an integral component of adaptation in the Arctic; it provides the body with proper nutrients that will aid in metabolism. It is in the extreme northern conditions that the nutrition of the peoples who migrated there intervenes with the local traditional forms of nutrition as a result of intercultural contact with the local population; thus, new types of nutrition are formed. The rhizome of nutrition culture of the Turkic-speaking Sakha nomads intervened with the local nutrition and this intervention was mutual. Resilience, popularity, and extinction as well as the transformation of specific dishes of the contacting cultures can only be explained from the point of view of rhizomes.

The ethnographic and historic literature contains a significant amount of data on the history and culture of the peoples of the North, where traditional nutrition is regarded as an inseparable component of the peoples' culture. Nutrition, its contents, methods of every day cooking, festive and ritual meals, typical for any kind of peoples, reflects the conditions and landscape of the peoples of the North's permanent place of residence. One of the main requirements to sustain human life in extreme climatic conditions is good quality food, which compensates the negative climatic impact on the body system, which was completely achieved at the expense of centuries of the existing system of nutrition. For these reasons, the northern people have long since devoted a great deal of attention to healthy nutrition. Due to their economic activities, meat and fish products form the basis of nutrition for the Sakha people and the indigenous peoples of the North; however, the method of consuming these products varies from one local group to another, and moreover, fish products used to be unpopular among the steppe Sakha nomads.

The chaotic nature of rhizomes demonstrates the unpopularity of some products. In the nutrition culture of the indigenous peoples of the North, venison, the most popular meat among the nomad Sakha people, did not become widespread, even though many other products were consumed extensively. Their nutrition mainly comprised of reindeer since reindeer in the North provided people with all the vital necessities, including the variety of nutrition. Deer meat is a universal nutrition product for the peoples of the North. Tender and easy to boil, meat is quickly processed by the digestive system. In terms of its nutrients, deer meat is more valuable compared to other kinds of meat. For the Sakha people, horse meat, and mare meat in particular, is a first-priority product; this tendency intervened into the nutrition culture of the new settling nations, Russians, in particular, who settled in Yakutia. *Stroganina* (or frozen fish/horse meat) is especially valued; it is prepared by slicing it into long, thin pieces. It is seasoned with salt or local herbs and served with pickled or crushed Arctic berries. This product was adopted in all the nutrition cultures of Yakutia.

Today, in the process of a transformation in the method of serving it, stroganina is served at the table with onions, peppers, and vinegar. The indigenous peoples of the North prefer deer meat. The main preference in the northern nutrition is given to meat, which is commonly served in three ways: a specially steam-cooked meat, stroganina, and dried. Dried meat is made using a special thermal processing technique; it is simply dried outside in the frost and wind. If it is cooked at a food-producing factory, the cooking technique is different. Dried meat is becoming an integral part of all nutrition cultures. Today it is considered a delicacy.

Fishing is an ancient activity among the local population. In Indigirka and Kolyma, fish was served as a substitution for bread: Russian old-timers lost the habit of eating bread and many people in that region do not even know how it tastes. Fish was boiled in the summertime and conserved—it was dried, pickled in pits, and stored in the layers of permafrost; it was made into stroganina (frozen raw fish *ukola* [dried raw fish]), and even mashed into powder. Fish bellies and burbot liver were eaten raw; the insides and caviar were fried. Fish caviar was also used to make flat cakes.

In the summertime, people cooked fish by wrapping it into willow leaves for a day. The healing properties of fish fat are well known. It is fully digested and provides the human body with vitamins that are not contained in other products. Fish products firmly established themselves in the nutrition culture of the Sakha people. Thus, *balyk* (fish products) became an integral part of nutrition culture of the people who migrated to the North. The Sakha people living in the Viluy River regions have mastered the technique of pickling syma fish. This is a result of the rhizome penetrating the northern nutrition. N. G. Vasilyev states that properly cooked syma is healthy, rich in vitamins, and nutritious.[12]

Intervening into the Sakha nutrition culture, fishing brought with it prohibitions and rituals, which are still followed. For instance, a person who participates in a funeral ceremony is considered *kirdekh* (filthy) during a forty-day time period; for this reason, this person could not take part in fishing. Fishing for carp/sobo is popular nationwide and is especially valued by the Sakha people. Sobo became one of the most popular fish products in nearly the entire territory of Yakutia. The introduction and further spreading of the fishing culture is also seen in the Russian nutrition culture among the representatives living in Yakutia: the popularity of fish products and fishing in general is a very popular activity among the Russian population that migrated here.

Food collecting was a secondary activity for the indigenous peoples of the North. The northern peoples did not purposely attempt to store berries, nuts, or edible roots for the winter. Everything they collected was consumed as a fresh product. Using wild-growing herbs to cook meals became a part of the nutrition culture among the Sakha people who settled here. Apart from the imported tea, they would drink flower, briar berry, and fireweed leaf tea. They collected edible, herbal, and household plants. The tradition of storing berries, mushrooms, and onions was not typical for the peoples of Yakutia; the indigenous peoples of the North considered mushrooms to be the "ears" of the evil forces.

By the end of the nineteenth and the beginning of the twentieth century, the indigenous peoples of the North and the Russian populations (who arrived in the seventeenth) had a diet mainly comprised of products collected and self-produced in the household: deer meat (in the North), horse and beef, fish, deer milk (in the North), cow milk (in the central and western Yakutia and in the northeast), and wild-growing edible plants. Starting from the seventeenth century, flour, bread, and vegetables began to spread sporadically under the influence of the Russian rhizome, thus, becoming a part of the traditional nutrition. However, the traditional meat-and-fish method of nutrition preserved itself as the key method for quite an extensive period of time, including during the Soviet period. For instance, until the 1960s, the Evens from the region of Beryozovka rarely consumed bread but stored flour.[13] In the seventeenth and eighteenth centuries, owing to the Russian-Yakut trade relations, the northern peoples gained access to flour, grains, salt, tea, sugar, tobacco, and vodka. Nevertheless, the level of consumption of these items was insignificant due to the high cost for both wealthy and poor families.

Meat, fish, and berries form the basis of the indigenous peoples' nutrition in the circumpolar zone; a typical feature of their nutrition is the absence of first course meals and dairy products. First course meal consumption gradually entered the Sakha and Russian nutrition cultures. The Sakha have a large variety of soups that have their own names in the Yakut languages: *sulumakh min* (or *min*)—broth—*selieidekh min*. This soup was introduced later with the introduction of flour, and its Russian name adopted in the Yakut language serves as proof to this. *Seliei* is an adapted Russian word for jelly of non-native origin (in French *gelée*). Seliei also became a part of the indigenous peoples of the North nutrition.

Penetrating the peoples' nutrition culture, the rhizome leads to an adaptation to particular nutrition preferences; in the course of this process, some of the products are replaced or transformed, a phenomenon that manifests itself in the language. Presently, the vocabulary reflecting the no longer existing and unpopular nutrition products has become archaic. The following examples illustrate this in the Yakut language: (1) *Koyu kymys* (*konnyu kymys koyurgen*) is a fermented dairy drink, with a larger concentration of alcohol and gas. Consumed in large amounts, it can cause minor intoxication. (2) *Samal kymys* is a fresh, lightly brewed kumis. (3) *Hara kymys*, a kind of kumis, which is not flavored with butter, cream, or milk in the process of fermentation. In the old times, kumis was flavored with cream or melted butter before serving. This kind of flavoring was called *arakh*. Just like the variety of formerly popular drinks, these words have entered the passive vocabulary.[14]

However, making a drink out of fermented cow's milk is called *byppakh* or *byyppakh* and it is a popular drink. Today, this drink has become more popular than mare's milk because its preparation requires less work.

The ritual porridge *salamat*, which is used to appease all the gods of the Yakut pantheon, is still popular today; it is also made by the northern peoples, influenced by the Yakut culture. It has its variations, which are often differentiated: *Aiyyhyt salamaata/Salamat* of the Goddess of Fertility, *Aiyyhyt*, which was presented to the goddess and to the woman who just gave birth to a child and *Uruu salamaata*, a wedding salamaat. The fermented milk and other dairy product names are used frequently: *suorat* (a variety of kefir), *korchekh* (whipped cream), *iedzhegei* (cottage cheese), *chohon* (*kobuor* and bohukye). The other names that were used to denote whipped cream are being forgotten, such examples include: *dagda, koppoku, koppooku, moruos*. The following word units are also archaic: *sumekh, tar, bolonokh, urumye, Viluy style agharaan* (*tar* or *suorat* with berries), *ongurgestekh uut* (milk with sinew), *Sardaanalaakh koppooku* (fresh whipped cream with the Sardana [lily] flower and berries), *tar koppooku, itiirdekh uut* (milk with beef abdomen fat). There is a large variety of archaic vocabulary denoting meat dishes. As for the languages of the indigenous peoples, in the 1960s, such words had become archaic and passive in the modern Evenki language: *nokcha, kolbo, taki, urgan, charda*, and *barcha*.

The transformation of the non-native peoples' nutrition rhizome among the indigenous peoples of the north manifested itself in the qualitative and quantitative improvement of the nutrition ingredients. Food distinction, based on its national origin, was no longer considered.

The most prominent examples of nomadism are hunting tools and dishes prepared with game. There are many beliefs in the Sakha culture connected with eating bear meat; these beliefs were adopted from northern cultures. An entire play unfolds in the process of eating meals prepared with bear meat. People pretended that a raven was eating the bear meat and imitated the sounds of the raven calling. While preparing the dish called bear paw," it is boiled and fried whole and served on a large dish to the hunter himself and to the honorable guest. *Luorpakh*, a dish made of bear meat and intestines, is served during a ceremonial and semi-ritual lunch after a successful bear hunt.

Many traditions connected with hunting interweave with different cultures so intensely that it explains the indigenous peoples of the North and non-native peoples' rhizome interpretation. In its general sense, nomadism, which displays situational circumstances and the unpredictability of the hunting culture, finds its lexical representations in the Even language, for example: allusions, which were previously used as taboo during bear hunting, clearly illustrate the nomadism philosophy. The lexicon itself proves situational and in addition to the case because the nomad never knows what he will find. He is always in uncertainty. Extraction depends on what will happen during a nomadic hunt, "what the earth will bestow,", "what land has given to the debt," etc. The component of the word *mărăm* ("killed") or *bakrăm* ("retrieved," or literally, "found") can be expressed using the following expressions: *tordu an'iviyăttam* ("killed," literally, "The Earth granted it to me, I am granted something by the Earth"); *toringd'I bakarkimn;attam* ("killed," literally, "I made it slip and fall over the Earth"); toringd'I ngenukemrem ("killed," literally, "The Earth [my land] gave it to me"); *tordu bovrem (boviyettem)* ("killed," literally, "The earth gave it to me, it was given to me by the earth"); *toringd'it ilăriviyăttam* ("killed," literally, "My earth looked at me"); *toringd'I onumevrem* ("killed," literally, "My own land loaned this to me").[15]

Nature is also personified in the Sakha language: *eh'eken uchugei haraghynan kordo* (Nature [the spirit of hunting] looked upon me with a blessing), *eheken belekhtete* (The Nature [spirit of hunting] has granted me a gift). Hunting is a situational phenomenon, the result is unpredictable, and its success is difficult to explain. Hunting holds a special position in the nutrition culture of the people living in Yakutia. Today, hunting is not the main source of northern nutrition, however, it does play a significant role in the culture, entering the culture of the Russian-speaking population.

In the age of globalization, the nutrition culture rhizome interpenetration is taking place at much more accelerated rates than ever before. Our informants from the Tomponsky region told us that the nutrition lifestyle of the nomad reindeer herders had changed; although reindeer meat remains the basic source of nutrition, the peoples also use grain crops, macaroni, instant noodles, canned dry powder, and condensed milk instead of reindeer milk as well as canned meat and fish. The indigenous peoples were generally supplied with these products in the 1970s under the leadership of the director of the Tomponsky Soviet agricultural farm, V. M. Kladkin. (informants: Vera Neustroeva and Antonina Sleptsova).

"Reindeer herders' food is undergoing changes; their nutrition largely includes Chinese instant noodles called Doshirak" (informant: Andrei Valeryevich Nesterov). However, there are also traditional products that have passed the test of time, for instance, intestines pickled inside a deer's abdomen that is then filled with blood, fermented, and dried, which can be transported and added into food. Drying meat is still considered a special cooking method even today. Reindeer spinal cord meat is cut into thin thirty-centimeter-long slices, dipped into salted water, and dried hanging over a fire.

Nomad reindeer herders carry dried meat with them and eat it as a snack. Semisettled Sakha horse breeders consume modern food that they have become accustomed to: grains, macaroni, instant noodles, tinned condensed and dried milk powder instead of natural milk, tinned meat, and fish. While reindeer herders sometimes slaughter the reindeer, horse breeders are not accustomed to slaughtering horses for food. This is due to the fact that deer is much smaller in size, weighing 26.5 to 63 kilograms (slaughter weight from 45 kg). Horses become quite large as they get older. By six months old a horse reaches 105 kilograms, by two years old it weighs 150 kilograms. An adult horses reach 230 kilograms. The cost of 1 kilogram of venison is from 300 to 350 rubles, horse meat from 500 to 650 rubles.

In their everyday routine, there is a complete process of interweaving nutrition cultures. It is not only nutrition cultures that contact and intervene with each other; the same process takes place in western and eastern nutrition. Moreover, in accordance with the nomadism theory, there is no specific tendency of this interpenetration; it is a sporadic process. With Deleuze's rhizome, the rhizome of any food sprouts in any direction and in any configuration. A dish of any people can become integrated into another's culture of food and become transformed in connection with the replacement of components by local, accessible components; old and difficult is replaced by convenient and fast. For nomadism, some dishes and their penetration into any culture have no borders, no laws. The penetration and interpenetration of dishes of peoples living in the same territory as well as those that are remote geographically, occurs precisely according to the laws of rhizome. For example, the survey held within the scope of our study included 1,600 respondents and revealed that the population perceives Italian pizza, Central Asian plov, Russian pirozhki, Asian sushi, and so forth as traditional food.

DISCUSSION

One of the main conditions for a sustainable human life in extreme conditions is good-quality nutrition, which compensates the negative climatic effects. For this reason, the Evens have long since devoted special attention to healthy nutrition. Traditional cuisine of the peoples of Yakutia is justified by the traditional household and way of life as well as the natural environment and season of the year, fishing and hunting seasons, month and traditional activities cycle. In Yakutia, populated by the representatives of more than one hundred nationalities, food tastes and preferences migrate and enrich themselves owing to the mixture and interweavement of the different cultures.

Until the 1930s, food products connected with hunting, reindeer herding, and fishing prevailed in the meat-and-fish nutrition model. The local scope of food products has always been complemented by imported products (flour, grains, salt, tea, sugar, tobacco, and vodka) and its variety expanded by the middle of the twentieth century. Product exchange and trading emerged from the time of the first contacts, predominantly with the Russian population from the beginning of the seventeenth century. Undoubtedly, the process of integrating into the Soviet economic structure played a key defining role in the life and sustainability system changes, including the nutrition culture of the peoples of the North. Soviet culture and the Soviet type of management with centralized supply and delivery of products unified all regions of the Soviet Union and became a rhizome that transformed traditional food.

It is widely known that social factors play a significant role in forming nutritional choices. In the prerevolutionary period, meals that included local and imported products prevailed in the nutrition of wealthy families, while the less fortunate made use of a lesser variety of foods and in small quantities. After the 1930s, there was a tendency toward a unified nutrition system, when the peoples of the North began to fulfill the main nutrition necessities of the population. The initial integration into urban civilization, culture, various meals, and recipes of other peoples dates to the same time period.

A diverse change in the local peoples' nutrition took place at the end of the 1940s, that is, in the post-war period when in connection with the reasons listed below, there was a unification and sovietization of a food culture that has penetrated and sprouted (rhizoma) into all food cultures. A considerable impact was caused by the development of food production in the country as well as factors such as trade and economic relations, centralized provision of the population and the expansion of the following spheres: the social nutrition factory branches, public services, power electricity, and gas supply, and so forth. All these aspects had a significant effect on the variety of products and food preparation methods.

Meanwhile, in the 1950s to 1980s, there was a balance in the consumption levels among diverse social groups; this was a result of a unified social and economic housing basis created for all citizens of the former USSR. This led to a leveling in the regional nutrition zones.[16]

Presently, there is enrichment in the cuisine of the peoples of the North with other peoples' national dishes. Given this, however, traditional cuisine retains its popularity in the form of delicacy and solemn food. Our field research data shows that there is still a preference toward meat and fish dishes among the population. The main imported products, such as flour, bread, salt, tea, pasta products, and sunflower oil became everyday items by the middle of the twentieth century.

The analysis of the materials shows that the mutual intervening process into the nutrition system of the peoples of Yakutia took place in the following aspects:

- Improvement in economy management techniques
- Expansion of agricultural, economical, and ethno-cultural contacts (cultural interdependency, goods trade, foreign borrowings)
- Social and economic changes (economic reforms in the 1980s, etc.)
- Negative effects in the traditional nutrition of the peoples of Yakutia after the natural ecological changes connected with industrial development of the northern territories took place (e.g., pollution of the rivers Vilyui and Lena; some northern rivers had a reduction in the number of fish, animals, and pollution of drinking water).

At the end of the nineteenth and the beginning of the twentieth century, nutrition comprised of a traditional set of products connected with hunting and reindeer herding economics and cultural norms (i.e., meat-and-fish nutrition model). The local set of nutrition products has long since been combined with imported products, the variety of which expanded in the middle of the twentieth century. Starting from this time, there has been an improvement in the nutrition system that is based on the traditional system.

From the beginning of the 1980s, changes in the way of life resulting from radical economic reforms played an important role in the transformation of the nutrition culture. As a result of these processes, many traditional dishes, which had managed to retain themselves until this time, disappeared; this phenomenon can mostly be observed in the nontraditional living environment.

Despite the fact that the national dishes, rituals, and traditions have not been preserved in the traditional nutrition culture of the peoples of Yakutia, and the national cuisine underwent a process of adapting to the cuisine traditions of other nations, nevertheless, it still retains itself owing to the fact that it holds a special place in the modern festive ceremonies. Thus, it is one of the symbols of ethnic uniqueness. All these ethnic groups want to preserve their cultural uniqueness in the era of globalization.

On the other hand, the Westernization of world culture, the utilization of its values in the consumer society is one of the key nomadism factors in the nutrition culture. In Yakutia, new cafes and restaurants with Asian or Western menus are being created extensively. The development of international cuisine complicates the forms of self-identification in one's native ethnic and culture environment; this process takes place through the persuasion of the consumers to try various exotic dishes such as sushi, fugue fish, crocodile meat, etc. Despite the fact that traditional food is preserved as festive and delicious, the development of international tourism also promotes the abandoning of national nutrition traditions in the everyday life of people, especially the young. "A cosmopolitan people" bring home not only a variety of impressions but also favorable nutrition products and recipes to surprise their friends with exotic meals.

At the same time, diet experts tend to believe that it is precisely the native product made of native food resources that is truly nutritious. The nomadism phenomenon is not appreciated by diet experts as far as nutrition is concerned.

The Yakut and the neighboring peoples' traditional system of nutrition mainly comprises of meat (horse and reindeer) and fish, dairy and herb products, as well as dairy products and herb infusions; this kind of nutrition was also the main health-care source owing to the fact that it provides a balanced diet. In the conditions of a neighboring territorial position and the connectedness to the world globalization process, the traditional nutrition culture together with the other cultural phenomena, intervene, intercept, and complement each other in accordance with the law of nomadism. One of the laws of nomadism—rhizome—explains these processes.

Nomadism in the nutrition culture of neighboring peoples is a natural process that is governed by adaptation to living conditions.

Nomadism in the globalization process is governed by the increasing rate of information exchange owing to the worldwide web and to the growing levels of population mobility.

However, nomadism in the nutrition culture is transforming the long-standing traditional nutrition preferences that cause the following problems:

1. Some traditional forms of nutrition are ceasing to exist or are transforming.
2. Due to the increasing rate of population growth, the transformation of nutrition, and the degrading ecology of the environment, the problem of providing the population with natural nutrition products is becoming a vitally important issue.
3. In severe climatic conditions of the North, the replacement of natural products with artificial ones and the violation of the protein-lipid nutrition type of nutrition leads to constantly increasing numbers of individuals with cardiovascular disease, diabetes, and endocrinological and oncological diseases.

Given such conditions, there is an increasing role in popularizing the traditional, long-standing experience in nutrition culture. In recent years we have seen a growing interest in traditional nutrition; however, due to their high cost, ecologically clean local products are not available to most of the population.

ACKNOWLEDGMENTS

This research was published with the financial support of the Russian Foundation for Basic Research, and "The Problem of Valorization and Popularization of the Nutrition Culture of the Peoples of the North in Modern Conditions (through the Example of Yakutia)," No. 17-21-08001. The authors give their gratitude to all participants in the research.

INFORMANTS

Nikolai Semyonovch Khabarovsky, born in the village of Berozovka, Srednekolymsky Region, Sakha Republic (Yakutia), a representative of the Doida family.

Vera Neustroeva, reindeer herder/reindeer skin tent worker, born in the village of Topolinoye, Tomponsky Region, Sakha Republic (Yakutia).

Antonina Sleptsova, a teacher of culture, Tomponskaya Comprehensive School, born in the village of Topolinoye, Tomponsky Region, Sakha Republic (Yakutia).

Andrei Valeryevich Nesterov, reindeer herder, born in the village of Berozovka, Srednekolymsky Region, Sakha Republic (Yakutia).

BIBLIOGRAPHY

Deleuze, G., and Guattari, F. Rizhome. *A Thousand Plateaus: Capitalism and Schizophrenia—An Online Almanac*, Vostok Press, 2005.

Deleuze, G., and Guattari, F. Rizhome. *Nomadology*, New York: Semiotex, 1986.

Robbek, V. A., and Robbek, M. E. *Evensko-Russkiy Slovar-Evedy-nuchidi toreruk* (Evenki-Russian Dictionary). Novosibirsk: Nauka Press, 2004, 356.

Robbek, M. E. *Traditsionnaya pisha evenov* (Traditional Food of the Evens). Novosibirsk: Nauka Press, 2007, 164.

Seroshevsky, V. L. *Yakuty* (the Yakuts), Vol.1. St. Petersburg: 1896, 315.

Somers-Hall, Henry, "Deleuze's philosophical heritage: unity, difference, and onto-theology." The Cambridge companion to Deleuze / Daniel Smith, Henry Somers-ll (eds.). Cambridge: Cambridge University Press, 2012, 337–56.

Yakutsko-russkiy slovar (Yakut-Russian Dictionary). Moscow: Sovietskaya Entsiklopedia Press, 1972.

5

Circulating Food Practices and Food Representations of Senegalese Inhabitants of Bordeaux and Dakar

Chantal Crenn

Exploring the food practices of Senegalese[1] individuals from Bordeaux who begin traveling again[2] after retirement is an effective means of bypassing certain preconceived notions regarding the food cultures of immigrants and minorities in France, which are typically confined to the continuity/discontinuity dichotomy.[3] In effect, the retired Senegalese men (and occasionally women[4]) discussed in this chapter, who have lived in Bordeaux for thirty or forty years as factory workers or janitors, have, over the course of their lives, created new styles of food consumption. They have imported foods in their luggage (millet; *tiof* fish; *bouy* juice, a beverage made from baobab fruit; *hako* leaves from the *niébé* bean, etc.), have promoted the development of so-called African food stores in order to obtain broken rice from Thailand, fresh or dried fish, peanut butter, peanut flour, palm oil, millet or corn groats, niébé leaves, spices, bouillon cubes, etc., and have been vectors of culinary innovation (corn-based couscous, *cëe bu jen* made with Arcachon fish, *tiakri* made from wheat couscous, *yassa* chicken with mussels, etc.). By settling in France, Senegalese (or Serer, Fulani, or Wolof) culinary practices have thus reinvented themselves. Generally speaking, when it comes to food practices, nothing remains the same over time, and nothing circulates or travels without becoming transformed. But for the retired Senegalese discussed here, the process of food transformation does not stop there. When they retire, these men (and, more rarely, women) follow the same path in reverse by moving to Senegal temporarily, where they begin another food hybridization process and then return to France to begin yet another. These retirees proceed to "put down new roots"[5] in a cyclical manner because they alternate between multiple moves and stays in familiar places, each time putting into play the connections between nativeness and place of origin. Thus, I propose the hypothesis that their dietary practices are nomadic because these retirees do not stay in the same place throughout the year but circulate between fixed points and are therefore confronted by dietary practices that

are simultaneously different, recurrent, and changing. By following the food journeys of older individuals who I will refer to as "intermittent-combined cosmopolitan
travelers"[6] and their wives (who most often reside permanently in Bordeaux), this
chapter will show how their repeated journeys and moves consist of nomadic dietary
practices and representations that, over the course of their personal timelines (notably ageing, divorce, and unemployment), adapt to the different social, economic,
familial, and political contexts that they encounter.

After establishing the methodological and theoretical framework, I will first examine how, by their presence in Dakar, these immigrants participate in the construction
of a distinctive Senegalese identity integrating "Western food" that has been validated since colonization and reinforced by globalization. However, this part of the
chapter will show that, even though while in Dakar these individuals demonstrate
the economic success achieved through their *adventure* abroad, the "high cost of
living" characterizes their everyday experiences. The chapter will then analyze how
mobility and travel engender dietary practices and reflexive discourses about food
that mark the transition from one world to another (the end of some practices and
the beginning of others) and, particularly, at the point of departure, in non-places[7]
including the airplane, the layover in Casablanca, Madrid, etc. I engaged in a serious
consideration of the eating experiences that occur in the "non-places" of airports,
which are just as much a part of their relationship to the world and to Others than
the most traditional forms of territorial belonging. Even more so, the complex link
that places and non-places maintain with dietary uses and representations seems fundamental to me. It provides an opportunity to think about localization and mobility,
identity and relationships together.

FROM A PRIVATE AND NOMADIC ETHNOGRAPHY
TO THE CONCEPT OF A *FOODSCAPE*

To follow these transnational food practices, I engaged in nomadic ethnography. The
questions that I encountered were knowing how to determine, outline, or construct
fields for studying the dietary practices of retirees who have become mobile again,
and how to "practice" as an anthropologist in this atypical field. Atypical because,
for a long time, researchers have explored migratory phenomena based on where
the migrants arrive and, more recently, where they depart from. They therefore
observed fixed places and fixed time points. In contrast, the idea here was to envis-
age migratory food practices as a process, a social fact characterized by the notion
of "movement," and to reflect on what this could mean on a methodological level.
If migration is above all movement from one point to another, which implies that
migrants settle in a single place, then my study, which is more concerned with people
who circulate from one international territory to another, must postulate the intrinsic instability of the food practices that this flow generates. In other words, it must
include a consideration of different eating practices, changes in the social status of

the eaters, the permanent (re)negotiation of their relationships with fellow diners, the repeated adaptation of their eating behaviors, and the changing nature of their feelings of belonging. Thus, given that the goal was to gain an overall understanding of retirees' travels as a combination of different moves and phases, it seemed to me that it would not be useful to study their eating practices solely from a single fixed point. In contrast, it seemed necessary to vary the contexts of observation and expression. This approach presupposes that the observer is mobile. Here, mobility can be understood in two ways: mobility *between* areas and "mobility" *as* an area. I chose to consider both modalities. For several years (2010, 2011, and 2015), I therefore immersed myself in the "circulating territories"[8] traversed and constructed by these men and women who were between sixty and eighty years old at the time of the study. By visiting the two places where they lived, as they did, and by traveling with them in the third place (between different destinations), I became immersed in their international migratory space. In kitchens in Dakar and Bordeaux, meal preparation was punctuated with the sharing of secrets and confidences. By observing marketplaces in Dakar where provisions are purchased on a daily basis, I also grasped the extent to which food had become central to their new everyday existence. More than thirty accounts of eating practices were collected from these migrants and their family members between 2010 and 2015, in France as well as in Senegal. Being a good ethnographer, I kept field notebooks recording my many culinary, emotional, and lived experiences derived from personal immersion.

From a theoretical point of view, rather than Jean-Pierre Corbeau's "eating triangle,"[9] which posits that eating practices are the result of the meeting of a "socially identified eater," a "food," and a "situation," the concept of a *foodscape* seemed best suited to exploring how the *nomadic foodways* hypothesis proposed by Isabelle Bianquis and Jean-Pierre Williot characterizes the eating practices of retirees from Bordeaux. In my opinion, the most stimulating understanding of the concept of a foodscape is that proposed by the philosopher Rick Dolphijn.[10] According to Dolphijn, a foodscape shows how, from a micro-sociological point of view, unique eating events create and re-create themselves at each meeting between eater and food. The foodscape concept thus permits a complex analysis of the place that eating occupies in our contemporary worlds, marked by the reinforcing influence of relocation (urban migration, expatriation, tourists side by side with individuals who have been exiled due to wars and dictatorships), the rise in nationalist ideologies, and economic globalization. With reference to the work done by Arjun Appaduraï, it seems crucial to me to take into consideration that fact that the lives of these elderly Senegalese retirees are undoubtedly transformed by their rediscovered mobility, but also by the disconnect between an increasingly global production (virtual family neighborhoods facilitated by the internet, daily consumption of "foreign" or familiar products due to intensive agriculture, transport, etc.), and localist or even nationalist rhetoric and frameworks for existence, in which food plays a central role. Nevertheless, taking an anthropological interest in the global food landscape (which is often impossible to grasp) needs to be approached carefully. Thus, the material dimension of eating allowed me to bring some reality to Dolphijn's food landscape metaphor and to re-anchor it in the everyday life of these retirees. This allows the movement of ideas, values, and economic systems, as well as the circulation of foods, tools, and cookbooks, which accompany these individuals in a way that is not solely abstract, to be integrated into the analysis of nomadic foodways in a concrete way. In addition, products, dishes, and recipes circulated and circulate independently of migrants via commercial networks. Taking into account the social life of foods as merchandise[11] shows the extent to which they necessarily undergo change when they are moved. They metamorphose from a symbolic point of view because once they have left their point of departure, once they have (re)started to travel, foods can be consumed for new reasons and elicit different emotions than those that they produced in the context of their place of departure (contexts that vary as a function of location, in this case, France or Senegal). The foods are also transformed from a nutritional point of view due to different cooking styles, changes in serving sizes, and the use of new utensils for cooking or eating them. Therefore, does finding identical foods at one end or another of a journey necessarily indicate similar consumption?

With regards to Mexicans living in the United States, Françoise Lestage[12] shows that the regional food specialties originating in Mexico and sold in the United States reestablish links between families in both places but are transformed into an identity-based and political argument during the migration process. Similarly, the Senegalese, by transporting and selling one type of food or another in Senegal, do not reproduce an identical social order but perform it for a new public: "people from Bordeaux," who may be white Africans, diners in search of a new exotic option, left-wing militants, and so on.

In the same way, similar to the equatorial migrants studied by the British anthropologist Emma Abbots,[13] I will show the extent to which these retirees are undoubtedly influenced by the dietary practices of their family members and the foods present in Senegal and also how, in their turn, they indirectly influence practices in the North (notably through restaurants) within the framework of globalization. Food mobility, in its diversity between societies and cultures, participates in globalization in the same way (at a smaller scale) as work, leisure activities, or tourism do. In this sense, could the practices of Senegalese retirees enable a more general analysis of the mobilities, dietary changes, and social relationships associated with them?

SENEGALESE RETIREES FROM FRANCE IN A SENEGALESE SOCIETY AND FOOD UNCERTAINTY

The relationships between these retirees and their families are profoundly influenced by the disadvantaged Senegalese economic context, in which getting enough to eat every day is a problem. They are distressed to see their elderly brothers and sisters have to continue working to earn enough money for their households' daily expenses (*dépense quotidienne*, DQ). Their nephews or nieces are typically unemployed and live under the same roof as their parents (with their own children), whereas when they migrated to Europe in the 1970s, the liberation of young couples was manifested by living away from the family. The riots "against the high cost of living" that they sometimes participated in in Dakar, at the end of the 2000s, persuaded them of the absolute necessity of their financial aid. The increase in the price of wheat led to an increase in the price of bread (*toubab* baguette), which, since colonization, has become a key food for residents of Dakar. However, they also struggle to provide for their families' needs in France (rent, food, children's studies, etc.). Thus, when they return, they are expected to distribute the riches that they have supposedly accumulated in France since they have had access to enough food to allow them to have a "full stomach," or *Biir bu fes* in Wolof, and are also expected to reproduce what their family members consider to be Western food norms, which are symbols of modernity. The family hopes to find fries, canned green beans or sardines, jarred mayonnaise, pasta, chocolate spread, margarine, Maggi brand bouillon cubes (from Bordeaux), broken rice from Thailand, juice, carbonated drinks, etc. in their glasses and bowls, that they can then tell wonderful stories about. "French" ways of eating—Tijane in response to the extraversion model that is still underway in Senegalese society—remain distinctive and highly valued, especially in relation to the neighbors. Tijane, who formerly worked for Ford in Bordeaux, routinely sits out front of the corner store at the end of the day to watch television and chat. He understands that the street is not only a means of getting from place to place as it is in Bordeaux, but also constitutes the main space for socializing, where there is an obligation to exchange greetings, avoid certain topics, and modify your behavior depending on which people are present and what groups have formed. The road and its neighborhood shops (often owned by people from France) are a place for gossiping, where subjects such as the price of food and people's cooking skills are discussed. It is here that people's behaviors, and especially those of people from France, are commented on as well as their solidarity. In Pikine and Guédiawaye, suburbs of Dakar, almost every family has a member from France, Italy, Spain, and so forth. Tijane listens to his neighbors explain the cultural aspects of the West through a description of the abundant and modern food that can be purchased even on the pensions[14] received by retirees who have returned from France. He notes the extent to which the presence of "the returned," according to the common expression, allows those who stayed behind to share their journey and their success in their imaginations through food. But even though "food modernity" is thus validated through neighborhood relationships and by members of the extended family, it is more important to these family members that the migrant's financial means to be able to feed that whole (extended) family and that the migrants demonstrate an "African solidarity" that does not change the established social order. For example, this involves (especially for men) accepting the choices made regarding the communal meal (amount of meat, rice, and oil, number of bouillon cubes, use of hot peppers, etc.) by the woman in charge of the kitchen that day, and being generous during religious ceremonies (*Korité* [end of Ramadan], *Tabaski* [*Aïd El Kébir*, important religious event], *Gamou* [celebration of the birth of the prophet], etc.), which allow the maximum number of people to be invited and fed in a country where it is also extremely important to "be able to show up without being invited." The retirees from France soon invest in huge pots and ladles that enable them to cook for hundreds of acquaintances as well as party tents and hundreds of chairs that allow them to fill the street and entertain their guests "at home."

Thus, by buying a sheep for *Tabaski* and delegating a nephew to butcher it in the street, which is considered "backward" by their own children in France, they ensure that their position as the eldest and their generosity are recognized. By engaging in a second religious marriage with a female cousin who will cook for them (and who will sometimes be "told off" by these retirees, who are often diabetic due to their use of certain qualities and quantities of oil and sugar), they are considered "consolidators" of family links. They thereby demonstrate their (expected) economic success as well as that of the entire family. In the same way, by orchestrating the arrival of their children from France (for a baptism or for *Tabaski*), who are then fed and housed by the extended family (reimbursed by the retirees from France), they give physical form to the fiction of familial solidarity (or the supposed culture of Senegalese hospitality). All these eating codes, Tijane, Samba, Ibrahima, etc. are (re)learned and adopted by them.

They create unique food pathways by choosing to combine their own food practices with those of their family members at specific times. Combining these practices provides a unique affirmation of their role as food purveyors, while also freeing them from familial control. Effectively, once these obligations have been fulfilled, they can realize themselves in different ways, in other areas, and at other times. For the retirees from France, combining these approaches signifies submitting to the values of the extended family while still allowing them to lead a life that fulfills their values and their personal aspirations as much as possible, and to direct their efforts in a way that makes sense and that will be become part of their story, a coherent story that holds them together.

Thus, the meticulous ethnography of refrigerators that I performed (refrigerators that these retirees buy as soon as they get settled, fearing for themselves and their health, due to the absence of cold food storage options) reveal the secrets of their subjective positions. They quickly learn that the shopping habits[15] that they are used to in France do not make sense. The women of the household (sister-in-law, niece, cousin, maid), who take turns being responsible for purchasing supplies and overseeing the kitchen, adapt the kinds and quantities of purchases made to the number of diners expected and their social rank.[16] In addition, buying vegetables, meat, fish, condiments, and oil depends on the DQ that is available each day (which can vary dramatically) and on being able to keep them fresh. Feeding between fifteen and twenty[17] people per day makes it difficult to store food, on top of which owning a refrigerator is a luxury. Few people own one due to the expense and the cost of electricity. For this, they depend on brothers and sisters, uncles or aunts who have returned from France.

In this regard, Harry's sliced bread and Bonne Maman apricot jam brought over from Bordeaux indicate the presence of people from France. Nevertheless, these products disappear quickly from refrigerators, and over time are replaced with fish waiting to be gutted from the neighbors. In the same way, the women of the family give camembert and individual yogurt pots purchased at Casino supermarkets in the wealthy areas of Dakar to the first important visitors who stop by. The control over their individual eating practices that is exerted every day by the women of the family seems, over time, insurmountable. They quickly cease to make any personal purchases. However, most of them believe that they have become "old men" whose bodies have specific nutritional needs, and that they have *toubab* health habits that they can no longer change, for example, eating a healthy diet. The absence of inspection stamps on meat (which is often unrefrigerated and covered with flies) purchased in the marketplace worries them. They are reassured—to a certain extent—when the stamp is visible, even though they know that counterfeiting is common in the abattoirs. But it is also the desire to eat steak-frites while seated on a chair at a table from an individual plate that is impossible to fulfill in the poor suburb where they have built their house (and where they provide lodging, as we have seen, for multiple family members), that makes them realize that they have fully become foreigners. "I go to my room to have a snack and every five minutes someone comes in asking me if I'm alright. Of course I'm alright! But I'd be even better if people left me alone!" (Samba, sixty-four years old, retired from Ford). In contrast to the responsibility that falls on them to "fill the bellies" of family members who are supposedly big eaters, many tell me that their "stomach, too, wants what it's used to." Does the need for a "full belly," which is described as an ethnic permanence and that retirees in Bordeaux must absolutely satisfy thanks to the money earned in France, is not rather related to the context of the 2000s (the context of this study)? At that time Dakar experienced urban manifestations "against the high cost of living" and in particular the prices of basic food products. Could this "belly," which is specifically "Senegalese" and must be filled by the people from France who have become "light eaters," perhaps conceal the daily increase in the price of foodstuffs that the family members are confronted with, while the quantity and the presence of each ingredient required remain important? On the contrary, the physical emotions of the act of eating alone, eating a single[18] measured portion (for the diabetics), one serving of rice with fish, a hamburger, or a yogurt, triggers for these retirees, reveal how these practices allow them to break with the food norms that are dominant in the family context. The feeling of enjoying food when eating alone, in the city, is experienced intimately when face-to-face with the food, eyes closed, as if in a private ceremony that allows the self to be rediscovered, so much so that silence falls. In urban Dakar, restaurants, taxis, and supermarkets allow them to reclaim some freedom for themselves. My first meeting with the retirees from Bordeaux took place over fast-food at Ali Baba, an "institution" in Dakar.[19] These retirees, who are considered fortunate[20] compared to the rest of the Senegalese population, make a hobby of eating at fast-food or barbecue restaurants and, like other middle-class consumers in Dakar, participate in the urban creativity in Plateau (Dakar's historical and colonial quarter), thereby validating trends toward extraversion in Dakar. For their family members who live in this difficult economic context, which is even more difficult in a poorer suburb like Pikine, eating an expensive meal does not constitute a family "betrayal," but a form of agency.

Gastric pain (always stomach pains due, according to them, to the unsanitary water, hot peppers, and the saturation of dishes with mustard and pepper, also make their "returns" extremely reflective. Have they become physically maladapted to their families' living conditions? For the next trip, their suitcases will be filled with water filters, water purification tablets, spices, "French" Maggi cubes, olive oil, and protective stomach medication, while little by little sofas and low tables (even tall tables and chairs) will replace carpets and "meals on the floor"[21] in order to circumvent the feats of physical endurance that these different stays require of them.

For these men, retirement, which signifies their entry into old age, should be accompanied by a sort of "letting go" that is considered possible in Senegal because older people are, according to them, supported and pampered. Before "returning," they imagined that the women of their family would be entirely at their disposal, particularly from a culinary point of view, in response to their status as older men. This is a form of devotion that their wives in Bordeaux, who are younger than themselves and still working, do not display any more. On the contrary, it may even be said that the gender roles are reversed in France. Now that they do not have any work-related obligations, when they are in Bordeaux they must take responsibility for providing food, sometimes preparing meals, making sure their school-aged children are fed, taking them to doctors' appointments, and so forth. As they consider this situation to be demeaning, they hope that, by moving to Senegal, they will occupy the recognized status of *magget* (old man or old woman); but, as we have seen, this is not always the case.

In fact, having become inheritors of a wage-earning French society in the 1980s and 1990s, when the emergence of a positive individual was possible thanks to the protector state, in Dakar (where the state is almost absent) they are confronted with the rejection of the "individualist individual" and find that the community constraints remain very strong. Thus, family reunions—sometimes after many years of separation—are critical moments that may awaken ambivalent feelings and have effects that are contradictory, or at least unexpected, for the people from France, who believe at first that they will be taking up their "rightful place" as elders. Thus, the expression *yaa ngi lekk xaalis bi* ("you eat money"), which is commonly used by Senegalese in Bordeaux to say of a family member that he has had a good life and that he has wasted the money that he earned in France through hard work, can be used against him. These migrants, who are considered to be rich and often not generous, are also accused of "eating money" while "they," who have to remain, are limited to a rudimentary food consumption (most notably since the increase in wheat prices in 2008). Thus, these retired migrants are obliged to "make do" with these financial constraints, within which there is little place for dietary advice (with regards to their diabetes), counseling, and restraint.

Nevertheless, from a dietary point of view, they perceive that forms of help other than those linked to the family may exist. More horizontal forms of help are organized based on friendly relationships[22] that they succeed in forming with a nephew or a niece, or even a neighbor. They thereby put into place more creative means of organizing the daily food expense and invent a system of selective redistribution (e.g., by helping the young *talibés*[23] who beg for their marabouts in the street). Similarly, drinking alcohol is a dietary practice that is engaged outside of the family circle. Alcohol plays a central role in some of the life stories of retirees from Bordeaux and is associated with their youth and liberation from the older generation. Alcohol also contributes to the feeling of having lived in a historic time, which some individuals associate with the Indépendances and May 1968. Drinking alcohol is banned in Senegal as a Muslim country. To depart from this rule is to emancipate oneself from those who hold the power of the Muslim norm: the elders. Drinking alcohol in France also had the function of making possible the participation in the way of life of the globalized youth, which was impossible in Senegal during colonization.

However, in Senegal, "partying with alcohol" is now frowned upon.[24] While the practice of "drinking" is maintained by some individuals, it involves multiple tactics: visiting French restaurants with people from France to drink a bottle of Bordeaux, discreet get-togethers at a friend's house to have a before-dinner drink, and the creation of a network centered around Senegalese restaurant owners from France who sell alcohol (such as Citron Vert in Hann Pêcheur). Though alcohol may be banned by the most religious individuals from France in an attempt to gain notability, when they move to Dakar, these individuals perceive their engagement in religious asceticism not only as a symbolic coming together with Senegalese Muslims, but also as a means of staying in good health while preparing for their own deaths as honorably as possible, as they feel themselves getting older.

THE AIRPORT BETWEEN PLACES AND NON-PLACES

The nomadic ethnography undertaken here took on its full significance when following their migrations by plane. I was able to see how the farther we got from Bordeaux and the closer we got to Dakar, or vice versa, their fears crystallized into discussions about "ageing well" or about food. Nevertheless, it is by using airports that they fulfill the value of being cosmopolitan and mobile (able to pass from one food world to another). But, as seen in the waiting areas of airports in Casablanca, Madrid, or Lisbon, they are also aware that this value, even if it is understood by their children in Bordeaux and by the most well-off residents of Dakar, is less well understood by their families in Senegal. Rather, these families consider this value to be a "physical" ability that enables them to resist eating "African" food since they have become *toubabisé* (Europeanized). It is considered to be a sort of achievement, uncoupled from its ideological value. By participating in a sort of shared traveling brotherhood,[25] I was able to understand how norms regarding "eating well" changed as a function of approaching toward or withdrawing from the country that we had left, whether France or Senegal. On a related note, Madrid is the place to have what may be the "last hamburger." Abdoulaye (sixty-three years old, retired from Ford) does not hesitate to run to Terminal 2, at the risk of missing his flight, to experience "one last time" the inimitable taste of McDonald's sauce and the golden glow of the stainless steel fixtures and advertisements. McDonald's "golden arches" are like a metaphor in Bordeaux, and even more so a protective image, a talisman, against the fear losing his sense of "self" in the familial food requirements that he knows he will have to adhere to in Senegal. He is aware that fast-food restaurants have a negative image as a poor-quality meal with no social aspect in the French mind and a negative image of individualism in the Senegalese mind. Nevertheless, at this stage in his life,[26] eating at McDonald's in the Madrid airport reassures him that it is possible to avoid the family order[27] and to reverse it at any time by departing again for Bordeaux. The "parenthetical anonymity" of airports, which offers a provisional identity, is experienced as temporary freedom by those who know that they will have to maintain their position, live up to their status as elders, and, for the women, watch over what they eat and/or cook.

In the other direction, from Dakar to Bordeaux, *soccou*,[28] *dibi* meat (grilled lamb), peanuts, and kola seeds, stuffed into bags and boubous, acquire an elevated status at the airport, even though they might be looked down on in Senegal. As we approach Bordeaux, munching and sucking on these snacks while waiting for flights to destinations around to be announced, the world maintains the culinary and emotional link to the country that we have just left. These foods represent the family that is left behind, the country that is already missed even while one savors eating in solitude, which the airport makes possible. The duty free shops are also visited frequently, less so for buying a cheap, immense bar of *Milka* chocolate to take back to the children in France than for fully proving the reality of his momentary freedom, his indisputable quality of being a passenger about to depart, freed from all of the responsibilities of daily Senegalese life.

This noisy, agitated, and uncomfortable place of passage also, and paradoxically, allows the sharing of intimate secrets. As a mediator or confidante, after long hours of waiting and traveling throughout the night, I listened to stories of despair from men in the process of getting divorced in France who "no longer had anyone to cook for them," thereby justifying their return to their native country to be fed as an "elder."[29] In these non-places, I collected confidences from individuals who carried the secret (difficult to admit in Bordeaux) of imposed (or chosen) polygamy that introduced them to a cyclical pattern of culinary and sexual (re)discovery. At other moments, through their disagreements about food, couples attested to their disenchantment with the conditions that met them upon their return to Senegal. Particularly for the retired women, preparing large quantities of food every day and having to be available for visits from family members at any time of the day is trying, while in France they consider themselves to be free from these obligations. In France, refrigeration and more advanced cooking technology enable everyone to serve and feed him or herself, independently of the women. In addition, their professional activities and their schedules regulate their daily life, unlike in Dakar where family, religious, and neighborhood social activities are more important, thus denying their individuality. For the women, the gender roles regarding cooking obligations are significantly different in Dakar. Preparing meals and purchasing daily supplies have become thresholds for uncertainty and indecision for the few women who have decided to live in Senegal part time in their later years.

In all of these life histories told in the Casablanca, Lisbon, or Madrid airports, the couple and the cooking (sharing tasks: buying food, preparing dishes, eating) proved to be a nexus of change at retirement, overturning a social order in favor of another lived order. Marriage, pots, and crises become intermingled in the functionality of airports. In effect, these non-places, which do not have any true spokespeople (other than moral people or institutions) use images, words, and prescriptive, prohibitive, or informative texts. In this landscape of innumerable signs, screens, and posters expressing neutrality, the retirees' process of food reflectivity is reinforced. "Assailed by the overwhelming abundance of images presented by transportation companies or businesses, the individual traveling though non-places simultaneously experiences the perpetual present and the encounter of the self."[30] Finally, airports constitute a familiar "cloakroom" (recognition of waiters in the restaurants or members of the airline ground crew, who are often Moroccan) where one gathers forces before entering an arena in which one will have to adapt to the food over the course of several months by returning to one destination or another.

In conclusion, this technique of considering multiple angles of approach allowed me to study the progressive dietary transformations in the mobility of:

- discussions with migrants regarding the reasons for their departures. By questioning the same eater at different times and places in their migratory path, it became clear that, effectively, dietary discussions can change as they become more and more distant from the country of departure (France or Senegal) or as they approach; the impossibility of caring for diabetes or being on a diet in Senegal, or the solitude in Bordeaux, can justify departure.
- their economic behaviors as a function of their apprehension about what comes after the trip: the daily expenditure for the food budget in Senegal requires saving up in Bordeaux, and when this budget has all been spent, they believe that they must "return" to France to "build themselves back up again" and remain "new."
- their feelings of belonging, which change depending on the culinary situations encountered at each step. For example, the growing apprehension of confronting the repeated family meals (the obligatory shared and very spicy meal in Dakar/the freezer meal eaten alone in Bordeaux) and the otherness/identity (the restaurants in the different airports crossing France, Senegal, Spain, Morocco),

perceived differently as the migrants get closer and closer to Europe or Africa. At the same time, these different mobile food experiences reinforce the feeling of belonging to the world of travelers who transcend nationalities, religions, and languages.

• their migratory plans. Here again, engaging in repeated discussions with the migrants, individually or in small groups, at successive steps along their Bordeaux–Dakar trajectories, revealed that migration plans are not fixed but are constantly revised, bit by bit over time, according to the information that the migrants receive, the opportunities that present themselves to them, and the constraints that are encountered.

This chapter reveals the social, individual, symbolic, economic, and political motivations that underpin food nomadism, which are reflections of our contemporary societies in general (and not only those of migrants), trapped between localization and mobility.

BIBLIOGRAPHY

Abbots, Emma. "Approaches to Food and Migration: Rootedness, Belonging and Exchange," In the *Handbook of Food and Anthropology*, J. Klein & J. Watson (eds.), London: Bloomsbury, 2015.

Appaduraï, Arjun. *Après le colonialisme. Les conséquences culturelles de la globalisation*, Payot, series: Petite Bibliothèque Payot, 2015.

Augé, Marc. *Non-lieux*, Edition du Seuil, 1992.

Bredeloup, Sylvie. "L'aventurier, une figure de la migration africaine." *Cahiers internationaux de sociologie*, vol. 125, no. 2 (2008): 281–306.

Corbeau, Jean Pierre, and Poulain, Jean-Pierre. *Penser l'alimentation. Entre imaginaire et rationalité*. Paris: Ed Privat, 2002.

Crenn, Chantal, and Hassoun, Jean-Pierre. "Introduction: Repenser et réimaginer l'acte alimentaire en situations de migration," *Anthropology of Food*, no. 7 (December 2010): http://journals.openedition.org/aof/6672.

Crenn, Chantal, and Hassoun, Jean-Pierre. "Dakar. Four ages of fast food," *Ethnologie française* 2014/1 (Vol. 44), p. 59–72. https://www.cairn-int.info/article-E_ETHN_141_0059--the -four-ages-of-fast-food-in- dakar.htm.

Desjeux, Dominique. *Alimentations contemporaines*, "Préface," Paris: L'Harmattan, (2002): 9–13.

Dolphijn Rick. Foodscapes. *Towards a Deleuzian Ethics of Consumption*. Eburon, 2004.

Lestage, Françoise. "De la circulation des nourritures," *Anthropology of food*, S4, May 2008: http://journals.openedition.org/aof/2942.

Martiniello, Marco, Puig, Nicolas, and Suzanne, G. "Editorial: Créations en migrations," *Revue Européenne des Migrations Internationales*, 25, no. 2 (2009): 7–11.

Tarrius, Alain. "Territoires circulatoires et étapes urbaines des transmigrant(e)s," *Regards croisés sur l'économie*, vol. 8, no. 2 (2010): 63–70.

Warnier, Jean-Pierre. *La mondialisation de la culture*. Paris, La Découverte, 1998.

6

Space-Food

Food in Mobile Technological Environments of Late High-Modernity

Alwin Cubasch

If you plan to travel the endless expanses of space, you must bring food from home—if you do not want the stomachs of the astronauts to remain as empty as space itself.[1] Therefore, NASA provided US astronaut John Glenn provisions while he orbited Earth three times on February 20, 1962, on the Mercury-Atlas 6 space flight mission. Glenn enjoyed applesauce, beef and gravy, and pureed vegetables from aluminum tubes that had been developed after lengthy tests by a team of engineers and physicians.[2] The first "space dinner" of the US space program marked the beginning of the history of US space-food.

TECHNOLOGICAL ENVIRONMENTS OF LATE HIGH-MODERNITY

The history of space-food begins in the epoch of late high-modernity. But high-modernity is not only a certain epoch in the sense of Ulrich Herbert, but a specific and powerful ideology.[3] Essential for this ideology, according to James C. Scott, was the unconditional belief in technical observation, modernization, and optimization of all areas of life down to daily nutrition.[4] For this techno-scientific mode of ordering the world,[5] spacecrafts were the ideal laboratory, as they actually represented a world, an environment, that had to be created from scratch by technical means and in which the technocratic high-modernity could prove its wide-ranging claims. High-modernity also encompassed an ideology of unconditional acceleration and movement, which expressed itself through technological means and resulted in the contraction of physical space.[6] Planetary in scale, modern technologies of movement—from railways to digital communication—have given rise to populations in constant motion that are sometimes referred to as "new nomads."[7] But these new nomads are not nomads in the ethnographic or historical sense.[8] The nomads of the arid belt lived in natural spaces with limited resources and difficult climates that made pastoral and mobile modes of subsistence necessary to optimally use these scarce resources and allowed for their regeneration.[9] The modern and technology-driven mobility of the new nomads, on the other hand, relies on sedentary structures like states, administrations, and industry. Modern mobility takes place in technological, not natural environments. It was and is itself an internal phenomenon of sedentary cultures, albeit sedentary on now a global scale.[10] Still, this modern mobility was not something that was adapted easily. New mobile and technological forms of life need to be learned and trained.[11] The acceleration of technological and social change necessitated new adaptations, mentalities, and cultural techniques of mobility toward the ever-changing circumstances of the twentieth century. NASA's development of space travel from the 1950s onward is a particular example for this training of new, technology-driven lifestyles of mobility and its accompanying techniques. A spacecraft as a total technological environment that traveled at tremendous speed was the ultimate projection of high-modern mobilization and environmental mechanization.[12] Where better to test new technologies of mobility and accompanying cultural techniques than in space? How better to develop astronautic lifestyles suited to technological environments than with actual astronauts?[13] One technique to be tested was space-food. How could food be made completely mobile in a total technological environment? And how, NASA asked itself, could this new food technology be applied on Earth for the new, highly mobile nomads of the future? The "spaceship food-system," as called in NASA parlance, was central to the creation of an artificial and moving environment in space. "Manned space flight requires accurate control of the environments in spacecraft to maintain life. Food is an indispensable part of that environment."[14] According to Walton L. Jones, director of NASA's biotechnological research center, food-system engineers hoped to combat world hunger with space-food.[15]

Space-food as a technological invention ran into difficulties, however, due to the unexpected resistance that astronauts had toward food engineering. Highly motivated astronauts who flew to the stars in the most complex machines to date, did not want to eat food that was as technical as their spaceships. On the other hand, social, psychological, and gender-specific aspects of the Western culinary system prevailed in space against technical requirements, while attempts to establish space-food on Earth's plates succeeded only partially. The history of space-food outlined in this chapter will show how incursions of a culinary future and visions of a mechanized diet collided with conservative structures within the Western culinary system and were thus rejected. Being a new nomad in technological environments didn't mean giving up one's sedentary cultural tastes and food habits.

MOBILIZING FOOD: FROM LABORATORY TO SPACE

The history of space-food began with fears of insurmountable difficulties and potentially life-threatening dangers. For the engineers and physiologists who designed space-food, the human body was first and foremost a fragile and defective construction. Their concept of the human body and its needs was primarily based on the explicit and quantifiable knowledge of medicine, biology, and physiology. Space engineers thought of humans in the sense of a cybernetic machine with calculable input/output relations and several distinct metabolic subsystems.[16] But the environmental envelop of this organism was limited. A report published in 1963 feared, for example, that overheated astronauts could not regulate their electrolyte balance.[17] Unhygienic excrement of the astronauts appeared to be at least as dangerous, and flatulence threatened to poison the atmosphere of the spaceship: "The effect of flatus can be serious, particularly at low absolute pressures. Also, since the composition of flatus is not innocuous, it is conceivable that, in time, considerable concentrations of toxic gases may accumulate."[18] This also applied to illnesses. NASA experts feared little more than astronauts struggling with food poisoning in space. Diarrhea and vomiting would have put an end to any of the expensive space missions.[19] On the other hand, the technical environment of the spacecraft was far from perfect. The low thrust of the rockets allowed only minimal load, and food, therefore, had to deliver the desired number of calories as efficiently and weight-savingly as possible. The packaging of the food had to withstand the reduced pressure and the pure oxygen atmosphere of the spacecraft. The food itself was not allowed to crumble, which would have otherwise endangered the spaceship's air filters and the astronaut's lungs.[20]

Despite these diverse and sometimes contradictory requirements, the working group responsible for the 1963 report had a simple solution at hand: "formula food," that is, compressed pastes, cubes, or powders of precisely specified composition of all nutrients they deemed necessary.[21] Chicken sandwiches, biscuits, and bacon were diced, freeze-dried under high pressure, and coated with gelatin and starch. The advantages were obvious: compact cubes could be optimally stowed in the spacecraft. Consumption of the cubes took only seconds and could be managed in the space suit. The cubes were further able to prevent the dangers of digestion: minimizing the content of fiber reduced the frequency with which astronauts had to go to the toilet and prevented flatulence. To amplify the effect, the astronauts were supposed to eat only space-food in the weeks prior to launch.[22] To rule out any disease during flight, NASA microbiologists set strict limits on the allowed microbial contamination, which meant nothing other than completely sterile foods.[23] To comply with its own strict contamination limits for flightworthy food, NASA and food industry representatives developed a system of hazard analysis and critical control points that were implemented into the production process and enabled permanent monitoring of microbiotic parameters at various points. In some cases, food production was moved to cleanrooms.[24] Finally, these bite-sized cubes were to facilitate the performance of nutritional and medical experiments by ensuring exact control of nutrient intake.[25] The final stage of this line of thought was applied to envisioned long-duration flights to Mars. Not being able to prepack meals with the necessary shelf-life for prolonged times, NASA planned to grow algae on the spacecraft to feed to snails and slugs, which themselves would form the basis of the astronaut's diet.[26]

The working group disregarded objections that food could be monotonous or unappetizing; after all, according to the authors of the report, many parts of the world population ate monotonous and bad-tasting food their whole life without harm or illness: "Good nutrition can be adequately maintained for an indefinite period through the use of a properly constituted formula diet, variety in food is primarily a matter affecting the morale rather than nutritional state of crew members."[27] But morale was of no concern, the authors argued. The reward of being among the first men in space was supposed to override any inconveniencies of astronautic life: "Since highly motivated individuals are chosen for the initial space flights, it is unlikely that they would object to the monotony of a formula diet and would probably prefer its simplicity."[28]

From the NASA engineers' point of view, it was therefore possible to integrate all the requirements of man, technology, and space into the "formula food system," but only because the astronauts themselves were understood as delicate but ultimately controllable metabolic machines. Crew morale and eating preferences were minor and negligible. But this idea was untenable, as became apparent only two years later during the Gemini missions. When the first manned *Gemini* spacecraft was launched on March 23, 1965, under the command of Gus Grissom, the real era of space-food began. For the first time, there was enough time to dine extensively in space. During the second orbit pilot John Young was to spend exactly fifty-five minutes on the "primary objective 6.j," the preparation of space-food and the disposal of food residues. The aim of this experiment was to evaluate the functionality and user-friendliness of the "Gemini Food System" with the planned Apollo missions in mind. Additionally, the resorption of nutrients and the work of the digestive tract in weightlessness were to be investigated by physio-metric examinations before and after the flight.[29]

At least that was the plan the food engineers, physicians, and physiologists had drawn up. But they had not considered the effects of weightlessness and the stubbornness of the astronauts. Although the eating trials started on time, one hour and forty-four minutes after launch, problems arose just a few minutes later. One of the bactericidal pills for leftover food came loose and flew away. Lunch bags floated through the cabin. Pilot John Young ruined the experiments when he handed Gus Grissom a corned beef sandwich he had smuggled on board in his space suit.[30] When Grissom bit into it breadcrumbs spread quickly throughout the capsule. Grissom stowed the sandwich away hastily in his own space suit. The intended physiological data collection was useless as all measurements of nutritional intake pre-, during-, and post-flight was compromised by corned beef calories. Instead, the sandwich demonstrated that the astronauts were not willing to compromise their diet in space. Gus Grissom complained that pork chops were missing to accompany the applesauce from the tube. John Young stated at least, "That's not bad for applesauce."[31]

John Young was not the only astronaut to challenge the nutritional regime of engineers and physiologists. According to General James Humphreys Jr., director of space medicine, the astronauts of Apollo 7 under Walter Schirra complained "rather vociferously" about the taste and texture of the food. According to the astronauts, the water was also unpalatable. It was provided by the fuel cells as a by-product of electricity production and tasted of plastic and chemicals. Additionally, bubbles in the water from the fuel cell made it difficult to rehydrate freeze-dried foods in microgravity because bubbles prevented the thorough mixing of water and food powder. Even after extensive kneading, parts of the meal were still dry and unpalatable.[32]

Furthermore, the astronauts demanded to be involved in the selection of food. Prior to this, only a committee of "food experts" was responsible for the organoleptic evaluation of taste, texture, and smell, but not the astronauts.[33] Another tactic of the astronauts was to exchange food according to their personal preferences. In principle, the food and its sequence had been determined about six months in advance for each crew member. In order to enforce the correct sequence of withdrawals, each menu was linked to the next. However, this did not prevent the astronauts from disregarding the order and exchanging individual menu components. This exchange was not always recorded in the logbook—probably to avoid further discussion with ground control. The astronauts defied the central planning of the nutrition experts because it didn't fit their individual preferences. But from the point of view of physicians and physiologists, this practice led to data distortions and rendered their anthropometric surveys inaccurate.[34] Researching how the human metabolism reacted to microgravity was impossible as long as the variables of food intake were uncontrollable. Throughout all missions the astronauts ate too little and came home with unopened food rations. In the absence of efficient feedback loops, the astronauts demonstrated their disapproval by refusing to eat. Humphreys expressed his irritation accordingly during a NASA conference in 1969:

> One item which has not been widely mentioned is that in our system the food discipline of the crewmembers has been poor. I have said this to them, so I will say it in public: Food and water discipline is something that soldiers learn early or they do not survive. The space crews have not been very disciplined about their eating—they have picked, traded, and done as they pleased. That is permissible if no scientific metabolic information is to be obtained but food discipline must be enforced in flight if we are to determine whether a system is good and how it should be changed. It is particularly important in those flights in which we have experimental protocols that must be complied with.[35]

CULINARY INTERFERING: FROM HOME TO SPACE

With the astronauts viewed as disciplined soldiers—real men—who should endure monotony and hardships, cultural narratives became apparent that were deeply entrenched in the US space exploration program.[36] According to Howard McCurdy, American society's expectations of the space program were structurally conservative. The technical means of space travel were thought to revitalize and consolidate conservative values of American society. This also included the frontier myth of the hardships and heroism of westward expansion. Americans hoped that space would open up a new frontier where core American virtues such as adventurism, endurance, and resilience could be revived. Within this system, the role of the settlers was given to the new all-American heroes, the astronauts. Like the settlers of the frontier, the astronauts were to exemplify traditional American virtues and transport them into space.[37] And that meant, of course, getting along with monotonous and tasteless food without complaints. The astronauts, however, behaved more like wealthy inhabitants of the white Anglo-Saxon Protestant suburbs in which they lived and whose ideas of appropriate food they took to space. Shrimp cocktail was therefore not only popular at upper-middle-class parties in the 1960s, it also enjoyed great popularity in space.[38]

One reason for these conflicts between the technological requirements of space-food, the physician's expectations of astronautic masculinity, and the astronauts' resistance to space-food is to be found in the culinary system. Food is always more than the sum of its nutrients; it is embedded in a culinary system. The culinary system describes the cultural and semantic dimension of eating and works as a system of differential signs.[39] This code of eating regulates what food is to be eaten, at which time, at what place, and finally—by whom. Thus, the culinary system regulates, for example, the combination of certain foods and determines the limits of composition through semantic markers such as taste, nutrition, and social status, but also religion and gender. Other semantic markers of the culinary system enforce the time of consumption. These time markers can organize small time periods like morning, afternoon, or evening, but also large-scale social time periods like childhood, illness, or pregnancy, for instance. The culinary system is also closely linked to codes of sociopolitical hierarchy, normativity, and to the cultural construction of environment and time. The culinary system reflects those other cultural code systems and reaffirms them in its execution.[40] Another important feature of the culinary system is its autopoiesis and therefore its more or less independent development over time. Not every cultural, natural, or technical change is integrated into the culinary system. In case that integration happens, the adaption usually occurs with delay. Visions of futuristic science and technology driven nomadicity may be accepted by the culinary system and its carriers or not. Political expectations of masculinity and heroism can collide with the culinary system when they are no longer integrated into to actual culinary habits. Even the hard, technical requirements of the spacecraft are not set to be accepted unconditionally. In all these cases of environmental pressures on the culinary system, friction, disturbances, and outright resistance, as seen with the astronauts, have to be expected.

The collision between technological requirements of the spacecraft and the culinary system becomes even clearer in the case of the Skylab missions from 1973 to 1974. Experiments with nutrition played a central role in mission planning from the outset as the prolonged flight times of up to eighty-four days allowed for more comprehensive studies of the effects that microgravity might have on the human body and its metabolism. Again, strict control of the variables was thought to be paramount to the success of the nutritional experiments. Therefore, the physicians planned to serve every astronaut exactly the same food every day. But this concept was quickly abandoned due to protests from the astronauts and their training staff.[41] Instead, complex methods were developed to measure personal food intake, weight development, and amounts of leftover food. To uplift crew morale, which had been a food-related problem in earlier missions, the mission planners complied with the astronaut's demand for ice cream. They also were provided a dining table where they could dine together that was designed by psychologists.[42] However, the astronauts did not eat their ice cream at the table but chose to eat it floating in front of the window of the space station in the evening after work.[43] This illustrates the capacity of culinary systems for establishing structures, which assign certain times of day and certain activities to corresponding foods, even if it was no longer feasible to speak of different times of day in space while seeing the sun rise and set several times a day.

Gender roles shape culinary systems that in turn stabilize gendered activities of cooking and eating. Space-food was not immune to this and affirmed traditional as well as conservative role concepts of the 1950s and 1960s and translated them into space. That tendency was already visible in popular TV shows home on Earth. "Cooking is women's work!" Jeannie announces in an early episode of the television show *I Dream of Jeannie* as her master, the astronaut Tony Nelson, attempts to prepare frozen meals. But she fails in the preparation of the frozen high-tech food, too, and sets the kitchen on fire as she puts peas and gravy on the gas stove while they are still in their protective plastic wrap. The prefabricated gravy, she exclaims, is the most horrible she ever tasted.[44] She was the ideal housewife of the 1950s and 1960s with her household capabilities and her invisibility to the outside world. But ideal housewives weren't supposed to use too much technology (or magic in her case) during their housework.[45] Food had to be authentically homemade and this meant handmade by the loving and caring housewife. Technologies of nomadic food like frozen foodstuffs and ready-made gravy were contrary to the time-consuming sedentary lifestyle women were supposed to maintain.

The role of the caring housewife of the astronauts was assumed by NASA physician Rita Rapp, who—starting with the Apollo missions—baked cookies for the astronauts and the ground crews before launch.[46] Her cookies served the astronauts as comfort food and as trade goods of a microeconomy of individual nutritional wishes and unloved tasks in space.[47] Even though the preparation of the cookies soon took on industrial dimensions in order to satisfy the astronauts' insatiable hunger, they were considered "homemade," which was probably not insignificantly connected with the fact that they were produced by a woman.[48] "I like to feed them what I want, because I want them healthy and happy," Rapp announced in a newspaper interview, comparing her work with the preparation of baby food, although she led a team of thirty highly specialized nutritionists during the Skylab missions and published more than twenty articles.[49] Rapp was still able to care for the astronauts during their short trips around Earth while being ground-based herself. But on long-term missions at the latest, the *New York Times* found women had to fly into space too: "If man is to colonize the planets, if celestial housekeeping is ever to be instituted, the 'second sex' must have booking on future space flights."[50]

Finally, religious codes of the culinary system found their way into space. For the moon orbit of the Apollo 8 mission on Christmas 1968, NASA made a special Christmas dinner available to its three astronauts: turkey with gravy. After dinner, the three astronauts read aloud excerpts from Genesis in a live broadcast on television.[51] The notion behind this was threefold: For the nutritionists the experiment confirmed the usability of normally hydrated food in space. To the crew that orbited the moon in distance of 238,900 miles from Earth, it gave a feeling of Christmas normality. To the Americans viewing it on their television sets at home it signaled that NASA took Christian-American traditions seriously, even in space.[52] In a now famous anecdote from the first moon landing, Buzz Aldrin, second man on the lunar surface and deeply religious, took bread and wine with him, spoke John 15:5, poured wine into a chalice he had brought with him, and administered communion in the lunar landing capsule.[53]

Gradually, NASA became aware of the cultural and psychological constraints on technology driven food:

> What could have gone wrong? With 20-20 hindsight, it has become obvious that a part of the problem lies in our lack of complete understanding of the psychophysiology of eating. Man and his eating habits are not easily changed. Good nutrition begins with good food presented to the consumer in a familiar manner.[54]

Beginning with the Apollo 8 mission, NASA experimented with food that didn't need to be rehydrated but was able to retain its original water content. Even more important, spoons were provided for the first time for the aforementioned Christmas dinner. Although the meals in those spoon-bowl packages tasted more or less like their rehydratable forerunners, which the astronauts squeezed directly into their mouths, the use of an almost earthly spoon made an outstanding psychological difference for the astronauts because it conveyed a certain sense of normality. The engineers' fears that the food would come off the spoon and endanger the spaceship did not come true.[55] The airline industry was already further ahead.[56] At the same conference where J. W. Humphreys complained about unmanly astronauts, J. P. Treadwell from Pan Am told NASA flat out the problems of their food-system:

> "Welcome Aboard Flight 1 to London. Our flight time today will be 3 hours, and, immediately after takeoff, we will be offering cocktails and dinner. Included in your choice this evening, may we suggest a dehydrated, low-residue, easily disposable, unappetizing, and misshapen meal. Water guns on request." What's wrong with that? [. . .] One of the basic differences between the airlines and space travel is that, at least at this stage, the airlines are selling something, and we need to pamper people in order to sell tickets. What kind of creature comforts can we provide? [. . .] How many seats do you suppose that opening announcement I made would sell? None. Food is not something that is just eaten. It's also seen, and it's felt, and it's heard. It is a textured item and we are used to it in its current earthbound form.[57]

It was these creature comforts that NASA had difficulties with. Although every measurable external factor was under control and the technological environment of the spacecraft was stable, the technologies of nomadic food didn't function completely because there was still an uncontrolled environment the engineers hadn't thought of. This was the sedentary culture and its culinary system in which the astronauts were situated. Out of this environment food got its semantic significance and structure but also its power for causing disorder and unpredictability. At the end of the Apollo mission, NASA's nutrition engineers surrendered to this multitude of cultural demands on food. Those aspects of nutrition that they considered negligible—personal preferences, cultural expectations, and gender roles—also demanded their place in space. Futuristic food, which openly signaled its technical origin, failed because of the structural conservatism of the Western culinary system and its carriers. Sedentary food habits trumped the semantics of total mobility when it came to food. Disillusioned, the Apollo mission food-system engineers discovered the limits of their engineering approach to nutrition:

> Experience with the Apollo Program demonstrated that successful development, fabrication, testing, and spacecraft integration of food systems required unique technical management efforts to coordinate and establish priorities between and within biological and engineering considerations. This situation is caused by several factors inherent to foods in general and foods for manned space flight:
>
> 1. most foods are dead biological materials that have lost the original capabilities to adapt to environmental changes;
> 2. food habits and prejudices are highly individualized and deeply ingrained in the tastes of the intended consumers (the astronauts) and the interested non consumers (the program, system, and subsystem managers);
> 3. foods are inadequately defined in biological terms, and this situation is compounded by the need of aerospace system management to have absolute definitions of foods in engineering terms; and
> 4. criteria and configurations usually are required long before specific knowledge of the final consumer is available. Generally, food systems for manned space flight consist of a group of poorly defined components (foods) that can be infinitely variable and that are designed to satisfy the absolute physical criteria for the spacecraft. The fact that criteria for the adequate support of the physiological and psychological processes of man are poorly defined results in a natural tendency to place a lower priority on the development effort needed to meet the nutritional requirements of the individual crewmember.[58]

NASA formulated new goals for its space-food accordingly. Although the food should continue to meet the technical requirements of the spacecraft and the medical demands of physiologists, it should also have the same psychological effects as food back home. This required a semantic shift. Space-food—as Rita Rapp's cookies demonstrated—had to appear authentic and homemade, as if it were not part of a complex high-technology that advanced into previously unimaginable realms.

A "good" spacecraft may be bigger, faster, more versatile and safer than the previous one. A "good" spacecraft food system is one which meets system requirements but is built around good foods that stimulate and satisfy hunger, that are readily prepared, that have a familiar flavor and texture, that provide diversion, relaxation, security, and adequate quantities of nutrients to maintain metabolic balance in the particular environment.[59]

IMPLEMENTING MOBILITY: FROM SPACE TO HOME

While the semantics of the homemade inscribed itself in space-food, there were also reversed tendencies back home. The futuristic semantics and the technology of space-food also left their mark on the nutrition of those left behind. Tang, a commercial orange juice powder that the astronauts used in their space capsules to mask the taste of fuel cell water, was quite successful and is still remembered as the quintessential space-drink.[60] The manufacturer of Tang skillfully used the nimbus of the US space program for grand-scale advertising campaigns that left their mark on American food culture. In more than twenty TV commercials with simulated *Apollo* moon landings and countless print ads, the food company behind Tang, General Foods Corporation, referred to NASA's use of the beverage powder, but concealed the actual reasons behind Tang's use in space. Instead, they emphasized the scientific relevance of their own product for healthy nutrition in space: "Because of the limitations of space, only the most vital earth elements can be taken aboard," announced one of the ads, referring of course to Tang as one of these vital elements. Another commercial claimed that Tang contained more vitamin C than actual orange juice and was therefore healthier.[61] General Foods Corporation even cosponsored the live coverage of the moon landing on ABC.[62] The Tang ads with fictional images from the landing site ran during the commercial breaks but General Foods had shot some space-free commercials too as a contingency plan in case the moon landing would turn into a catastrophe.[63] Selling commercial products on the appeal of future utopias, however, always becomes problematic when the future recedes into the past. This happened to Tang. When the interest of contemporaries in the success of the space program waned and there were no more spectacular manned space flights between Skylab and the Space Shuttle, the enthusiasm for Tang also faded. The same fate befell Space Food Sticks, which Pillsbury had originally developed on behalf of NASA for use in spacesuits. With the end of the Apollo missions, these early energy bars also disappeared from the supermarkets.

The earthly use of space-food was more successful where no consumer wishes had to be satisfied but only the technical characteristics of space-food were important. In the 1970s, for example, NASA's concept of the "formula-food system" was experimentally used in psychiatric wards under the name "balanced synthetic diet." Here the reduced fiber content of the astronaut food was of interest and in a two-and-a-half-year trial it was possible to cut the defecation of the psychiatric inmates down to once every nine days.

[T]his led to a significant simplification of the care of the patients, who had previously soiled themselves frequently. The cleaning costs for bed linen and clothing, for room care and, finally, accident rate in the department decreased accordingly. Laxatives and enemas, which had previously been administered regularly, became unnecessary. Patients who had previously been painstakingly fed with spoons could now drink the balanced synthetic diet with little assistance. The patients were no longer annoyed by intestinal gas formation. The severe odor of perspiration and urine receded, and skin irritations disappeared. All in all, the patients were more sociable and had a better sleep. This was documented by a reduction of the noise level in the department to about 50% of the original level, an end to the administration of otherwise often necessary sleeping pills and a reduction of the tranquilizer usage to one sixth.[64]

NASA's nutrition department itself developed "space-food for the elderly" during the intermediate phase of Skylab and the Shuttle program.[65] The intention was to send the freeze-dried meals, which could be kept at room temperature in their plastic overwraps, to seniors living alone, by mail in monthly rations. They would then rehydrate the food at home with hot water and eat it with minimum effort.[66] However, a test with 10,000 of these food rations led to no consequences because in the late 1960s and early 1970s there was an increasing resistance to these visions of engineered and rationalized nutrition.[67] Oil price shock, recession, and especially the experience of the Vietnam War, led increasingly broad sections of the population to adopt a skeptical attitude toward large-scale engineering projects initiated by authorities or corporations that were seen as highly technocratic institutions.[68] From the perspective of critical contemporaries, large technical solutions to supposed nutritional problems in particular seemed to constitute an illegitimate incursion into ordinary daily life. John Keats, author of several critical books on the American food industry, scolded NASA's plans in the *New York Times* in 1976:

NASA's new project is certainly well-intended, but it strikes me as being just another example of scientific bureaucracy's frequently misplaced enthusiasms, because there is nothing about it that is in any way humane. [. . .] God knows that when I become an old man, I do not want to live alone in an apartment and receive in the mail a box of plastic bags packed in man-per-day overwraps that will enable me to fulfill my daily mission menu requirements, particularly when the only daily mission left to me will be to wait for death in silence. I believe that old people need company more than they need systems. I believe that there is much more to food than nourishment, and much more to a meal than the food.[69]

Science fiction films of the 1970s as well abandoned depictions of a joyful technocratic utopia of the future together with gleeful expectations of future food. While the astronauts in Stanley Kubrick's *2001: A Space Odyssey* (1968) joyfully consume a wide range of imagined space-food, only four years later, the environmentally conscious and space-travelling protagonist of *Silent Running* (1972) slaughters his space-food-loving co-astronauts and instead eats his own homegrown melons. Even more radically, the horror film *Alien*, released in 1979, reversed the semantics of space-food. In a scenery that is certainly not by chance reminiscent of the dining table of the *Skylab* space station, the crew of the freighter convenes for dinner only to end up on the menu of the extraterrestrial but in symbolic terms highly capitalist alien itself. From then on, most science fiction films depicted space-food as lumps of grey-brown protein mass.[70] In 1970, Lewis Mumford lambasted the spaceships as "air-conditioned pyramids" with which barely living technological mummies undertook the last ascension to heaven.[71] But, according to Mumford, the real danger was that these mummified astronauts tested concepts of living for the industrial nations of the future and made them suitable for the masses:

> Unfortunately, the earth dwellers may prove more gravely endangered by space travel than the chosen astronauts; and there is every prospect, if the current methods of processing and conditioning the human organism are not modified, that the mass of men will be forced to endure the penalties of space travel for a whole lifetime without enjoying any of the rewards that are showered on a favored elite. So the ultimate gift of space technics, it now turns out, is to establish in experimental small-scale models the requirements for imprisoning, conditioning, and controlling large populations. To universalize this under-dimensioned model and make it a permanent feature of human existence would be one of the grossest miscarriages of megatechnics.[72]

NASA was not completely uninvolved in this epochal transition to reflexive modernity.[73] The images of the "blue marble" Earth, which the *Apollo* astronauts photographed, developed unexpected and wide-ranging effects and became, according to Wolfgang Sachs, the "real epiphany of American space travel."[74] Together with James Lovelock's Gaia hypothesis, which also originated from NASA research, the photographs of Earth gave an enormous boost to the environmental movements and the contemporary counterculture by making the object of concern—the Earth—visually perceptible as a material object in its entirety for the first time. Simultaneously, the pictures conveyed the supposed fragility and delicacy of the terrestrial ecosystem.[75] In the subsequent discourses on the ecosystem and the biosphere, questions of nutrition played a prominent role. Nutrition was now being repositioned around the semantic dimensions of sustainability and homemade authenticity contrary to an industrialized food culture that seemed to threaten the foundations of life on Earth.

CULINARY COMBINATION:
THE MENU OF POSTMODERNITY

While on Earth the concept of industrial food for futuristic and engineered environments increasingly developed into a vision of horror and space-food gained the pejorative connotation that it still holds today, NASA likewise tried new approaches to space-food from the Space Shuttle program onward: "Engineers should probably stay out of the kitchen," the head of the shuttle food program, Charles T. Bourland, remarks in his recently published recipe book.[76] The focus now lay on food from the supermarket, fresh produce, and ready meals,[77] which were coordinated in multiple feedback loops with the astronauts and thus constituted, according to Belasco, a "recombinant (or postmodernist) menu."[78]

But certain aspects of space-food and NASA research have found their way into the daily diet routines of Western countries. The hazard analysis and critical control points quality control regime developed by NASA and Pillsbury for space-food constitutes the current basis of the FAO/WHO Codex Alimentarius and the EU guidelines for food production.[79] Packaging techniques that diffused from NASA kitchens into food factories and supermarket shelves are the tangible result of the close interweaving of NASA and the food industry.[80] Most recent research recommends the use of NASA's space-food concepts for cattle farming to reduce land-use and global warming.[81] Nowadays, there are hardly any foods left that rely solely on semantics of a utopian technological future for their marketing or inscribe themselves in the culinary system of the West via such semantics, even if in many cases food is manufactured by technology-driven companies that realize food in the mode of NASA's system-engineering. This highly technological food that can be eaten wherever, whenever, by whomever still adheres to older semantics of the homemade and authentic. As Miggelbrink et al. point out, the difference between nomadic and sedentary lifeforms never plays out exactly along borders of smooth and striated space.[82] Pockets of nomadic smooth spaces persist in striated sedentary spaces and vice versa. People change seamlessly between nomadic strategies of coping with the environment and sedentary strategies of controlling the environment. The same goes for food. Space derived technologies of food production are intertwined with the culinary system's conservative semantics. The technological mobility of modern sedentary cultures mobilizes food but the food doesn't become necessarily nomadic food because of its mobilization. On the contrary, the technological environment of the spacecraft means that astronauts are always at home—in their enclosed capsule. This is also true for the earth-bound population. For them, being highly mobile means being mobile in technologically constructed but fundamentally sedentary spaces. Everywhere is home now. Thus, food for these new nomads up in space and on Earth had and has to retain some semblance to homemade food—at least on the cultural and semantic level.

BIBLIOGRAPHY

Belasco, Warren. *Meals to come—A history of the future of food.* Berkeley: University of California Press, 2006.

Bourland, Charles T., and Gregory L. Vogt. *The Astronauts Cookbook, Tales, Recipes and More.* New York: Springer, 2010.

Cawley, Diarmuid. 2017. "The Future of Food in *Blade Runner 2049.*" *Dublin Institute of Technology,* 2017. Retrieved September 20, 2018. https://arrow.dit.ie/tfschcafoth/29/.

Chaikin, Andrew. "Live from the Moon: The societal impact of Apollo." In *Societal Impact of Spaceflight,* edited by Steven J. Dick, and Roger D. Launius, 54–66. Washington, DC: NASA History Division, 2007.

Fellner, Christian, and Robert, Riedl. *HACCP*, Wien: Behr's, 2009.

Foss, Richard, *Food in the air and space: The surprising history of food and drink in the skies*, Lanham, MD: Rowman & Littlefield: 2016.

Gertel, Jörg. "Globalisierung, Entankerung und Mobilität. Analytische Perspektiven einer gegenwartsbezogenen geographischen Nomadismusforschung." In *Nomadismus aus der Perspektive der Begrifflichkeit. Beiträge der 1. Tagung am 11.7.2001*, edited by Stefan Leder and Bernhard Streck, 57–88. Halle: Orientwissenschaftliche Hefte 3; Mitteilungen des SFB Differenz und Integration, 2002.

Herbert, Ulrich. "Europe in High Modernity. Reflections on a Theory of the 20th Century." *Journal of Modern European History* 5(1): 5–21, 2007.

Humphreys, Kristi. R. "Supernatural Housework." In *Home Sweat home: Perspectives on housework and modern relationships*, edited by Elizabeth Patton and Mimi Choi, 105–22. Lanham, MD: Rowman & Littlefield, 2014.

Keller, J. *Neue Nomaden?: zur Theorie und Realität aktueller Migrationsbewegungen in Berlin.* Münster: LIT Verlag, 2005.

Kerwin, Joseph, and Rhea Seddon. 2002. "Eating in Space—From an Astronauts Perspective." Nutrition 18 (10): 921–25, 2002.

Korff, Gottfried. Mentalität und Kommunikation in der Großstadt. Berliner Notizen zur inneren Urbanisierung." In *Großstadt. Aspekte empirscher Kulturforschung* edited by T. Johlmann and H. Bausinger, 343–61. Berlin: Staatliche Museen Preußischer Kulturbesitz, 1985.

Lane, Helen W. and Daniel L. Feeback. "History of nutrition in space flight." *Nutrition* 18 (10): 797–804, 2002.

Latour, Bruno. "Give me a laboratory and I will raise the world." In *Science observed. Perspectives on the social studies of science*, edited by Karin Knorr-Cetina and Michael Mulkay, 142–69. London: SAGE, 1983.

Levi, Jane. "Conviviality in Microgravity." *Moving Worlds: Food, Culture & Community* 6 (2): 162–76.

Levi, Jane. "The rise of the gastronaut." In *Alphabet City—Food* edited by John Knechtel, 4–17. Cambridge, MA: MIT Press, 2008.

Levi, Jane. "An extraterrestrial sandwich: the perils of food in space." *Endeavour* 34 (1): 6–11, 2010.

McCurdy, Howard E. "Has Spaceflight Had an Impact on Society? An Interpretive Framework." In *Societal Impact of Spaceflight* edited by Steven J. Dick and Roger D. Launius, 3–18. Washington, DC: NASA History Division, 2007.

Miggelbrink, Judith, et al. "Nomadic and Indigenous Spaces: Paths and Perspectives." In *Nomadic and Indigenous Spaces—Productions and Cognitions*, edited by Judith Miggelbrink et al., 1–35. Farnham: Ashgate, 2013.

Montanari, Massimo. *Food is Culture.* New York: Columbia University Press, 2006.

Perchonok, Michele, and Charles, Bourland. "NASA Food Systems: Past, Present, and Future." *Nutrition* 18 (10): 913–20, 2002.

Pikaar et al. "Decoupling Livestock from Land Use through Industrial Feed Production Pathways." *Environmental Science & Technology* 52 (13): 7351–59, 2018.

Reser, Anne, "The Lost Stories of NASA's 'Pink-Collar' Workforce." In *The Atlantic*, 2017. Retrieved September 20, 2018. https://www.theatlantic.com/science/archive/ 2017/02/ ursula-vils-nasa/516468/.

Rosa, Hartmut. *Beschleunigung und Entfremdung—Entwurf einer Kritischen Theorie spätmoderner Zeitlichkeit.* Frankfurt am Main: Suhrkamp, 2013.

Ross-Nazzal, Jennifer. "'From Farm to Fork': How Space Food Standards Impacted the Food Industry And Changed Food Safety Standards." In *Societal Impact of Spaceflight* edited by Steven J. Dick, and Roger D. Launius, 219–36. Washington, DC: NASA History Division, 2007.

Sachs, Wolfgang. Der Blaue Planet—Zur Zweideutigkeit einer modernen Ikone. In *Moderne Zeiten—Technik und Zeitgeist im 19. und 20. Jahrhundert*, edited by Michael Salewski and Ilona Stölken-Fitschen, 197–209. Stuttgart: Steiner, 1994.

Sanders, Matthew. "The Woman Who Got Real Food to Space." *Smithsonian National Air and Space Museum*. Retrieved September 20, 2018. https://airandspace.si.edu/stories /editorial/ woman-who-got-real-food-space.

Scholz, Fred. *Nomadismus, Theorie und Wandel einer sozio-ökologischen Kulturweise*. Stuttgart: Steiner, 1995.

Scott, James C. *Seeing Like a State—How Certain Schemes to Improve the Human Condition Have Failed*. New Haven, CT: Yale University Press, 1994.

von Herrmann, Hans-Christian. "Der planetarische Maßstab der Technik." *Internationales Jahrbuch für Medienphilosophie* 2 (1): 53–66, 2016.

Spreen, Dierk. "Weltraum, Körper und Moderne—Eine soziologische Annäherung an den astronautischen Menschen und die Cyborggesellschaft." In *Soziologie der Weltraumfahrt*, edited by Joachim Fischer and Dierk Spreen, 41–88. Bielefeld: Transcript, 2014.

Streck, Bernhard. "Systematisierungsansätze aus dem Bereich der ethnologischen Forschung." In *Nomadismus aus der Perspektive der Begrifflichkeit. Beiträge der 1. Tagung am 11.7.2001* edited by Stefan Leder and Bernhard Streck, 1–9. Halle: Orientwissenschaftliche Hefte 3; Mitteilungen des SFB Differenz und Integration", 2002.

Tolksdorf, Ulrich. "Strukturalistische Nahrungsforschung" In *Theorien des Essens* edited by Kikuko Kashiwagi-Wetzel and Anne-Rose Meyer, 123–55. Berlin: Suhrkamp, 1976.

NASA Sources

NRC National Research Council. *Working Group on Nutrition and Feeding Problems*. Washington, DC: The National Academies Press, 1963.

NASA PK 65-81. *Press-Kit Gemini III*, 1965.

NASA CTG-GT3. *Composite air-to-ground and onboard voice tape transcription of the GT-3 mission*, 1965.

NASA SP-202. *Aerospace Food Technology Conference*, 1969.

NASA TN D-7720. *Apollo Experience Report—Food Systems*, 1974.

NASA Fact Sheet. *Space-Food Spinoffs*, 8/2004.

Ross-Nazzal, Jennifer. "Edited Oral History Transcript—Charles T. Bourland." NASA: Johnson Space Center Oral History Project, 2006.

General Sources

New York Times. October 21, 1962. "Why Not 'Astronauttes' Also?"

NBC. 1965. *I Dream of Jeannie*. Season 1. Episode 4. First aired October 9, 1965.

Washington Post. October 10, 1968. "Rehydrated Shrimp Dish Replaces Shoe Leather."

MGM. 1968. *2001: A Space Odyssey*. First released April 2, 1968.

New York Times. June 29, 1969. "Madison Ave. Takes a Trip to The Moon."

Los Angeles Times. July 17, 1969. "NASA Uneasy: Madison Avenue Capitalizing on Apollo Products."

Guideposts. October 1970. "Buzz Aldrin on Communion in Space."

Mumford, Lewis. 1970. *The Myth of the Machine—The Pentagon of Power.* New York: Harcourt Brace Jovanovich.

Los Angeles Times. July 26, 1971 "Heavenly Fare in the Pantry for Moon Crew."

UP. 1972. *Silent Running.* First released March 10, 1972.

Fekl, W. 1974. "Astronautendiät, ein Weg zur synthetischen Nahrung." In *Natürliche und Synthetische Zusatzstoffe in der Nahrung des Menschen* edited by Robert Ammon and Janos Holló, 256–67. Darmstadt: Steinkopf.

New York Times. April 4, 1976. "Cordon Blah."

20th Century Fox. 1979. *Alien.* First released May 25, 1979.

New York Times. January 16, 1985. "Dining á la carte in the Space Shuttle."

7

Eating on Corsica's GR Footpaths and Trails

Choosing between Hi-Tech and Tradition

Philippe Pesteil

A Mediterranean island known for its sunshine, beaches, and intensive summer tourism, Corsica is also a "mountain in the sea." In 2016, it was given the status of "mountain island," which acknowledges its multiple handicaps (insularity, isolation, demographic weakness).[1] While mass tourism in the coastal regions and at seaside resorts has been developing since the mid-1960s, the mountains, including the villages scattered across their elevations, have been home to enduring agro-pastoral activitivities, which thrived until the Second World War.

Long distances between residential areas (usually villages grouped together) and the agricultural and pastoral lands meant that Corsican farmers were often forced to make extended journeys to their fields and pastures every day. For the herdsmen seeking pastureland for their livestock, these journeys formed the framework of a so-called inverted transhumance. They would take their livestock high up the mountain from May to October and down onto the plains or the coast between November and April. The growers also often had to make long journeys, sometimes on a daily basis, to reach their fields, since land was parcelled and widely dispersed.[2] The custom of taking a quick break to eat, either as they walked while tending their herds or in temporary accommodation[3] during the summer or winter transhumance, stemmed from a long eating tradition. This was a culture of transforming and conserving food to be carried and consumed outside. Preserved meats (cooked and smoked), dried or fresh fruit depending on the season (grapes, figs, almonds, apples, pears), bread (chestnut flour, cereal flour), often soaked in olive oil, an onion,[4] and cheese were practical, nutritious provisions for the herdsman/grower.[5] Snacks could, of course, vary according to region and season. Today, however, it is usually native or tourist hikers who can be found walking the mountains. They follow the signposted routes specifically aimed at nature lovers and those wishing to seek out the most beautiful landscapes and vantage points or the best routes. This chapter will focus mainly on the famous GR20 route but will also include the lesser-known but more accessible and very popular variants of Da Mare à Mare (North, Center, South), Mare è Monti (North, South) and the Sentier de la Transhumance. It will also look at the development of hiking trails (in natural or urban environments) that are attracting increasing numbers on distances designed to appeal to everyone from the amateur hiker to the seasoned athlete.[6] This kind of physical exertion requires food that is suited to the demands of the hike. As a result, different food cultures, ranging from those relating to Corsica's agro-pastoral past to those developed by nutrition technologies, have developed and now coexist.

AN ISLAND TO EXPLORE

While seaside and city tourism has mainly been dominated by British nationals living in Ajaccio, the island's interior and its mountains were first popularized in Europe by the island's German visitors and then by other Europeans that came to enjoy its unspoiled natural environment. It is highly likely that all the "firsts" and "discoveries" among the highest peaks were actually made by the herdsmen and hunters who had roamed the island for millennia. We should, however, distinguish between hiking and climbing (with its routes). The most well-known figure in Corsican mountain history was Felix von Cube, who hiked through and climbed the island's most beautiful and difficult peaks from 1899 onward.[7]

The majority of routes today are located in the Corsica Regional Nature Park (CRNP), which was created in 1971. Initially covering an area of 220,000 hectares, including 40 villages, it has now grown to 350,510 hectares (approximately 40 percent of Corsica's surface area), incorporating 145 villages.[8] In addition to the other missions defined in its charter, the park has specialized in mountain tourism, the driving force of which has been hiking. It currently offers approximately 1,500 km of trails. The year after the park was created, the first GR20 route appeared, designed by Michel Fabrikant, whose books are still sought out by enthusiasts as references.[9] The main idea of the route was to offer seasoned hikers a trail that would live up to their expectations. For example, the mountain refuges that mark out the stages still evidence this guiding principle, with their modest structures and spartan comforts. The entire hike, which is approximately 167 kilometers long (with an 11,000 m elevation gain), was planned to last sixteen days (at the rate of one stage per day) at an average of seven hours walking per day. The amateur sport and performance sport versions of the GR20 consist of "doubling" or "tripling" the stages. Some experienced hikers can complete the route in just a few days. The current men's record of thirty-one hours and six minutes is held by François d'Haene (set in June 2016). The GR20 is often described as "the toughest trail in Europe," a reputation that has attracted thrill seekers from all over Europe. In addition to the winter version of the "Alta Strada" GR, there are other more original and less frequented routes that make up the Corsican mountain network. The most well-known of the guided hikes are the

Parc naturel régional de Corse

Légende

- Ancien périmètre 145 communes
- Périmètre d'étude charte Pnrc 180 communes
- Corte, Siège social
- Casa di a natura Vizzavona
- Centre de soins des rapaces
- Enclos Cerfs
- Réserve naturelle de Scandola
- Réserve MAB
- Casa marina Galeria
- Casa di u mele Murzu
- Casa Paoletti U Nucariu
- Musée archéologique Albertacce
- Village des tortues Moltifau
- GR 20 Fra li monti
- Variantes
- Mare a Mare Nord
- Mare a Mare Centre
- Mare a Mare Sud
- Mare e Monti Nord
- Mare e Monti Sud
- Sentier de la Transhumance
- Sentier U Sulaghju- Ghisoni
- L'Isula Rossa- Corti
- Refuges

10   0   10   20 km

Fond de carte: IGN
Données: Pnrc

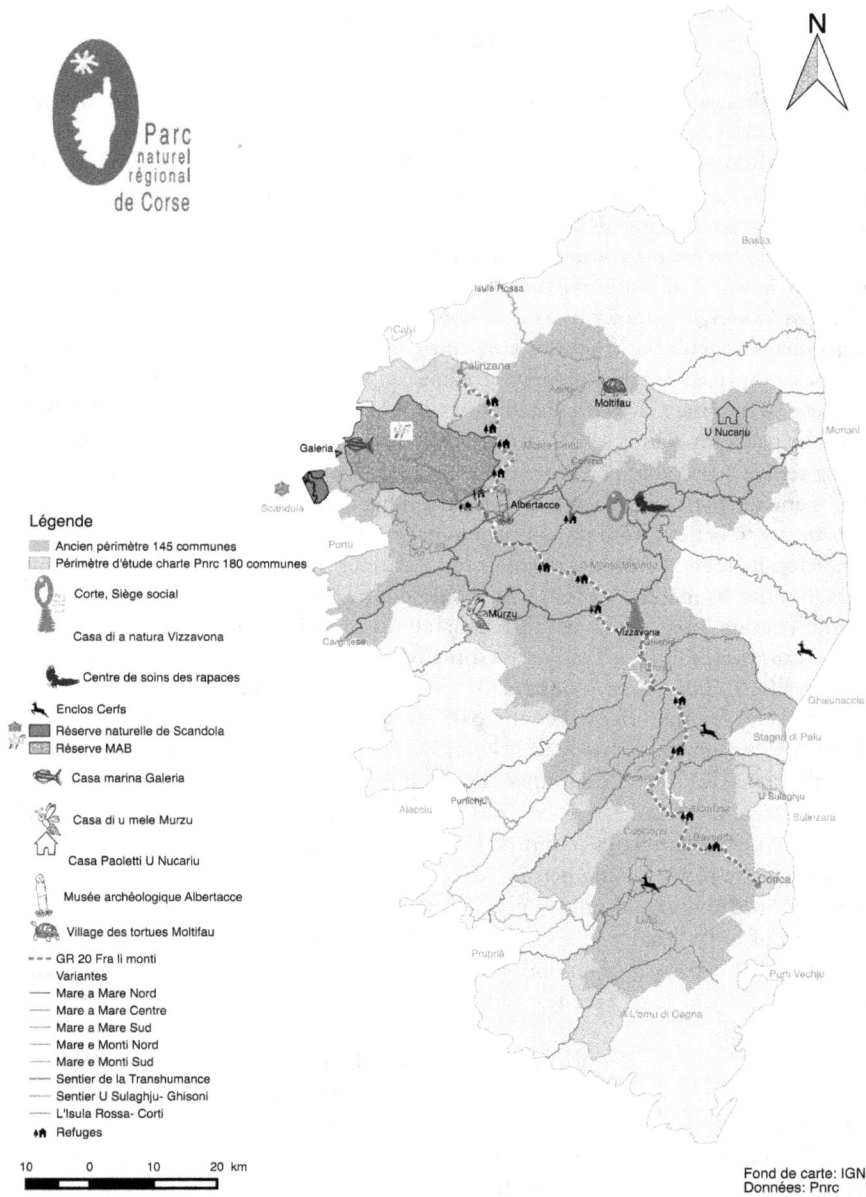

Figure 7.1. Territoire du Parc Naturel Régional de Corse = Corsica Regional Nature Park area

Maison d'information = Information center
Refuge Parc = Park refuge
Gîte d'étape = Tourist lodge
Sentiers de pays = Country trails
Parcours VTT = Mountain bike trails
Nord = north
Centre = center
Sud = south
Chemin de la transhumance = Sentier de la Transhumance
It is difficult to obtain figures for the hikers who use the various marked trails.

Source: http://www.pnr.corsica/cartographie/

different variations of the Mare e Monti (north, south) and the Mare a Mare (north, center, south). There are also shorter hikes, such as the Sentier de la Transhumance and the Île-Rousse-Corte trails, which are known as country or heritage trails, as well as loop walks. While these are still considered sports hiking routes, they are much less challenging than the GR20.

The GR20 has been an added attraction for tourists to the island since the 1980s. Although it was made more accessible when it was opened to the public, it still maintains its tough reputation. The autonomous routes, which once required either twenty-five kilogram backpacks or constant trips to the villages to obtain supplies, have been replaced by ten kilogram backpacks and in-situ provisions or tailored products. When the GR was created, the sale of food was prohibited, and this ban stayed in place for a long time even though the practice soon became widespread among refuge guardians. The more recently created routes are also based around the villages and are partly intended to provide the inhabitants of mountain areas with the opportunity to benefit from the tourism bonanza. The village grocery stores thus sell fresh,[10] local, "identity" produce (cold meats, cheese) to hikers who have strayed off the high-altitude, marked trails or who would not be happy if they crossed the island without coming into contact with the inhabitants of its interior.

The number of hikers has been estimated between twenty thousand (official estimate 2016) and thirty thousand (rectified estimate taking into account non-listed walkers) for the GR20. For the past few years some mountain professionals, and even some amateurs, have publicly criticized the saturation of the hiking trails, especially the GR20. In the summer there can be up to 160 hikers stopping in the refuges, which have not been designed for such numbers. Waste of all kinds (organic and otherwise) accumulates in situ. The owners of the gîtes d'étape refuge began providing waste-sorting containers in 2016. While the herdsmen's old pouches could hold very little and would only contain unpackaged, organic foodstuffs, the hikers' backpacks of today hold a minimum of fifty liters, with food in high-performance packaging that can last a thousand years. According to the people we interviewed, the vast majority of hikers are respectful of the environment, and the trail remains little impacted by waste.

In 1998, a new activity was launched that united mountain and running enthusiasts. It was the first organized trail run (Le Grand Raid Inter-lacs/The Great Inter-Lakes Raid) in Corsica. Its rapid success among a range of people (older adults, young people, women, etc.) led to the creation of an increasing number of routes of varying lengths, elevation gain, and difficulty. There are also urban versions in Bastia and Ajaccio.[11] These gatherings of hundreds of runners require substantial logistical effort to mobilize volunteers to help with putting out signs and cones, manning refreshment stations, security, medical assistance, etc. The most iconic of the trail runs, the Ultra Trail di Corsica, takes place over three days and two nights from July 5–7 each year. There are four versions of this trail run, 15 kilometers, 33 kilometers, 69 kilometers, and 110 kilometers, the latter involving an 8,000-meter elevation gain.

In 2017, a total of 916 participants succeeded in crossing the finishing line. In the 2019 trail run, a total of 1,094 participants were ranked on arrival.

All of Corsica's permanent paths and temporary trail runs require participants to have at least some dietary logistics tailored to the terrain, the type of activity (a walk, amateur sport, performance sport), and the ability and training preparation of each participant.

EATING TO WALK OR RUN

The question of diet directly depends on the way in which the journey is approached and executed. The difference between the trained competitor, who completes the route in four or five days, and the walker, who wishes to take advantage of the stop-offs and spend three weeks in the mountains, will be obvious from their food supplies. Those who just want to complete one stage over a weekend and spend a night in the mountains, relaxing and admiring the landscapes, can take as much food as they like. When the GR20 was opened, young Corsicans would freely indulge in this type of hiking as a means of social interaction and discovering the mountain. They would take with them cold meats and baguettes along with crisps, wine, and bottles of pastis. In spite of the weight and bulk of their backpacks, these were considered picnic essentials by the young Corsicans, who were more interested in partying against a majestic backdrop than they were in performance: "products like energy bars did not exist 30 or 40 years ago . . . a bit of sausage, a piece of cheese, what did we have? . . . we just took what we wanted, we would set off loaded like mules. In the evening, the tins, the kids would go fishing . . . we just took what we liked" (translated from French). Today, most people going into the mountains are foreigners, with some considering the GR a challenge. While the picnic has not disappeared, however, its contents have evolved. They now conform to more restrictive specifications.

The typical hiker who intends to follow the GR20's sixteen stages will not want to carry too much weight, but will want to eat correctly in order to complete the route and not suffer any ill effects as a result of poor nutrition management.[12] Breakfast, which will be eaten either in their accommodation or in the surrounding area, will be composed of coffee or tea, fruit juice, cereal with milk, and fruit. In addition, individuals will select extras that are in keeping with their usual eating habits in order to take into account their energy and digestive requirements. Some of the recommended foods for trekking (energy snacking)—in other words, products consumed while walking or during short stops—are cereal bars, energy drinks and biscuits, classic dry biscuits, chocolate (bars or squares), and dried and/or oleaginous fruits (apricots, bananas, apples, almonds, hazelnuts, dates, etc.). For those who do not want to get up at dawn to do the (minimum) seven-hour walk but prefer to take their time and arrive at the gîtes d'étape around midday to enjoy an afternoon rest, lunch is a picnic. Mixed salad remains a safe bet despite its weight and preparation time because it guarantees vitamin intake. This will consist of a mixture of seasonal vegetables, protein (tuna, hard-boiled egg, etc.) and rice, lentils, or cold pasta. Quinoa and bulgur wheat have also recently made an appearance in tourists' backpacks. This can be accompanied by cold meats (from Corsica or elsewhere), dried meats or sardines and, for dessert, soft cheeses (pressed or steamed), fresh fruit, or chocolate. Bread, for those who cannot do without it, will be in the form of packets of whole grain slices. Eating regularly after the first snack of the morning ensures that lunchtime intake will not be excessive because there are still several hours of walking ahead. Dinner in the evenings, which will be eaten either in or in the vicinity of the gîte d'étape, must remedy the hiker's fatigue and prepare their body for the next day's exertion. Dried soup mix, slow sugars (rice, pasta, potatoes, etc.), and fruit, accompanied by copious amounts of water, will restore the hiker's reserves. The physical aspect of the hike should not, however, completely overshadow the festive and convivial aspect, which is often part of the reason why people want to complete a GR hike. Meeting new people and relaxing are often synonymous with drinking alcohol. This usually happens during or after the evening meal, with all thoughts of dietary requirements going out the window. As is often the case in situations of constraint, the little extras make all the difference and are much appreciated in group hikes. Food "luxuries" such as salt, sugar, sauces, and spices will revive hikers and contribute to keeping up morale during challenging times.

Regarding the technical evolutions relating to portable foods and the context that facilitates their transport, freeze-dried food, once the preserve of the well-off and solo expeditionists, has evolved to offer ready meals to their fans. Although they are said to have certain practical advantages (reduced bulk, lightweight powder, very quick preparation time), the main criticism continues to be that the portions are ungenerous and that they soon leave you feeling tired. Most tend to enhance the original flavors of these freeze-dried food with a little something extra. As Romain Bragard notes in his study, walkers using freeze-dried food will often represent themselves humorously as living in a state of "savagery" because they are experiencing the constant feeling of "deprivation" from their diet, which they see as very basic:

> The basic dimension is reinforced by the fact that this food is functional, or medical, since its main aim is to guarantee a quantity of calories. It has something basic and utilitarian about it, denoting a minimalist symbolic dimension. Hence, the use of this utilitarian technology forces asceticism on hikers. It plunges them into a world of taste where there is no diversity or element of surprise, that is, no pleasure other than that of performing this ascetic experience. This is the experience they have when they consume this highly technological product. (Translated from French)[13]

Tins have clearly regressed since the 1970s and 1980s. Their weight and mass are a handicap for the brisk walker. Only sardines continue to be taken owing to their nutritional qualities. Water supplies en route are subject to the vagaries of the mountain island's climate and the state of its springs. The Camelbak[14] has proved a great success for a number of years now because it avoids having to stop to take your bottle out or having to rely on someone else to help you. Many hikers now use tablets to purify the water drawn from streams or springs.[15] Finally, BCAA[16] carbohydrate drinks have become popular over the past few years, as have energy supplements in the form of capsules or tablets. Mineral salts (sodium, potassium, calcium, magnesium) and the B vitamins present in food (milk, meat, cereals) can be taken in liquid form in drinks to avoid dehydration and ensure proper muscle function.

As a footnote to the food question, there is also the matter of the equipment used to carry, contain, and preserve foodstuffs during journeys. The equipment for preparing and eating meals includes the classic knife, fork, and spoon along with a hiking stove, folding cup, and saucepan. Today's high-tech offers backpacks that combine comfort, lightness, abrasion resistance, and waterproofness.[17] This kind of performance has been made possible by hybridizing different materials that have emerged from research in the chemical industry (nylon, polymer, tarpaulin, PVC, Dyneema, Cuben, silnylon, etc.).

Catering and groceries offered in the gîtes d'étape are another factor that merit consideration. These provisions allow hikers to travel with a lighter backpack because they do not need to carry as much. The question of eating en route therefore comes down to a choice between buying everything in advance or eating in facilities that offer catering. The extremely rocky nature of the higher peaks means hikers generally prefer to bring a bag that is as light as possible. The refuges offer hot or cold dishes depending on the season. In the mornings they serve food that is quick to prepare, such as omelettes, cold meats, pasta, soup (Corsican). In the evenings, when it is time to rest and recover from the day's exertions, they generally offer more substantial, gastronomic dishes. For many years it was left to the refuge guardians to organize the evening meals. CRNP management turned a blind eye to this unregulated practice that allowed tourists to enjoy a "real Corsican meal" and the guardians to supplement their salaries. Hikers must make a reservation as soon as they arrive at a refuge because demand can be high during the "season." The refuge will also have a grocery store where visitors can buy dry goods (biscuits, bread, cold meats) and energy foods (cheese). However, this new service has impacted small businesses in the villages, where hikers used to buy their supplies, which has has caused a certain amount of resentment among the shop owners. The prices charged in the refuges are sometimes considered excessive, especially by those who opt for full catering or who are relying on the grocery store for their provisions.

As far as the mountain trail races are concerned, it is important to distinguish between the short trails (around 15 or 20 km) and the ultra-trails (which can last more than forty-eight or seventy-two hours). Both trails require a specific diet corresponding to the energy required. For the short trails, it is best to bring glycogens[18]—powders to mix with drinks, bars, and gels—vitamins, and caffeine. The bars and all solid foods are carried in the backpack and eaten while walking, while the gels can be consumed while running.[19] Refreshment stations generally offer fresh bananas as well as cola drinks (despite gastric reflux),[20] dried fruit, prunes, and chocolate.

For longer distances, where more energy is required, sugars become insufficient and savory foods are preferred, including individual choices from a broad range of food plus the creation of ad hoc diets.[21] Food habits can vary from one competitor to the next. Our data show these include cold meats, vermicelli soup, eating a boiled potato while walking, and rice balls mixed with cheese, honey, and ham.[22] The need for protein for muscle strengthening can be met by local products. The Ultra Trail di Corte (110 km), for example, offers local cheese. Expressions of food cultures were found among all our interviewees, who talked of spicy rice balls and crystallized ginger. Since hydration is essential, water is often accompanied by isotonic products that pass directly into the bloodstream and BCCAs to compensate for deficiencies that can severely affect energy recovery.[23] Fans of natural products prefer agave syrup and almond milk. The longer running routes in Europe and elsewhere provide "life bases," where runners make proper stops and have full meals. During dry spells in summer there are a number of ways for runners to rehydrate, including drinking liquids[24] and eating fresh fruits such as melons, pomelos, watermelons, and oranges.

Energy demands and the rhythmicity of intake require participants to have at least some knowledge of nutrition,[25] calorific expenditure, and their own bodies in terms of reading reactions during exercise and anticipating "cravings" or "hot flushes":

> When you start not wanting to eat at all, it means it's all over . . . if you don't eat, you deteriorate . . . you can get to the end eating nothing almost but that would be all down to mental strength and you'd pay for it . . . if you eat well regularly, everything's okay at the start, it's easy . . . a sip of water every ten minutes, an energy bar roughly every hour . . . it's easy . . . eight or ten hours later though it begins to get more and more difficult . . . it's difficult to stick to the plan . . . if you stick to your food plan your race will be successful right to the end . . . but you shouldn't wait till you're hungry before you eat or thirsty before you have a drink." (Translated from French)

We cannot just look at the food question from a strictly physiological and energy point of view, however. In addition to its image as a fuel that drives our bodies, there is a more social dimension to food. Food intake is a conduit for meeting new people and social interaction.

EATING TO SHARE AND REMEMBER

Specialized websites and blogs maintained by hikers merit further study. Many candidates seek advice from those who have already done a particular trek, and many express their apprehension about their ability to take on the task. They do not want to make any mistakes when it comes to planning the stages, deciding what equipment to take, packing the right food, planning the meals, etc. Likewise, proud of their experience, they in turn advise future hikers. This double communication input contributes to consolidating the legend of the mountain island, and the GR20 in particular because, among the testimonies of success, there are also confessions of failure.[26] Ranking high among the failures are underestimating the physical challenge followed by errors relating to diet and backpack weight.

Reading the testimonies reinforces Le Breton's analyses concerning the "happy values"[27] of contemporary walking, which are respect for the environment and the territories crossed, meeting and respecting the populations encountered along the way, self-discovery, and discovering bodily sensations. The landscapes, which become immortalized in multiple photographic or video shots, allow people to transcend any difficulties experienced during the journey. Memories of conversations with other hikers, with refuge guardians, herdsmen, and villagers encountered in the few surviving shops reinforce the idea that what is important is not the end goal (the arrival) but the journey itself.

Encounters with "identity products"[28] do not just take place during the stage stops. On the GR20, as well as on the routes that cross the villages, the walker often likes to take a break from their daily foods and flavors, even those prioritizing energy consumption. They will seek out good cheeses, ideally with short distribution channels (direct sale from the producer to the consumer and purchased at the place of production). This, combined with that unique moment when they meet the herdsman producer/refiner, is a major motivational factor that does not exist in the purely nutritional treatment of performance. As the memory of their exertion, fatigue, or "nightmares" even, begin to fade away and are replaced by only pleasant memories and a valorization of personal achievement, the walker's encounters with the Corsican herdsmen will remain unforgettable moments, justifying all the difficulties they encountered. Hence, the websites and blogs mention all the places and pens where you can find not only cheese but also the quality welcome you would expect given the legendary Corsican hospitality. Over time, the regulars get to know the gîtes d'étape guardians as well as their culinary customs: "At the first refuge it's generally lentils . . . Marie it's lentils . . . and Pascal to Petra Piana as well . . . Pierrot it's pasta . . . it's pasta at almost all of them." (translated from French). Cold meats and/or Corsican soup as a starter with cheese for dessert complete this overview of comfort food that is provided by the island after a visitor's exertion. However, total immersion in the island's culture comes with a glass of Pietra beer that is made from chestnut flour and sold in situ. These sometimes-prolonged "aperitifs," shared on the terraces of the gîtes and prompting unbridled exchanges and flowing conversations, forge lasting memories.

The herdsman, who is now an emblematic figure of Corsican identity, has risen from the bottom of the social ladder to being the guardian of customs and memories. In addition to his activities as a producer/refiner, he is also a salesman to passing tourists. He must manage his stocks carefully as demand outstrips supply. Direct sales could wipe out his stock of long-keeping cheeses, for example, making it difficult to fulfill orders from restaurateurs and villagers. The solitary transhumants, whose pastoral conviviality used to fill their periods of rest, have now evolved into welcomers, advisers, and storytellers for tourists, who are in turn happy with the "authenticity" of their encounter and the products they purchase. There have been many doubts cast as to the origin of the food sold on the island, including the cheese (and cold meats).[29] According to some of our interviewees, the practice of transforming milk from another herd into cheese or even of selling cheese from another herdsman has now spread to the high summer pastures.

Not everything on the hiking trails meets with unanimous appreciation. Walking, which is an opportunity to confront one's own limitations, is an activity that takes place within an ever-present social and economic context. Supporting fellow walkers as you set off in groups, integrating with other groups at the stages or during walks, and enduring unexpected or difficult situations is all part of the experience and of the tourists' encounter with otherness. For example, food-related issues are high on the list of hikers' complaints. Walkers are torn between wanting to meet the inhabitants of the villages in order to consolidate a need for contact and "authenticity" and the desire not to spend money unnecessarily or excessively. The information shared online can encourage walkers to opt for a bivouac pitched near a refuge or gîte and take-away meals, rather than buying meals in situ at the end of the stages. It should be remembered, however, that "wild" camping is prohibited.

This is all irrelevant for the runners, who cannot afford to stay long at any gîtes. While racing is, by nature, a competitive and solo pursuit, there is still a convivial dimension:

> When you're racing you talk on the long trails, you run with people who go at about the same pace as you, on the short trails everyone's going for it, you can't talk, on the long trails you make running buddies, on the night stretches you tend to form into groups of two or three, it's nice . . . you can lend each other food." (Translated from French)

Our interviewees stressed the existence of a certain spirit specific to this discipline, which they hoped would continue despite the increase in the number of races. Camaraderie prevails in this rare nonprofessionalised sport, which offers no prize money to the winner. Everyone helps everyone else, and the best runners in the world can be seen competing alongside only occasional participants.

MOUNTAIN FOOD: AN ILLUSTRATION OF POSTMODERN PARADOXES

This mountain island reflects the trends accompanying the humanity versus nature changes currently underway. The slow journey of the herds and their herdsmen has been replaced by long lines of hikers or runners, sometimes to the point of exhaustion. The mountain has become less a space for production and more a landscape, a natural setting for spectacle, performance, and challenge. Green tourism, in all its senses, represents for many European regions experiencing population decline and productive extensification a compensatory solution that is envisaged to reverse the trend.[30] The economic and social redevelopment of the island's interior, carried out under the aegis of the CRNP,[31] has made it possible to maintain an evolved form of pastoralism that is appended as much to the tourist trade as to the "proto-farming" of bygone days, which responds to the herd's natural movements.

Valorizing the island's natural heritage, local production, and its image of quality and authenticity attracts an often-urban population, eager to discover a landscape lauded for its beauty and diversity.[32] These visitors enjoy savoring the unpackaged and unbarcoded cheeses and cold meats, motivated by the confidence they have in a supposed ancestral know-how that has been preserved. They also appreciate their conversations with the man from the mountains, which serves to reinforce their archetypal vision of the simple, welcoming herdsman if the interaction was positive and of the coarse "strong character" if it was more confrontational.

The herdsman has had to modify his routes, his ancestral customs, and his technical activities. Breeding and births must correspond with the influx of tourists in order to take advantage of the seasonal bonanza. He has no real "appetite" for contact with populations with whom he has little in common, but this financial contribution has become crucial to him. Hence, his often harsh judgment of tourists who travel (according to him) without money or with no intention of spending it. These tourists forget that one motivation for walking is to gain access to the most impoverished of peoples.[33] This situation reinforces in turn the herdsman's own stereotypes of the supposed greed of mainlanders.[34] This context, which is typical of a working misunderstanding, reflects the convergence of opposites. It contributes to turning hiking into a paradoxical object with uncompromising principles. The congested paths and gîtes, which are victims of their own success, and the scheduled encounter with the herdsman coexist with a desire for freedom, for the solitude of the summits, and for individual endeavor. It would be futile to try to dissociate the two characteristics of this ambivalent object, which is characteristic of the fluid recompositions and blurred paths described by Balandier on the subject of supermodernity.[35]

This oppositional montage fuels a debate that reveals a plurality of explanations. Can hiking and/or trail running be considered an archetypal expression of a consumer society that appropriates marginalized territories in its endless quest for new markets? Or is it, on the contrary, a protected niche, where modern humanity can escape its consumer destiny? Opinions diverge on this. For Soulé-Bourneton and Stumpp[36] the ultra-trail is the "avatar of a performance society," which is targeted at the educated middle classes, at "distinctive" ambition, although they argue this by developing a discourse of inner experience and encounter with the other.[37] In response, Codezero's[38] website promotes a return to a practice that is the distinguishing feature of human beings, viewing this sport as "a basic gesture of freedom." In this respect, we can draw on the words of Martine Segalen (1994; although she was writing on the subject of urban racing) who says that:

> These men and women have regained possession of their bodies. Inter-age and inter-class, racing allows the heavy, the slow and the young to say what they are. Reclaiming their bodies, they reclaim the city, taking it back just for a moment from the cars. They subvert it and re-humanise it through the oldest of anthropological *activities*.

Trail run enthusiasts clearly refer to a return to a basic need when they talk about their passion. Trail running has existed since the dawn of humanity, since the age of the hunter-gatherers, when endurance was part of survival and a daily way of life.

> Human beings were hunter/gatherers, it was every day, how did they hunt down the mammoths? . . . to exhaustion . . . so we have it in us . . we just have to work on it . . . we've become sedentary . . . there's a tribe in Mexico,[39] they run 250, 300 kilometers with sandals on, not shoes like us . . . it's existed for a long time . . . that person who died at Marathon, Philippides . . . he did 350 kilometers, before going to Marathon . . . after he died, he had a liver problem . . . 350 before running the 42 . . . take the Kenyans, even today they are strong. Why? Every day they do 20 kilomters to school on foot and 20 kilometers to come home from school at night . . . they do a marathon a day. (Translated from French)

This revival of walking in all its senses, in contrast to global mechanization (symbolized by the combustion engine), has its origins in the writings of all the most famous authors, from Rousseau to Rimbaud. More modern texts extol the many virtues of walking. You can savor a time that stretches out[40] before you when you are on a hike (a dimension that disappears with races and trail runs). It allows you to think, dream, or even be an activist[41] in a counterculture whose expression in food terms would be the slow-food movement.[42]

However, it is important to note that walking (even slowly) on an island means having to take a boat or plane to get there. Moreover, as we have seen, participants must choose between the island gastronomy and performance foods. Financial considerations cannot, therefore, be ignored. This is the less idyllic conception of the underlying realities that some authors prefer to highlight. The democratized cult of the body, a collective pushing ourselves to the limits, and the liberal values of performance also find their expression in hiking and its discourse of freedom. This is also acquired, however, by giving salaried employment to the labor force of the invisible masses. As Bragard reminds us, the Other is not just the Corsican that you meet in a gîte or a pen or by chance in a village; the Other is also the individual represented by hi-tech, in other words, the "producer of the material prerequisites for rambling pleasure. However, this worker is extremely remote because they become diluted in the flow of goods. The Chinese, Burmese and Indonesian workers employed by the big brand labels distributed in France have no political presence in the practice of hiking." (2009, 150) The "democratization" of hiking through its diffusion among an ever wider public[43] of products generated by the industry (including food) has led to the disappearance of the producer and the salaried workforce and aligned mountain hiking and trail runs with globalized production relationships and confirmed dominations.

Baudrillard asks: "What could be more enticing than a challenge?"[44] To respond to this question, he contrasts the conventional, secret, highly ritualized pact with immanent, explicit law. Advanced hiking and trail runs belong more in the first category (convention) than the second (law). Mountain walking or running is also appealing because it involves risk-taking, which includes diet as a key factor. The social actor seeks to reduce and anticipate any possible snags by using hi-tech equipment that is supposed to respond to all foreseeable high-risk events.[45] The technical quality of this equipment must therefore not disappoint. It must protect against any injury that might interrupt the activity or turn what should be a moment of happiness and communion with nature into a tragic reminder of our limitations and the body's vulnerability. Fully equipped and tuned into itself (to use Bragard's expressions[46]) the body unites some apparently contradictory dimensions. The individualized cult of the body promotes the relationship of self and the concept of being tuned into oneself (through sensations of both beauty and pain) through a new intimacy with matter (natural or chemical). As we have seen, food is a conduit for both dimensions. Both the contemplative and the hedonistic walkers play with and put together food according to their own plans and resources. Whether they choose health-conscious food (to avoid the vicissitudes of failure) or pleasure food (to enjoy the local flavors and the feeling of being full), controlling their diet is done as a means of reassurance.

Integrated within a socioanthropology of risk, therefore, diet becomes precautionary food, intended to preserve the body's integrity.[47] The mountain project thus involves calculation (calorific) and a codification of practices according to rationalized knowledge (nutrition) and an adaptation of behavior to needs as they arise (anticipation, regularity, recovery, etc.). In addition, it must take into account the influence of the participant's experiences as well as those of others (shared on the internet or in direct exchanges). Circulating information helps to warn participants of any dangers. Hence, the social realm bolsters the individual project while, at the same time, reinforcing reasons for coming together.

BIBLIOGRAPHY

Balandier, Georges. *Le dédale; pour en finir avec le XXᵉ siècle*, Paris: 1994, Fayard.

Baudrillard, Jean. *De la séduction*, Paris: 1979, Galilée.

Bragard, Romain. *Urbanité et sentiment de nature; Ethnographies comparées de la randonnée pédestre Corse-Chapada Diamantina (Brésil)*, PhD thesis, supervised by F. Laplantine, Université Lumière Lyon 2: 2009.

———. "Ensauvagement et héroïsme dans la randonnée pédestre," *Cultures-Kairós* [online], appeared in *Théma*, updated: 18/12/2016, URL: http://revues.mshparisnord.org/cultures kairos/index.php?id=1444.

Corse. "Le dynamisme du Parc régional," Encyclopédie Régionale, Paris: 1979. Christine Bonneton Ed., 269–88.

Fabrikant, Michel. *A travers la montagne Corse en 16 jours de randonnée*, Fédération Française de la Randonnée Pédestre, Topoguide GR, 2012.

Fourneau, Francis. "Tourisme rural et développement local dans les moyennes montagnes andalouses," in *Moyennes montagnes européennes, Nouvelles fonctions, nouvelles gestions de l'espace rural*, CERMAC, no. 11, Université Blaise Pascal Clermont-Ferrand: 2011, 575–87.

Gros, Frédéric. *Marcher une philosophie*, Paris: 2011, Flammarion.

Héritier, Stéphane and Laslaz, Lionel, (eds.). *Les parcs nationaux dans le monde; Protection, gestion et développement durable*, Paris: 2008, Ellipses.

Lacquement, Guillaume. "Le devenir des espaces marginaux dans les nouveaux Länder allemands: la moyenne montagne et l'exemple du massif de Thuringe," in *Moyennes montagnes européennes, Nouvelles fonctions, nouvelles gestions de l'espace rural*, CERMAC, no. 11, Université Blaise Pascal Clermont-Ferrand: 2011, 497–520.

Le Breton, David. *Marcher, éloge des chemins et de la lenteur*, Paris: 2000, Métailié.

Lhérété, Héloïse. "Le sens de la marche," *Sciences humaines*, August–September 2012, no. 240, 2–5.

Michel, Franck. "La marche à pied, un mode philosophique d'être, de penser et de voyager," *Les Cahiers Espaces*, no. 112, April 2012, 26–35.

Pécaud, Domonique. *Risques et précautions; l'interminable rationalisation du social*, Paris: 2005, La Dispute.

Pesteil, Philippe. "Les nourritures de marche; du berger au randonneur (exemples corses)," *Antrocom*, vol. 4–2, 121–26, 2008. http://www.antrocom.net.

———. *L'Emotion identitaire en Corse; Un territoire au cœur*, Anthropologie), Paris: L'Harmattan, 2010.

———. "Le territoire comme gisement de produits miroirs: exemples corses," in *L'assiette du touriste; Le goût de l'authentique*, (eds. J.-Y. Andrieux, P. Harismendy), Presses Universitaires de Rennes et Presses Universitaires François Rabelais: 2013, 83–99.

———. "Adhérer aux stéréotypes, le fatal destin des minorités?" In: *Les sociétés minoritaires ou minorisées face à la globalisation: Uniformisation, résistance ou renouveau?*, 2015, Yakoutsk Conference proceedings, 16–19 Oct. 2012, T.2, 263–83.

———. *Les productions alimentaires en Corse 1769–1852*, Ajaccio: 2016, Albiana.

Routier, Guillaume et Soulé, Bastien. "Jouer avec la gravité: approche sociologique plurielle de l'engagement dans les sports dangereux," *SociologieS* [online], Théories et Recherches, published online 01 June 2010, URL: http://journals.openedition.org/sociologies/3121.

Sansot, Pierre. *Chemins au vent; l'Art de voyager*, Paris: 2000, Payot.

Segalen, Martine. *Les enfants d'Achille et de Nike*, Paris: 1994, Editons Métailié.

Urbain, Jean-Didier. *L'Idiot du voyage; Histoires de touristes*, Paris: 2002, Petite Bibliothèque Payot.

Weiss, Michel-Claude. *Les bergeries traditionnelles de Corse*, Ajaccio: 2020, Albiana.

Websites consulted

www.expemag.com
www.le-gr20.fr
www.le monde.fr/idees/article/2017/09/10/1.
www.mdem.org/france/DT1344343697/page/Nutrition.html
www.pnr.corsica
www.randonnee-corse-gr20.fr

8

Italian-Sounding

A World Carrier of a Traveling *Cuisine*

Giovanni Ceccarelli and Stefano Magagnoli

IN SEARCH OF HOMELAND: *LITTLE BIG ITALY*

Francesco Panella is a restaurant owner famous in Italy and the United States. In Italy he and his family run a well-known restaurant in Trastevere in the heart of Rome called L'Antica Pesa that has become a regular port of call for those seeking an authentic culinary experience. In 2012 in Brooklyn, New York, he opened a sister restaurant serving the same dishes and ingredients. It quickly became a great success frequented by celebrities. Panella has established a reputation as an expert of Italian eating in the United Sates and has also published a restaurant guide to Brooklyn.[1]

Nove, the Italian general entertainment cable television channel owned by *Discovery* Inc., broadcast the first of eight episodes of Panella's foodtainment series *Little Big Italy* in April 2018.[2] This show is based on stereotypes as well as facts, shows "expat" Italians living overseas talking about the "taste of home," and features their favorite restaurants where they find real Italian food. In each city,[3] Panella interviews three Italians who are living there for work, or school, or family. They also eat at the person's favorite Italian restaurant. At each meal one dish is chosen by the expat, who does not vote for the best dish, one is chosen by the cook who shows off his or her "signature dish," and one is chosen by Panella, who orders a meal off the menu, representing the secret desire of an Italian abroad. The dishes are awarded between one and five points, and Panella also gives a score for the "Italianità," which is often decisive in the result. The winning restaurant obtains the Best *Little Big Italy* Restaurant award, which garners enormous publicity, and the expat wins a bonus card to eat at the restaurant for a year.

Little Big Italy reveals the emotive reasons for food nomadism. Although its main aim is to entertain, it is inspired by important themes and issues. The expats and the restaurant owners find themselves, for whatever reason, in a foreign land far away from

Italy, and their life stories, feelings, and opinions offer insight into the varied experience of migrants everywhere. The program features real-life scenarios and memories as well as nostalgia and what is often a positive experience of adaptation to the new country. Tastes and flavors from home telescope the distances, and home becomes closer as foods and meals alive in the memory are once again given tangible form.[4]

NOSTALGIA FOR THE HOMELAND

Little Big Italy is based on the nostalgia felt by every individual uprooted from their environment and forced to use new signs and systems. New colors, sounds, and smells are the phonemes of this new language that migrants gradually learn for their new daily existence and incorporate alongside the nostalgia for those that shaped their past existence. The memory of "the flavor of home,"[5] or the taste of the village, reappears alongside the new tastes and flavors of expatriate existence. Often the desire for traditional foods is amplified by the memory of family figures who are no more: parents, grandparents, and so forth. This desire can be strong and makes people search for a sensory and emotional experience in eating that will put them once more in touch symbolically with their past and the roots of their identity.

It is commonplace that the essence of an island is that it lives in itself and becomes a whole continent with its own customs, rituals, and language as well as its own economy. Islands often feature archaic forms of socioeconomic organization and tend to conserve tradition and folklore down the centuries thanks to their isolation.[6] Isolation is key to the protection of plants and animals in their original state of "purity," and the presence of risk of extinction in more heavily populated and anthropized areas is lower. It is significant, too, that species can evolve along parallel but different pathways compared to their mainland "relatives." The evolution of national or regional cuisines among diaspora can be seen in the same terms. Styles of cuisine may start out with the same tastes, techniques, and emphases, but these are all closely affected by the ways of the host country. Local customs will affect the tastes, techniques, and emphases as well as eating patterns and social and religious rules. The original cookery will be affected by food production and processing in the host country, as well as climate and soil quality, which will impact heavily on the organoleptic properties of the raw materials.

The outcome is that the two branches of the "ethnic cuisine," in this case Italian, in fact start to differ as they undergo these processes of evolution. Over time, in a process of divergent evolution,[7] differences become increasingly marked and the food becomes more like mainstream cookery in taste, serving, and presentation. The tastes of expatriates evolve as well when they stay overseas long term in the diaspora and become less able to perceive the true Italian nature of food. This is seen clearly in the program *Little Big Italy*; emigrants who have been away for a shorter time retain a stronger sense of traditional flavors. In a sense, the gradual shift away from smells and flavors that made them feel truly Italian counteracts feelings of nostalgia.

HOME SWEET HOME

The nostalgia of migrants usually goes hand in hand with a deep material and symbolic yearning for home, and this underpins the individual affective and emotional sphere. In this context "home" is a generalized synonym for what can be, for example, Heimat or Ithaca, places the migrant has left behind his or her roots with the idealized intention to one day return home.

In any migration process, long or short, there is normally a well-defined pattern. First is leaving one's own country, home, and familiar places where one is known and knows others. This separation removes all the certainties the migrant has hitherto lived with and accepted and is often followed by a nostalgia causing pain and distress, even leading perhaps to physical or emotional illness. Migrants must overcome thousands of obstacles and sometimes plans will fail and hopes destroyed, increasing the sense of drifting and loss. Nostalgia turns into disappointment and makes faraway home even more of a mirage. A place that offers familiar sensations can then become almost a surrogate for home and helps to reassure the migrant that he or she is not alone. A place such as this helps people keep in touch with their roots in terms of a country, a village, a building, square, or bench featured in the memory. And it reaches back to intangible roots of identity; close friends and family, embraces and handshakes of long ago. Such a place can transport migrants toward their own roots in beloved places and people as well as tastes and smells that complete the picture of the past and all the emotions and nostalgia it entails. Nostalgia becomes almost a therapy against feeling yourself without a home, family, or group to identify with. It protects identity and opens up existentialist questions that the stuff of poetry and songs are made of, like the Bob Dylan ballad, "How does it feel? How does it feel? To be without a home? Like a complete unknown? Like a rolling stone?"[8]

In the unbridled rolling of Dylan's ballad, nostalgia underpins both pain and relief; it is a comfort and refuge at the same time. A bright, clear memory provides comfort and a womb-like sensation provides refuge. It is widely understood that nostalgia is often awakened by objects and pictures and by smells and tastes that can be especially significant and give comfort to people feeling lost and frustrated. *Little Big Italy*, with its direct and indirect references to the concept of home, domesticity, and the overall sensations a place gives people, can be seen in this light. The sensations of reassurance and calm and our unconscious decodes the essence of these elements of domesticity.

CREOLIZATION OF TASTE

Creolization can involve hybridization, syncretism, metissage, blending, and fusion. There are other near-synonymous terms describing the process of meeting up between tastes, flavors, techniques, and memories that often unconsciously give rise to the blending found in "creolized" foods. Even spaghetti, the long strings of pasta that more than any other shape evoke Italian-ness, have themselves been "creolized" in at least two cases of food nomadism.

The first is the dish known as spaghetti bolognese, a flagship dish served in every Italian restaurant round the world, except in Italy. The dish is in fact an "invention" and has no tradition behind it. There is no record of its existence in the past, in spite of various attempts to "adopt" it being made in the Bologna countryside.[9] And neither is it on the menu in restaurants in the region today, even those that are trying to attract the growing number of tourists. Spaghetti bolognese is known only in the temples of Italian food outside Italy. The explanation is very simple. In cooking in the diaspora it was enough to put together spaghetti and meat sauce, two iconic ingredients from the Italian kitchen to make up a meta-recipe bursting with Italianness. The dish was supremely able to emphasize identity and counter any nostalgia for Italy. The two ingredients had never previously appeared together in traditional recipes. However, it was effective not only among expats, but also became a cornerstone of how Italian cooking was represented overseas. People probably imagined Italy as a land of plenty, the streets paved with pizza with original toppings, and barges full of spaghetti and mince sailing on rivers of cappuccino.[10]

The history of another creolization, meatballs and spaghetti, shows that it, too, is either a clever adaptation or an invention, depending on how it is viewed. There was probably no single cook responsible for the dish, but as in "Fuente Ovejuna"[11] it was produced by different cooks in different circumstances. This was probably mainly in home-cooking as well as in restaurants striving to follow tastes of Italian migrant networks as well as local people wishing to try the "true taste of Italy."[12] Emigration is clearly one of the main drivers of the "invention of tradition" in food. The process of creolization of course covers other areas such as language.[13] It is important to remember that one of Australia's national dishes, spag bol (i.e., spaghetti bolognese), is the legitimate offspring of migration, and the changing tastes characterizing the process that impacts so strongly on tastes, identity, and preferences.[14]

It has been noted that taste itself is not a natural ability but rather a "skill that can be learned, like walking or talking." If this is true, it is also true that "taste is not absolute but is based on *exposure* and long term sojourn in a context of landscape, aromas [. . .] spices and evanescence."[15]

Taste is thus relative and strongly affected by customs and habits. It is the outcome of habit in preparation and serving methods and accompaniments, and of education of sight, feel, colors, as well as the palate.[16] Spaghetti bolognese with a side of french fries brings to mind an Italian restaurant in Manhattan, with a checked tablecloth, a straw-covered bottle of wine, and fake heads of garlic and chili peppers adorning the walls. This is the Italy of Italo-Americans, born stateside for several generations. This is the image of Italy that other Americans expect to see, although their interest in Italian-inspired American dishes is entirely authentic. Italian-inspired food that has been the result of the evolution—in the American land—of Italian traditions. Initially giving rise to first pidginizations and then yielding a real creolized or hybrid Italo-American cuisine.

THE ATTRACTION OF THE FLAG

One of the factors in the success of Italy and Italian food around the world is the image of a "village" and a world "where public life is also private."[17] The Italian quarter of Manhattan appeared at one time to be sort of open-air market where immigrants performed the same rites and rituals as their home villages, and where there was little distinction between private and public. There was no boundary in the steps leading up to the door, the pavement, or the courtyard. Italian immigrants conquered all these spaces and turned them into areas that were public but colonized by domestic functions. Typically, they would be used for conserving tomatoes, aubergines, and onions and other Mediterranean specialities.[18]

Domestic life was thus brought out into the open in the form of housekeeping traditions taking over the collective spaces. Smells and colors from a distant domestic life in the Mediterranean basin became part of the horizons of the new world, a new model to alter its customs and standards. In the long term, they "conquered" many countries where prejudice against Italians at first discouraged interest in their food. But in many countries, like the United States, the hybridized cookery of the Bel Paese was to become the emblem of delicious, healthy, and fashionable eating.

The fact that Italian food was strongly "domestic" partly explains its enormous success in becoming a symbol of "the good life." Italian-ness, before being an ethnic belonging, is a "way of being" based on the centrality of domestic space. In this sense, "Italy" and "Home" overlap, giving life to a strong combination. There is a close association between "Italia-home." Italian-ness is based on the home and its symbologies, and this is especially important in the United States, the land of emigrants and the search for new frontiers.[19] The second point is that home represents the search for or reconstruction of a forgotten Heimat against a background of nostalgia. Italian-ness is a "way of life." The third point of the triangle is Italian food and dishes, which encapsulate the nature of being Italian. The Italian way of eating recalls the Italian way of life with its domestic rituals, from childhood to adulthood, all linked to close affections. These are what gives life its meaning, especially in the often-hard conditions of the diaspora. Just as the tango comes to signify regret and nostalgia in the sad barrios of Buenos Aires, Italian food offers relief for homesickness among Italians.[20]

However, Italian food made its name in the United States not only for its symbolic meanings.[21] Italian restaurants were common thanks to the quality they offered as far back as the 1930s. During the difficult years of the New Deal, they were a good way of eating cheaply,[22] and this was what gave Italian food, or at any rate the image of Italian food, its first push toward globalization. Pasta, pizza, and the *tricolore* flag became tangible symbols, alongside pasta, pizza, and Vesuvius, with maybe Pulcinella enthroned against the background of the Bay of Naples. Over time, such images were superimposed on one another and took on a life of their own as signs and sound and colors that either separately or in combination stood for the nature of being Italian. A red, green, and white colored box can be enough to make consumers think that a pasta product is Italian. In the same way, it can often be enough for a mediocre

Italo-American restaurant to take an Italian name for it to become a temple of Italian cuisine. The sound of words and names can be very convincing, and if these are combined with the colors of the flag and a picture showing Italy, consumer perception of Italian-ness is even stronger.

This in fact is the basic problem of Italian-sounding foods.[23] Around the world, one of the main fashion trends is Italian style, in food as in other areas, and in many societies food belonging to this ethnic group has become "haute cuisine."[24] For many reasons, eating Italian food has become a trend in both developed Western countries, among all social classes, and in developing countries, where for reasons of cost, it tends to be a marker of higher classes. In terms used by Pierre Bourdieu,[25] it has become a factor of social competition. In the search for social distinction and prestige by imitating behavior, the consumer has two options: (1) buy and eat authentic products imported from Italy, which may be hard to obtain and costly; (2) buy and eat products that are not really Italian but that seem so thanks to packaging, name, and pictures. There are cases where the label "Made in Italy" is used misleadingly, but the phenomenon of Italian-sounding products is much more widespread than fraud. It is interesting to discuss why consumers are misled by Italian-sounding products. For example, a New Zealand consumer who wants to eat Italian mozzarella will buy mozzarellae, clearly labelled as being made in New Zealand but with an Italian name and the Italian flag on the package.

The most obvious explanation, which is maybe the simplest and because of that the most unreasonable, is that the consumer is being deliberately misled. Therefore, producers of authentic mozzarella will be united in demanding stricter protection of their product. Such demands may be justified, but they often do not consider the behavior of the consumer, who is in reality free to choose the original product, transparently labelled as "made in Italy," if he or she so wishes.

Another reason, which is also simple, but perhaps not entirely unreasonable, is product freshness. Mozzarella "made in Italy" has a long way to go to reach New Zealand. The locally made product comes from a much shorter supply chain and is also more environmentally friendly. Today, the culture of "zero food miles" is increasingly important, and buying mozzarella produced in New Zealand is more environmentally aware and ethical, not simply utilitarian behavior.

The third explanation is based on the difference between fashion and taste. It is one thing to eat Italian food, waving the flag, and looking at a picture of the Bay of Naples, and another to go to a tasting session of "authentic" Parmigiano Reggiano or twenty-five-year-old balsamic vinegar. There is often a big gap between a distant consumer and an exported product. It would be entirely predictable if a Chinese consumer, for example, were unable to appreciate the strong taste of a mature cheese or the blue veins in Gorgonzola. Until recently, dairy products were not part of the Chinese diet, and in fact a pseudo-mozzarella "made in China" would be closer to Chinese tastes. Here, the value of zero food miles sometimes lies in the fact that tastes are closer to what is familiar and not only that the carbon footprint is smaller.

The fourth explanation closes the circle and confirms the first three. It is that the consumer is in reality aware of all these elements. It is the combination of all the explanations that makes the deception of Italian-sounding possible. Symbolic reasons can be even stronger than material ones, and Italian-sounding products are the area where symbols materialize and impact consumer choice. What happens is none other than what happens, in reverse order, for products bearing a geographical indication. A PDO (Protected Designation of Origin) label or something similar enhances a product with the idea that it is "made in history" and will clearly orient consumer choice. Products or brands that "sound Italian," maybe with Italian-looking colors on the package, are at an advantage in meeting consumers' desire to eat Italian food. It is the absence of education in recognizing real Italian food that emphasizes that it is not important to consumers whether their purchase is original or only Italian-sounding. The taste and flavor may be different, but the Italian-sounding product will encapsulate the same reputation as the original. It is a perfect substitute for the original in terms of social distinction and status. The Italian flag has become the emblem of a way of eating (and living), widely considered to be delicious, healthy, and nourishing but above all "trendy." It is not going too far to say that the appearance of the Italian flag on food packaging, authentic or otherwise, on tables around the world is a statement of identity, cohesion, and belonging. In fact, the flag is fulfilling its true function in symbolizing a joint sense of belonging to a sort of "small homeland."

Numerous virtues are associated with the tricolore flag and transferred to products "made in Italy." This is clearly important because the association of a product with a country has repercussions on market positioning.[26] As the reputation of a country is enhanced, all the products made in the country benefit from becoming more competitive. This is the "country effect," whereby every place where production takes place acquires a reputation that comes to affect all products made there. In the past these places were smaller areas or individual cities, but today it tends to be an entire nation that gains for itself this identity in quality and taste.[27]

THE TASTE OF HOME

Home is an element in the mind of every traveller and every individual who by choice or not stays away from it for any period. Ulysses thought constantly of Ithaca and his *nostos*. Italian writer Mario Rigoni Stern recounts how Italian alpine soldiers on the Don Front in the Second World War, peasants from the Bergamo area, anxiously asked their sergeant when they would return to their own mountain hut homes: "*Sergentmagiù, ghe rivarem a baita?*"[28]

The young conscripts of the past were feeling nostalgia, or the desire to feel the sensation, of being at home. Today, it can be the same for young people taking part in a student exchange program, although a short elective overseas is clearly more enjoyable. The flavors of home are clearly part of the sensations and emotions of travellers, migrants, and expats. This of course is only confirmed by Proust's observations on "involuntary memory."[29]

It is interesting to identify whether there is a measurable and classifiable "taste of home," but there is of course no clear answer to this question. Some say that the taste of home will always be recognizable in that every place produces a single individual taste, not a series of similar tastes. Others say that there is no single taste, and tastes are relative, and that links with taste are the result of an adaptation or an invention. In fact, both views are based on solid evidence and neither is mistaken. The question that most likely needs to be asked is the concept of taste, a variable element that is continually altered and reformed. This is particularly true in relation to place or territory, where propensities, culture, and human sensitivity as well as natural elements all undergo variation.

As has been noted, "absolute taste does not exist, but taste exists on the basis of familiarity, long-term sojourn in a context of landscape, excesses and defects, spices and evanescent factors."[30] In this view, tastes can be educated, particularly by surroundings. In fact, it is a question of educating not only taste, but also the other four senses of sight, touch, smell, and hearing. It also involves becoming used to customs in preparation, serving, and the order of presenting dishes. This implies that food preferences are constantly being altered, and that "nomadism" is a natural form of evolution. It is like the creolization of tastes and types of food discussed above.

It is important to note that the "taste of home" is variable. Not only do the recipes themselves alter, but so too the discernment of the people holding the memory of taste and who should be able to distinguish the real taste of home from imposters. Looking at what the *Little Big Italy* participants say, those who have been away from Italy for the longest tend to perceive Italian-ness in similar ways to people in the host country. Their tastes appear to have evolved naturally toward local flavors and they have become less able to distinguish between the tastes of their old home and their new home, and the new home taste is replacing the old one in their minds. Memory has adapted to reality, and the foods resulting from the hybridization come to represent the reassuring taste of home.

RISOTTO'S TURN: A NEW
HYBRIDIZATION OF ITALIAN CUISINE

"Risotto!" enthusiastically shouts Charlie Pace (played by Dominic Monaghan) to the other survivors of flight Oceanic 815 holding in his hands a box of provisions parachuted from the sky. It is not by chance that the star of an indie rock band is used by the writers of *Lost*—among the most celebrated (and cerebral) TV series of the 2000s—in introducing the audience to a new Italian cuisine, by then highly successful at a global scale.[31] A cuisine far away from the red and white squared tablecloth stereotype that was rediscovering ingredients and recipes until then peripheral in the food hybridization occurring in the twentieth century. Pasta and pizza now are coupled (if not replaced) by polenta, tortelli, minestrone, as well as risotto in a broader imaginary that will end up including mineral water, tiramisu, and espresso.[32]

To understand this process—that we name *risotto's turn*—one must go back to Italy and look at the deep changes occurring during the late 1970s. At that time, chef Gualtiero Marchesi used the revolutionary language of nouvelle cuisine by modifying, in-depth, the perception of Italian gastronomy. It is the destructionist approach put forward by Pierre Troisgros, Alain Senderens, and many others that makes it possible for a tradition, until then considered as simple and homemade, to achieve the status of haute cuisine. Marchesi became a three-star Michelin chef, embodying a dynamic idea of modernity that was very in fashion in Italy during the 1980s. Yet, he did it without rejecting the local rooting and care for the ingredients: the guiding ideas that, exactly in these years, were shaping the slow food movement Carlo Petrini was about to create.[33]

It is Italy's gastronomy that takes advantage of Marchesi's success, mimicking on a minor scale the worldwide triumphs of the fashion industry led, among others, by Giorgio Armani and Gianni Versace. An "Italian way of eating" that is promoting espresso and mineral water brands hungry for new markets, and at the same time sponsors regional cuisines, until then obscured by the ubiquitous renown of spaghetti and pizza. Once more, risotto is the icon of this double trend, the star of Marchesi's most famous recipe: Riso, Oro, e Zafferano. This popular dish (a true classic but from a lesser-known regional cuisine, that of Lombardy) undergoes a metamorphosis thanks to the topping of a thin gold flake that guides the eater to rediscover the sense of luxury that this recipe originally had.[34]

Outside of Italy it is, however, difficult to relate with this *nuova cucina italiana*, as it will be later defined. Alfredo Viazzi provides a case in point. Among the most celebrated Italian restaurateurs of New York since the late 1970s, he became a true point of reference for the US press, so much reputed that some erroneously assigned to him the authorship of the classic Italian American dish fettuccine Alfredo. Author of a memoir titled *Cucina e nostalgia*, Viazzi is everything but an exegete of food hybridization. His idea of gastronomy—totally in line with the one promoted by Marcella Hazan in her influential *Classic Italian Cookbook*—is philologically careful, and this leads him to counter some improvised followers of nouvelle cuisine who were experimenting with Italian food in the Manhattan food scene.[35] Interviewed by the *New York Times* in 1984, he bluntly says: "Cold tortellini salad with pesto . . . it's an outrageous thing." Dealing with a new language of gastronomy, Viazzi (and along with him a number of chefs and connoisseurs) reiterates that authenticity is the solution. This choice, if on the one side paves the way to the successful reception in the United States of the slow food movement, on the other side hinders the spread of a renewed image of Italian cuisine.[36] Therefore, while the "Italian way of living" trended in the early 1980s global pop culture thanks to Armani's jackets constantly appearing in the iconic TV series *Miami Vice*, food and gastronomy will need a longer incubation period.[37]

Properly speaking, risotto's turn occurs later, around the mid-1990s as the unexpected success of an indie movie about New Jersey and an Italian restaurant in the 1950s shows. *The Big Night* examines the cultural clash between the average American consumer and Italian chef-owner (Tony Shalhoub). Risotto symbolizes this conflict in a well-known scene in which customers expect to have it as a side dish with spaghetti and meatballs, receiving a firm refusal from the chef. His position may appear in line with Viazzi's defense of authentic Italian food, but there is an alternative interpretation as well. The film's writers (Joseph Tropiano and Stanley Tucci) are directly targeting their audience, namely a well-educated public accustomed to indie movies and Manhattan's trendy restaurants. The terms used to explain to the customers what is on their plate—"it is Italian Arborio rice"—reveal that the threshold between those who know and those who do not know the "Italian way of eating" is set at a higher level. In 1994, connoisseurs are expected not only to understand what risotto is, but also which type of rice is best to prepare it. The unforeseen success the film has reveals that it was not just a matter for a few, but a much broader public was ready for the *risotto's turn*.[38]

As a matter of fact, around the mid-1990s a growing number of products embodying this new "Italian way of eating" became part of a globalized American pop culture. TV series like *Sex and the City* and *Friends* introduced consumers, respectively, to a famous mineral water brand, and the new icon of the Italian patisserie: tiramisu.[39] One can observe this new trend also in the press and in a particular women's magazine. While *Cosmopolitan* provided wide coverage to *The Big Night*, *Woman's Day* gave greater consideration to dishes of a different Italian gastronomy like, among others, risotto, polenta, minestrone, and focaccia. The latter well exemplifies the formal recognition this alternative cuisine is receiving, with a cover story from 2000 in *Women's Day* titled "Ciao Italia." Photos of deserted farmhouses in rural Tuscany alternate with pictures of these classic dishes. It is a seemingly unnoticeable tip to stress that risotto's turn has now reached the popular press: to have a perfect risotto do not to use any type of rice but Arborio rice.[40] The United States, and Manhattan in particular, has become the stage of a new generation of chefs— Mario Batali, Nancy Silverton, Michael White (and even Massimo Bottura)—taking on the challenge to continue the transformation of Italian haute cuisine begun by Marchesi. Quite interestingly, most of them are not Italian, and some not even of Italian descent, paving the way to new and unexpected forms of hybridization.[41]

BACK HOME: NOMADIC FOOD, ITALY, AND GLOBALIZATION

Has the renewal of Italian cuisine coinciding with risotto's turn had an impact back home, where it all started? Is there any returning interaction that modified from abroad the "Italian way of eating" (and perceiving, or representing food)? Does Italian gastronomy preserve its original character of insularity in the age of globalized markets?[42]

Joe Bastianich's story summarizes best the recent trends occurring in Italy and worldwide. The son of Italian migrants who fled from Istria after the war, Bastianich grew up in Queens where he—exactly when risotto's turn was taking place—enters the food business. It turns out to be an extremely successful venture in the United States, as well as in Italy where he becomes a TV icon. Bastianich is not a chef, but he learns the secrets of cuisine from his mother, who runs a restaurant in Forest Hills and later appears in TV shows personifying the average Italian American cooking mamma. He embodies at its best the image of Italian food that is stealing the scene at a global scale, being able to combine the highest level of gastronomy with foodtainment and a dynamic business model.[43]

In the United States he runs more than twenty restaurants in partnership with celebrity chefs Nancy Silverton and Mario Batali, who surrendered his shares after reports of sexual misconduct. In Italy, he begins producing international "super-wines," only later arriving to restaurants; so in 2010 when Italian businessman Oscar Farinetti decided to expand into the United States, Bastianich is seen as the ideal partner for the new venture Eataly.[44] Worldwide renown comes however from the TV industry. It is a long-lasting relation starting in the 1990s, when his restaurant Becco was used as location for the sitcom *Friends*, and boomed in 2010–2011 when he was a judge on the first season of the reality show *MasterChef*, both in the United States and Italy. Following the reversed path that Panella made, Joe Bastianich becomes the standardbearer of a renewed Italian gastronomy looking back home not so much with the nostalgia of an expat, but rather with a sharp eye on the global consumer.[45]

Back home, a change of perspective was in the air in an iconic region for Italian food and wine: the Langhe in Piedmont. It is not by chance that Bastianich provides his voice for the off-screen narration of a documentary—the *Barolo Boys* (2014)— describing how it became possible for an Italian wine to achieve global success.[46] During the 1980s, things were happening in the Langhe, leading to new ideas about local viticulture and gastronomy. Associations like Amici del Barolo and Arci Gola became the incubators of a revolution that will lead to the slow food manifesto in 1987.[47] In this environment one could find Oscar Farinetti—who was already a successful entrepreneur, though not in the food industry—as well as a group of youngsters who aimed at bringing fresh air to wine making. As for Gualtiero Marchesi, his point of reference was France, a place to learn the techniques and strategies required to promote Barolo, a wine that outside Italy had no real standing. The change occurs, however, only when the group relates with the United States. Tastings arranged by an Italian American wine broker gives the "boys" the opportunity to present their Barolo in trendy restaurants of New York and Los Angeles. It was 1994, and the success was huge: the public, the connoisseurs, and the restaurateurs, everyone went crazy for the "new-style" Langhe wine. Back home, things went quite differently; a war begins between traditionalists and modernists and the attempts made to reestablish the previously existing cohesion appear worthless, even when made by influential persons like Carlo Petrini and Farinetti.[48]

The problems and inconsistencies that this further hybridization of Italian food triggers emerge; international success comes along with consumers having preferences quite different from the customary ones and pushes to replace traditional production and business in favor of a more modern approach. It is not just a matter of Barolo, but a much broader process. Shortly after, the same dilemma appears once again in Piedmont, involving another Italian classic, namely gelato. In 2003, the first Grom opened in Turin, it is a *gelateria* explicitly following slow food's main guidelines, such as short supply chains, use of local products, and fair-trade principles. The long lines customers are willing to face just to have a taste of this novelty seem to stress the triumph of the slow culture over fast-food and food corporations; a sensation strengthened by the public endorsement received from Petrini, shortly after the first opening.[49]

Increase in scale quickly follows this successful start, with more than thirty shops opening in New York, Paris, Los Angeles, Dubai, and elsewhere. The dilemma begins in the attempt of combining a business model suited to compete internationally— Starbucks is used as a point of reference—together with a sense of locally rooted, artisanal authenticity, really giving Grom its distinctive trait. Global consumers are provided with exactly the same freshly-made gelato, prepared with pistachios rigorously grown in a small part of Sicily, but travelling tens of thousands of kilometers to reach Malibu's beach or Osaka's city center.[50] The ending of this story takes place in 2015, when a well-known corporation purchases Grom and puts its gelato in a bucket to make it affordable to all.[51]

Italian nomadic food undergoes a new and unexpected type of hybridization embracing globally successful corporate models and making a further leap forward: it is no longer a matter of simply eating Italian food, but rather of experiencing the "Italian way of eating." The best-known case is provided by Eataly, a chain of quality Italian food halls that transformed into global products otherwise confined to local consumption because of their difficult availability (as well as for their high cost). The first opening in 2007 (once again in Turin), was followed one year later by one in Tokyo, revealing the international spirit of Farnetti's project. Currently, the number of Eataly locations almost totals forty, and is found in Europe, Asia, North, and South America.[52]

It is, however, in the realm of chain theme restaurants that this further hybridization becomes more open. Well known in the United States—with large and successful chains like Olive Garden and Carrabba's Italian Grill—this business is increasingly spreading in Italy, showing a process of convergence that is erasing previously existing differences. Following a marketing strategy developed in the late 1980s, these chains, rather than offering Italian food, are mostly selling the idea of an "Italian way of eating," using a reconstructed authenticity standardly reproduced in every outlet. Replication grants relevant economies of scale that in turn support a worldwide export of the model. Now the global customer can experience this "Italian way of eating" at an Olive Garden, for example, in Kuwait City or in São Paulo, in Malaysia, as well as in Peru.[53]

Rossopomodoro, a chain of pizzerias with a Neapolitan theme, proves that some form of Olive Garden–ization is currently ongoing also in Italy. Founded in the late 1990s, this company currently has almost 150 outlets—scattered in most European countries, Saudi Arabia, Japan, and Brazil—with the newest recently opened in

Manhattan. It is grounded on a dynamic corporate model—the ownership is in the hands of an English-based investment fund—that has no hesitation to equate a restaurant with a firm "where to make good money."[54] This business approach goes along with the *Napoletanità* (the Neapolitan character), which is not simply put forward in connection with food, but more broadly understood as "a way of being" the customer experiences while eating.[55] Hospitality is the guiding theme of it. If Olive Garden's motto is "We are family," at Rossopomodoro "Anyone, even a tourist" can try what it means to be a guest in "a Neapolitan home."[56]

With reference to the food offer, the call for authenticity is developed through themes recalling those successfully tested in the United States. While Carrabba's resorts to the recipes of "Mamma Grace" televized in the show *Cucina Sicilia*, in the Neapolitan version the traditional rooting is embodied by the products coming "from our terroir." As for Grom, this reference to Slow Food principles, typical products, and short supply chains can be at times contradictory, like in the case of water. Traditionally considered a crucial ingredient in preparing pizzas, and espressos, if the local one does not match the required standards, it is replaced by water directly brought from Naples.[57] The picture is completed by evocative architectures and interiors, like those taking inspiration from a Tuscan farmhouse hosting the Olive Garden's "culinary institute," or by "paintings describing Naples in a new and modern way," like Manuel di Chiara's pieces, which have become the real signature of any Rossopomodoro restaurant.[58]

CIRCULAR NOMADISM: A CONCLUSION

Having a closer look at what has been taken into analysis, insularity appears an image suited to depict the often-circular dynamics of Italian-sounding, as well as the Italian cuisine's worldwide hybridization process. The nature of such processes embeds circularity, and a tension that is bidirectional, if not multidirectional. Bastardization, crossbreeding, and syncretism often coincide with nomadism.

The latter is not just the result of cultural factors; socioeconomic forces have a large share in the itinerant history of Italian food. They did in the late nineteenth century globalization by spreading around the world millions of migrants, just like a century later when producing, retailing, and consuming food went global.[59] From the late 1980s, marketing strategies and corporate models have targeted customers with multiple identities and expectations about Italy and its cuisine. To meet them, food was not enough and a broader consumption experience was marketed. Selling the "Italian way of eating" is the key solution, an option particularly suited for producers and retailers operating worldwide and benefitting from standardization and economies of scale. Anyone can experience anywhere a replica of genuine *mangiare all'italiana*, adjusted to satisfy the multifaceted expectations of the global consumer.

But what is authentic Italian cuisine?[60] Any attempt of providing an answer runs the risk of being pointless. While searching for an apparent genuineness that rests on centuries-long skills and expertise, one must not forget that a notable share of tradition comes from invention, even when rooted in veridical or at least credible circumstances.[61] The incessantly evolving grammars of cuisine and semantics of taste reveal the nonsense of framing the issue in these terms. Language and fashion provide a clear case in point. Looking at how blue-collar workers or students were dressed during the Italian economic miracle of the 1950s, one discovers the major differences between then and now, almost as if geological eras had passed by. Likewise, one can compare the language currently used on TV by the news with that of fifty years ago: vocabulary and grammar are considerably different as well as rhythm and inflection. These are just small examples, but they recall that, when addressing food, we are on ever-changing ground.

One should always keep it in mind when referring to any tradition, but more if discussing Italian gastronomy, whose recent worldwide expansion intersects with massive diasporic historical movements.[62]

It should also be noted—as Carol Helstosky did—that the building of a national Italian cuisine has been driven not only by tradition and thus by history, but also by political choices and particularly by scarcity, a deeply rooted problem in Italy.[63]

This latter remark, often peripheral in discussions regarding terroir and place-based food, is in our view crucial. It reveals how the cultural approach, prevailing in most "grand narratives" on typical food, is nothing more than a storytelling disguising ordinary features, like the lack of given products due to environmental causes, or political and economic decisions, either willingly taken or not.[64]

In conclusion, another important matter must be stressed: the "comeback effect." Italy is no longer a sheer "exporter" of its food culture, experiencing at most, like in the "pizza effect" described by the anthropologist Agehananda Bharati, the return of its own dishes modified by the Italian diaspora.[65] In the last twenty years, increasing migration fluxes have deeply changed Italian food identity, and the process is still going on. School cafeterias and other catering services had to cope with cultural and religious diversity adapting their menus to new food paradigms. Likewise, a rise in demand of Halal products improved the meat processing chain, contributing to the spread of Middle Eastern cooking techniques.

Globalization is dismantling food borders while fusion and hybridization are becoming the pillars of twenty-first-century cuisine. No island can protect its own national gastronomy, and even the most reputed chef considers this as inevitable.

What will then be the meaning of "typical," "traditional," and "authentic"? Will they become key words of storytelling, or will they continue to represent something real? In the twenty-first century, how will globalization remodel the relation between food and terroir, and what will be the fate of all the little big Italies around the world?

BIBLIOGRAPHY

Adamoli, Ginevra. "The Slow Food Movement and Facebook: The Paradox of Advocating Slow Living through Fast Technology." In *Representing Italy through Food*, edited by Peter

Naccarato, Zachary Nowak, and Elgin K. Eckert, 55–73. London: Bloomsbury Academic, 2017.

Ahlborn, Kate, and Frelinghuysen, Louisine. "Sex and the City: A Product-Placement Roundup." *Vanity Fair*, May 30, 2008. https://www.vanityfair.com/news/2008/05/sex-and-the-cit.

Albala, Ken. "*Italianità* in America: The Cultural Politics of Representing 'Authentic' Italian Cuisine in the U.S." In *Representing Italy through Food*, edited by Peter Naccarato, Zachary Nowak, and Elgin K. Eckert, 205–17. London: Bloomsbury Academic, 2017.

Albrecht, Michael Mario. "'When You're Here, You're Family': Culinary Tourism and the Olive Garden Restaurant." *Tourist Studies* 11, no. 2 (2011): 99–113.

Andrews, Geoff. *The Slow Food Story: Politics and Pleasure*. London: Pluto Press, 2008.

Arthurs, Jane. "Sex and the City and Consumer Culture: Remediating Postfeminist Drama." *Feminist Media Studies* 3, no. 1 (2003): 83–98.

Balboni, Valeria. *Evolution ed evoluzionismo*. Milano: Alpha Test, 2002.

Bastianich, Joe. *Restaurant Man*. New York: Penguin, 2012.

Battilani, Patrizia, and Bertagnoni, Giuliana. *Il restyling di una vecchia icona pop: la storia transnazionale degli Spaghetti alla bolognese*. Conference paper presented at VII AISU Congress, *Food and the City*. Padua 3–5 September 2015.

Bharati, Agehananda. "The Hindu Renaissance and its Apologetic Patterns." *Journal of Asian Studies* 29, no. 2 (1970), 267–87.

Boiardi, Anna, and Lyness, Stephanie. *Delicious Memories. Recipes and Stories from the Chef Boyardee Family*. Hong Kong: Stewart, Tabori & Chang, 2011.

Bourdieu, Pierre. *La distinzione. Critica sociale del gusto*. Bologna: il Mulino, 1983 (or. ed. *La Distinzione. Critique sociale du jugement*. Paris: Les éditions de Minuit, 1979).

Braudel, Fernand. *Civiltà and imperi del Mediterraneo nell'età di Filippo II*. Torino: Einaudi, 1986[3] (ed. orig.: *La Mediterranée et le Monde méditerranéen à l'époque de Philippe II*. Paris: Librairie Armand Colin, 1949).

Carrabba's Italian Grill: Recipes from Around Our Family Table. Hoboken, NJ: John Wiley and Sons, 2011.

Ceccarelli, Giovanni, Grandi, Alberto, and Magagnoli, Stefano. "The Avatar: An Economic History Paradigm for Typical Products." In *Typicality in History. Tradition, Innovation, and Terroir/La typicité dans l'histoire. Tradition, innovation et terroir*, edited by Giovanni Ceccarelli, Alberto Grandi, and Stefano Magagnoli, 69–86. Bruxelles: Peter Lang, 2013.

"Ciao Italia!" *Woman's Day*, October 3, 2000.

Cinotto, Simone. *The Italian American Table*. Urbana: University of Illinois Press, 2013.

Codeluppi, Vanni. "Evoluzione e caratteristiche del Made in Italy." In *Il Made in Italy. Natura, settori e problemi*, edited by Ampelio Bucci, Vanni Codeluppi, and Mauro Ferraresi. Roma: Carocci, 2011.

Corti, Paola. "Emigrazione e consuetudini alimentari. L'esperienza di una catena migratoria." In *Storia d'Italia, Annali, 13, L'alimentazione*, edited by Alberto Capatti, Alberto De Bernardi, and Angelo Varni. Torino: Einaudi, 1998.

Dickie, John. *Delizia! The Epic History of the Italians and Their Food*. New York: Free Press, 2008.

Di Giandomenico, Mauro. "La scienza, il cibo, il gusto." In *Educare al (buon) gusto. Tra sapore, piacere e sapere*, edited by Franco Bochicchio, 35–48. Napoli: Giapeto, 2013.

Ducrot, Victor Ego. *Los sabores de la patria. Las intrigas de la historia argentina contadas desde la mesa y la cocina*. Buenos Aires: Grupo Editorial Norma, 2009.

Frankel, Martha. "Stanley Tucci," *Cosmopolitan*, October 1996.

Gibelli, Antonio, and Caffarena, Fabio. "Le lettere degli emigranti." In *Storia dell'emigrazione italiana*, vol. I, *Partenze*, edited by Piero Bevilacqua, Andreina De Clementi, and Emilio Franzina, 563–74. Rome: Donzelli, 2001.

Girardelli, Davide. "Commodified Identities: The Myth of Italian Food in the United States." *Journal of Communication Inquiry* 28, no. 4 (Fall 2004): 307–24

Grom, Federico, and Martinetti, Guido. *GROM Storia di un'amicizia, qualche gelato e molti fiori*. Milano: Bompiani, 2012.

Helstosky, Carol. *Garlic and Oil: Food and Politics in Italy*. New York: Berg, 2006.

Jenkins, Nancy. "Italians State the Case for Authentic Pasta." *New York Times*, May 9, 1984.

La Cecla, Franco. *La pasta e la pizza*. Bologna: il Mulino, 1998.

Lindenfeld, Laura, and Parasecoli, Fabio. *Feasting Our Eyes: Food Films and Cultural Identity in the United States*. New York: Columbia University Press, 2017.

Lope de Vega, Félix. "Fuente Ovejuna." In Id., *Teatro*. Firenze: Sansoni, 1963.

Magagnoli, Stefano. "Reputazione, *skill*, territorio." *Storia Economica*, no. 2 (2011): 247–74.

Magagnoli, Stefano. "*Made in Eataly*. Identità e falsificazione." In *Contraffazione e cambiamento economico. Marche, imprese, consumatori*, edited by Marco Belfanti, 71–97. Milano: EGEA, 2013.

———. *Le futurisme au service de la révolution. Artistes, politiciens, et une assiette de Spaghetti . . .*, Conference paper presented at 2ᵉ Conférence Internationale d'Histoire et des Cultures de l'Alimentation. Tours, IEHCA, 26–27 May 2016.

———. "Eating Tradition. Typical Products, Distinction and the Myth of Memory." In *Consuming the World: Eating and Drinking in Culture, History and Environment*, edited by Michelle Mart and Daniel J. Philippon, special issue of *Global Environment—A Journal of Transdisciplinary History* 11, no. 1 (2018): 154–72.

Magagnoli Stefano, "The Italian Way of Eating Round the World: Italian-Sounding, Counterfeit, and Original Products," in Kazunobu Ikeya (ed.), *The Spread of Food Cultures in Asia*, Osaka, National Museum of Ethnology (Senri Ethnological Studies 100), 2019, pp. 173–95.

Marchesi, Gualtiero, and Valli, Carlo G. *Marchesi si nasce: questa è la mia storia*. Milano: Rizzoli, 2010.

Matamori, Blas. *La ciudad del Tango (Tango histórico y sociedad)*. Buenos Aires: Editorial Galerna, 1969.

Melotti, Marxiano. "Oltre la crisi. Il turismo culturale tra riscoperta delle radici e lentezza rappresentata." *La critica sociologica* 185 (Spring 2013): 51–66.

Morris, Jonathan. "Making Italian Espresso, Making Espresso Italian." *Food and History* 8, no. 2 (2010): 155–83.

Naccarato, Peter, Nowak, Zachary, and Eckert, Elgin K. "Editors' Introduction: Presenting Food, Representing Italy." In *Representing Italy through Food*, edited by Peter Naccarato, Zachary Nowak, and Elgin K. Eckert, 1–13. London: Bloomsbury Academic, 2017.

Naccarato, Peter, Nowak, Zachary, and Eckert, Elgin K. "Afterword: Italy Represented." In *Representing Italy through Food*, edited by Peter Naccarato, Zachary Nowak, and Elgin K. Eckert, 263–65. London: Bloomsbury Academic, 2017.

Ortoleva, Peppino. "La tradizione e l'abbondanza. Riflessioni sulla cucina degli Italiani d'America." *Altreitalie*, no. 7 (January–June 1992).

Panella, Francesco. *Brooklyn Man. La guida insolita alla cucina di New York*. Rome: Newton Compton, 2014.

Parasecoli, Fabio. "Deconstructing Soup: Ferran Adrià's Culinary Challenges." *Gastronomica* 1, no. 1 (Winter 2001): 60–73.

Parasecoli, Fabio. "We are Family: Ethinic Food Marketing and the Consumption of Authenticity in Italian Themed Chain Restaurants." In *Making Italian America: Consumer Culture and the Production of Ethnic Identities*, edited by Simone Cinotto, 244–55. New York: Fordham University Press, 2014.

———. *Al Dente. Storia del cibo in Italia*. Gorizia: Leg edizioni, 2015 (or. ed. *Al Dente. A History of Food in Italy*. London: Reaktion Books, 2014).

Petrini, Carlo. "Il vero gelato con latte di vacca d'alpeggio." *La Stampa Tutto Libri Tempo Libero*, July 6, 2003.

———. *Slow Food: The Case for Taste*. Translated by William McCuaig. New York: Columbia University Press, 2004.

Ray, Krishnendu. *The Ethnic Restaurateur*. New York: Bloomsbury USA Academic, 2016.

Rigoni Stern, Mario. *Il sergente nella neve*. Torino: Einaudi, 1953.

Sartorio, Anna. *Il Mercante di Utopie. La storia di Oscar Farinetti, l'inventore di Eataly*. Milano: Sperling & Kupfer, 2008.

Tardi, Alan. "Postmodern Barolo. The War that Never Was." *Sommelier Journal*, July 15, 2012.

Teti, Vito. "Emigrazione, alimentazione, culture popolari." In *Storia dell'emigrazione italiana*, vol. I, *Partenze*, edited by Piero Bevilacqua, Andreina De Clementi, and Emilio Franzina, 575–97. Rome: Donzelli, 2001.

Tonelli, Marco. "Friuli Uniti d'America." *Spirito di Vino*, July 2010.

Turner, Frederick J. "The Significance of the Frontier in American History." *Annual Report of the American Historical Association (1893)*: 197–227.

Valdiserra, Piero. *Spaghetti alla Bolognese: l'altra faccia del tipico*. Bologna: Edizioni Edi House, 2016.

Viazzi, Alfredo. *Cucina e nostalgia: A Gastronomic Memoir by the Master Italian Chef with More Than 130 Recipes*. New York: Random House, 1983.

Wong, Aliza S. "Authenticity all'italiana: Food Discourses, Diasporas, and the Limits of Cuisine in Contemporary Italy." In *Representing Italy through Food*, edited by Peter Naccarato, Zachary Nowak, and Elgin K. Eckert, 33–53. London: Bloomsbury Academic, 2017.

Zoglin, Richard. "Video: Cool Cops, Hot Show." *Time*, September 16, 1985. http://content.time.com/time/subscriber/article/0,33009,959822-1,00.html.

9

Imaging Culinary Nomadism

Food Exchanges Shaped by Global Mixed Race, Diasporic Belongings, and Cosmopolitan Sensibilities

Jean Duruz

> The economic and social marginalization of African diaspora immigrants is compensated for by the richness of their culinary traditions [with] food as a trope of culinary nomadism.[1]

> I am interested in the way memory works, in what we do with it, and what it does with us.[2]

> Yesterday I was into Tai Chi, today I am into Yoga, and tomorrow I may try Zen.[3]

This chapter arises from the remembered tastes and smells of my travels, actual and virtual, at home and elsewhere. It is haunted by the fragrance of posole prepared by a German friend skilled in Mexican cooking in her Manhattan kitchen, the almond flavor and grainy texture of a piece of sugee cake bought from a Eurasian bakery in Singapore, and the sour, fermented taste of injera, a flatbread staple for scooping up spicy curries from a communal plate at an Ethiopian cafe in Adelaide, South Australia. Sense-experiences like these inscribe personal culinary landscapes with lingering tenacity and form the basis of much of my writing to date. Centrally, this chapter addresses food as critical to everyday cultures of global cities and begs the question of how different people in these "mongrel cities" manage the task of eating and living together.[4] This chapter, however, while reflecting on earlier writings to some extent, also sets out in a slightly different direction in search of intimations—of journeys, places, people, cultures—that might pose questions for understandings of contemporary nomadism. For this project, I want to engage food as a powerful "trope of culinary nomadism,"[5] its meanings mapped in cycles of movement, memories, and sensory imaginings between the locus of home and the world beyond. Or rather, it might be argued, by virtue of new technologies, these meanings with all their resonances, are mapped simultaneously as home and the world, now not-so-beyond. After all, says David Morley (citing Paul Virilio, discussing the rapidity of electronic transmission), "the individual is, in effect, in two places at once, and the element of the journey across space is lost."[6]

For the project of rewriting nomadism as imaginary landscapes of culinary cultures, the chapter traces two intersecting routes. First, nomadism itself, particularly in its postmodern iterations,[7] needs some unpacking for its usefulness in analyzing twentieth- and twenty-first-century cultures of global movement and belonging. Then, drawing on potential theoretical tools, I travel the second of this chapter's routes. This involves a return to interview fragments I've continued to puzzle over for some time but now intend to examine these and others through a different lens.[8] Here, I argue that the phenomenon of global mixed race (e.g., as in interracial marriage) presents an unusual perspective on nomadic relations and foodways. Does one marry into cultures of nomadism, for example? How are food exchanges negotiated within mixed relations, given the likely asymmetries of gender, ethnicity, citizen-belonging, language, and so on, that such relations produce? I am hoping that these twin perspectives on postmodern nomadism—mixed race relationships and the challenges of differing food cultures in the microcosm of specific households—will stretch nomadism's meanings and find a more complex interstitial space between, or beyond, the binary of freedom and exclusion, beyond spectres of global rootlessness and their opposite, a relentlessly pursued defence of territorialization.[9]

So, before embarking on resonant tales of people living "together-in-difference,"[10] we'll now proceed with identifying conceptual tools for their analysis. These tools fall into the following categories: the variable meanings of nomadism, ranging, for example, from the supposed freedoms of digital nomadism to the grimness of homelessness and displacement among refugee communities; culinary nomadism or, in my own term, ingested nomadism, in which the materiality and meanings of food provide more textured, and possibly different, stories to mainstream accounts of migration, diaspora, and displacement; and global mixed race as a phenomenon of increasing hybridization of cultures and identities associated with nomadic movement across space and time, across boundaries of ethnicity and within relations of intimacy.[11]

NOMADIC MOVEMENT: "TOMORROW I MAY TRY ZEN"

Today, we all want to be nomads. We travel like nomads, we shop and surf the internet like nomads, our technologies of communication release us from locality, and, when we use them, we defy the physical worlds that tie us to territory. So it would seem.[12]

The borderless world of limitless travel—over land, sea, through air, cyberspace—is a popular metaphor of freedom in twenty-first-century rhetoric. In fact, recent manifestations of the sharing economy (such as couch surfing, Airbnb accommodation networks, and Uber car transportation and food delivery systems) extoll the virtues of creative consumer choice governed by lifestyle values and affordability. Airbnb, for example, is lauded not only for the usually cheaper cost of staying in private accommodations (a room in someone else's home or an apartment temporarily vacated by the owners) compared to the tourist industry's hotels and commercially-run serviced apartments, but also for "[t]he experience of living in a [private] residence. . . . [This] offers guests the chance to have a more 'local' experience by living more like a local, interacting with the host or neighbours, and possibly staying in a 'non-touristy' area."[13] The impact of this sharing of resources on urban life, of course, is subject to public debate. Claiming gentrification of the built environment results in certain inequities and exclusions; critics of Airbnb, for example, focus on its supposed disruptive effects. These, it is claimed, range from short-term tenants' colonizing neighborhoods and apartment blocks with all-night parties and pop-up brothels to their "destroying affordable housing for immigrant, minority and low income families."[14]

As John Noyes implies, this explosion of nomadism of a sort—this de-territorialization of everyday activities such as travel, shopping, and information seeking—is intimately tied to the growth of electronic communication and its devices—computers, smartphones, iPods, iPads, laptops, and supporting systems such as Facebook, Twitter, and Instagram. Digital nomadism now becomes a lifestyle in itself, with its more substantial versions extending beyond surfing the net and occasional online purchasing to following the digital trail with other nomads to countercultural gatherings in exotic locations—to the island of Ibiza, for example, for the season of "Goa trance parties," or to Bali, Byron Bay, San Francisco, or Pune. According to Anthony D'Andrea, these are places that, in collective imagining, "have become especially charismatic tourist centers, *subsequent* to the arrival of gays, beatniks, hippies, New Agers, ravers and clubbers."[15] These, too, are promoted as sites of cultural transformation where "digital and orientalist elements congeal into a ritual assemblage that enables alternative experiences of the self."[16] Techno and New Age cultures, then, with their capacity to embrace the exotic, signal not only possibilities for escape from conventional Western materialism and its disciplinary order, but also possibilities for self-renewal.

Meanwhile, drawing inspiration from Walt Whitman's "Song of the Road," Rolf Potts's *Vagabonding*, a self-help guide to nomadic travel, declares: "Vagabonding involves taking an extended time-out from your normal life . . . to travel the world on your own terms."[17] Vagabonding Potts-style, however, is not simply concerned with time-out and leisure activities in this postmodern, post-industrial age but also with providing sources of income to sustain nomadic lifestyles. Apart from the presence of cultural capital possessed by many of those dropping out (as their insurance for returning to former urban centers of employment), D'Andrea also reminds us of the significance of nomads' countercultural business practices at exotic locations. The production of art and handicrafts or the provision of wellness and therapy services for purchase by holiday-makers, well-off local residents, and fellow nomads, for example, contributes in turn to the project of nomadic lifestyle sustainability.[18]

Perhaps in its purest form, however, digital nomadism marries the portability of electronically-controlled work practices with the lure of the exotic. Enticingly, electronic skills and forms of online, transnational employment are promoted by websites as the gateway to mobility to warm climates, breathtaking landscapes, and third world economies of living cheaply, and, for these flight-from-first-world nomads, of living well. The following is a typical example.

> The best thing about being a digital nomad is undoubtedly the genuine freedom. . . . You have an epiphany, you want to learn Spanish in Colombia. No talking, no social media bravado, no false dawns—you're off next week. Being a digital nomad means you can really live your life. You can volunteer in obscure places, you can watch the wildebeest migration, visit tribes, ride in hot-air balloons, and climb mountains. You can party till sunrise and you don't have to feel guilty about it. Life is meant to be lived. Digital nomadism allows that in abundance.[19]

In spite of the seductive romance of "freedom," "epiphanies," "really living," and digital "abundance," a doubtful note is bound to creep into our discussion. Noyes's "So it would seem" continues to haunt. It appears that grasping the benefits of sophisticated technologies, together with fostering a spirit of adventure, is all that is required.[20] After all, "'Yesterday I was into Tai Chi, today I am into Yoga, and tomorrow I may try Zen.'"[21] Meanwhile, questions of unequal access to resources for this yesterday-today-tomorrow existence remain unanswered.

Economies of travel—who travels, who doesn't; who travels well and who doesn't—is not a new insight in the literature. In the early days of debates regarding time-space compression prompted by geographers such as David Harvey, Jon May, and Nigel Thrift, Doreen Massey's image of a pensioner in a bed-sit (a one room combined bed/sitting room with minimal cooking facilities) in any British city, "eating fish and chips from a Chinese takeaway, watching a US film on a Japanese television, and not daring to go out after dark," is a poignant one in discussions of the unequal relations of mobility in the information age.[22] Likewise, Pico Iyer, watching passengers move through LAX in Los Angeles, claims that it is "dangerously tempting" to differentiate people in airports in class terms by their amount and style of luggage ("people from rich countries . . . travel light; those from poor countries come with their whole lives in cardboard boxes imperfectly tied with string").[23]

In the twenty-first century, this binary of rich and poor nomads intensifies with the ascendancy of global capital in structuring modern life, the continuing legacies of colonialism and imperialism, and the increasing numbers of displaced populations seeking asylum from war and ethnic conflict. While D'Andrea represents the drop-out beneficiaries of the information age as "neo-nomads"[24]—"a minority of high-modern renegades involved in hypermobile formations that seek to evade mainstream regimes," a darker portrait of "other" nomads is contributed by Iain Chambers. Calling for a re-mapping of Italy, the Mediterranean, and Europe beyond the fixity of national borders to acknowledge, instead, the region's "hybrid inheritance," Chambers says:

This other Mediterranean emerges in significantly sharp focus in the figure of today's (illegal) migrant who carries within herself the complex inheritance of a *colonial* past, crossed with the longstanding historical processes that make the modern world the site of perpetual mobility and migration.[25]

In a similar vein, Noyes ties debates regarding meanings and forms of nomadism to "the dual productivity of mobile subjects . . . the mobile rich and the mobile poor" and concludes: "Mobility casts subjectivity between the ideal freedom of the disembodied wanderer and the brute reality of the refugee."[26]

As ways of bringing culinary nuances to Chambers's "modern world . . . of perpetual mobility and migration," here I would like briefly to reflect on two popular assumptions to which we'll return later in a more grounded fashion using narrative fragments. The first, and perhaps the more obvious assumption to challenge, is that nomadism inevitably implies bodily movement across space. In *By Way of Nomadism*, Rosi Braidotti, drawing on Deleuze and Guattari,[27] injects a different meaning into nomadism from the traditional one of specific communities' cyclical patterns of movement associated with crop-growing and herd-tending. Instead, Braidotti conceptualizes nomadic movement philosophically, as a form of deviant discourse—as an ensemble of resistant moves within conventional texts of thought and action:

> Though the image of "nomadic subjects" is inspired by the experience of peoples or cultures that are literally nomadic, the nomadism in question here refers to the kind of critical consciousness that resists settling into socially coded modes of thought and behaviour. Not all nomads are world travellers; some of the greatest trips can take place without physically moving from one's habitat. It is *the subversion of set conventions that defines the nomadic state, not the literal act of traveling.*"[28]

"[T]rips . . . without physically moving," "the subversion of set conventions"— phrases like these are extremely generative for pondering the ways that nomadism might become, in turn, *culinary* nomadism. It is not simply a question of food's actual movement following particular historical and political trajectories, following particular patterns of trade, migration, and diaspora. Instead, it is the subversion of meanings of taste on the tongue, in the stomach—the ingestion of difference, the refusal of the grip of "socially coded"—that secretly slips into prominence. Writing about Gisele Pineau's novel *Un Papillon dans la Cité*, in which favorite dishes are re-created by Caribbean migrants in Paris kitchens, Brinda Mehta says:

> [T]he familiarity of the birthland is both conjured and physically actualized through fragrant whiffs of memory. . . . The frying pan has the power to melt boundaries by creating an undifferentiated territoriality between France and Guadeloupe, a "sensorial interstice" that suspends spatial hierarchies through culinary reconstructions.[29]

This "sensorial interstice" is, of course, an imagined space positioned between actual memories of the scents of cooking in Guadalupe and the evocative smells from the

frying pan in this "other" place and "other" time. Elsewhere I refer to this space, using Low and Kalekin-Fishman's terminology, as a "sensorial interface," as "a 'meeting
point' of different kinds of sensory knowledge (and emerging from different locations) [that] implies negotiation of these differences, and possibly, the production of
something 'new' in their stead."[30] Critically then, this is a form of nomadism ranging
through imaginary landscapes of belonging and not-quite-belonging (memories of
the "home" left behind; dreams of the marginalized, caught in spatial and culinary
hierarchies) yet with its own materialities—tastes, smells, textures, sounds, sights of
familiar foods, and actual processes of their ingestion. After all, it is food's very corporeality that becomes significant here, and strikes a different chord for meanings of
mobility and stasis: "It is the *sensorial* experience of food that endures in one's memory bank, long after the context in which it is consumed disappears or changes."[31]
This sensoriality I attach to the textual moves of postmodern nomadism to produce,
in turn, my own conception of ingested nomadism—a heady combination of
memories, imaginings, sensory knowledge, and corporeality that traces, discursively,
mobilities of cultural and culinary meaning in the subversive "tactics" of everyday.[32]

For the moment leaving aside questions of actual versus virtual mobility, or of
traditional versus textual mobility, we'll now focus on a second popular assumption.
This involves unravelling, conceptually speaking, binaries of the moving and the
settled, or in Deleuze and Guattari's terminology, of the "sedentary" and the "nomadic."[33] Cultural theorists may stress the semiotic interdependency of these terms,
together with their complex manifestations in everyday life—the ways neo-nomads
create imaginaries such as "Byron" and "Bali" for armchair travellers and actual tourists, for example.[34] Nevertheless, the moving-settled distinction, as we remember
from Massey's pensioner eating take-out and watching television in a bed-sitting
room, might seem clear-cut. Or is it? Even though positioned within the confines
of a bed-sitting room and constrained by fears of the streets at night, this pensioner,
in acts of consuming global commodities and meanings, muddies the separation of
sedentary and nomadic. Drawing on recent commentary on the European Union
(prior to the political and cultural disruptions of the Brexit poll), Aldea summarizes
Baridotti's arguments of the reshaping of global cities:

> [T]he political and practical reality of living in the European Union is one that chal-
> lenges the traditional notions of national belonging. . . . We inhabit a world where a
> simple relationship to the place we live in no longer exists, not either for ourselves or
> for our neighbours. We are exposed daily to people that cross national boundaries, defy
> language barriers and unsettle cultural traditions. In order to fully inhabit this world, we
> need to shift own our sense of identity."[35]

Aldea continues by arguing that global flows of people and goods and the downplay-
ing of national boundaries—or rather, identifying different boundaries, different
meanings of belonging—produce a startling shift in nomadic understandings: "Cru-
cially, the change from a sedentary to a nomadic order affects the subjectivity and
identity not only of those who move, but of all the inhabitants of an area."[36] In global

cities, then, given increasing migratory movement and diasporic displacement, people's everyday brush with different languages and cultures (especially those associated with food), together with their exposure to different "others," seems inevitable. Under these conditions, Ien Ang's project of living "together-in-difference" becomes more than utopian dreaming but a project of global necessity.³⁷ Citing McLennan, Ang says that "we have to learn 'how to live awkwardly (but also wisely and critically)' in a world in which difference and sameness are inextricably intertwined in complicated entanglement."³⁸

This does not mean, of course, that everyone is happy with these new fluidities of home territories, identities, and cultures. The rise of "Us-and-Them" politics (as evidenced by the outcome of the 2016 Brexit poll dictating Britain's departure from the European Union, by the increased visibility of the UK Independence Party with its anti-immigration stance, and by Donald Trump's America First policies in the United States) indicates a reactionary turn in Western popular imaginaries.³⁹ Nevertheless, despite resistances to foreign foods in global cities, such as those I've documented in the ethnically-mixed spaces of London's Green Lanes,⁴⁰ "multicultural" eating is achieving acceptance as a form of ingested, culinary nomadism. It seems that while national boundaries and identities are sources of intense debate and of gate-keeping practices, cultures of food and eating, particularly those attached to ethnic meanings, often manage to slip under the radar.⁴¹ Beyond the public face of trade, protectionism, policies of food security and sustainability, a quiet revolution in urban food spaces and food publishing continues. Increasing numbers of ethnic cookbooks, restaurants, supermarkets, and specialized food shops, for example, crowd the everyday of global cities. This reaches the point that these businesses and their products are no longer considered exotic. Consuming such foods, together with the rich cultures of diversity they represent, simply becomes intrinsic to educating the palate of the modern citizen. In fact, as Donna Gabaccia points out, for the United States these rich culinary cultures contribute to the definition of what it means to be American (though, as Gabaccia also reminds us, the United States does not comprise "a multi-ethnic nation but a nation of multi-ethnics").⁴²

Food then, together with its sensory resonances, creates not only a virtual-visceral performance of elsewhere, but also normalizes these resonances as home. Once again, we find "the individual is, in effect, in two places at once, and the element of the journey across space is lost."⁴³ However, this time, ingestions of food, memories, and sensory experience, together with the interfaces where these meet, take center stage, although conventional digital technologies of travel and communication, obviously from the wings, assist in this process. As well, it seems that nomadism, as imagined here, is threaded through with complex meanings both of movement and stasis—in journeys through poignant memories and imagined landscapes as well as their re-settlings deep in the gut.

A last theoretical tool to add to the mix for this section is perhaps the most significant one for analysis of everyday food exchanges. Ang, commenting on the "fundamental *uneasiness* inherent in our global condition of togetherness-in-difference," also emphasizes that such global uneasiness also might be relocated closer to home. Within the intimacy of domestic interracial relationships, for example, she continues, little is known about the ways couples and other members of households negotiate their differing value systems in private.[44] We presume here that Ang is referring specifically to values associated with dimensions of race, ethnicity, geography, and religion, although, obviously, values tied to class, gender, generation, and citizenship status also might be added to the mix. Obviously, too, in modern democratic states, while individual members in any domestic relationship or household might differ in varying degrees from each other in terms of social and cultural positioning and values held, the assumption here is that the category of race/ethnicity, implicated in the production of intimate mixed relations and those of descended mixed generations, sharpens these dimensions of difference. Eating together-in-difference then is not only a case of different ethnic groups sharing the same urban spaces for public eating but also a case of the dynamics of this commensality at close quarters—the microcosmic intensity of explicit differences in cultures of race/ethnicity as these are lived out *within* familial/sexual relationships.

As a point of clarification, I intend to use the term "mixed race," as Small and King-O'Riain do, as a way of referring to "people who feel they are descended from and attached to two or more socially significant [racial/ethnic] groups,"[45] even though it should be acknowledged that "race" is a socially constructed category.[46] My particular project is to examine the ways that intimate mixed race relationships (as in marriage, sexual-domestic partnerships, and child-rearing) mesh with this chapter's conceptualization of ingested nomadism. Here we recall some of my original nagging questions such as: Does one marry into or, for that matter, out of cultures of nomadism? How are food exchanges negotiated within mixed relations, given the likely asymmetries of gender, ethnicity, citizen-belonging, language, and so on, that such relations produce? And to these we might add: What is the significance of injested nomadism, particularly in contexts of mixed relationships? What contribution might these value-added meanings of postmodern nomadism offer, conceptually, for Chambers's re-thinking of the "fragile" project of "multilateral modernity?" Does food provide a different, less usual, conduit toward the end of Ang's "awkward" and "ambivalent" "together-in-difference?" And returning to the heart of the kitchen, we might speculate that such "hybridity talk,"[47] in turn, brings particular examples of nomadic cuisine into being, including its distinctive dishes as "the food of a community."[48]

COMING HOME: FROM AN AFRICAN HUT ON THE HIGHWAY TO A BOWL OF SPAGHETTI BOLOGNESE

Imagine it is 2010 and I am sitting with Mel Wondimu in Addis Ababa Café in Adelaide, South Australia, just before the evening meal service begins.[49] This Ethiopian restaurant, located in a small suburban location on a major highway to the port, is one that later I was to write about on several occasions for the distinctiveness of its food and cultural traditions. Addis Ababa Café was established in 2004 for Yenenesh Gbere by her sons, and since then it has provided a taste of home for Adelaide's African communities. As well, via neighborhood, social media, and local food promotion networks, the restaurant has offered hospitality to all "others" keen to belong to the "Addis family."[50]

It is tempting to narrate this as a typical feel-good refugee story. Briefly, it could be told like this: In 1979, after her second husband's death from wounds in Ethiopia's continuing civil war, Yenenesh entrusts her sons to the care of relatives and leaves the city of Addis Ababa for Kenya. Here she is to spend the next fourteen years in a refugee camp. Wanting her sons to avoid compulsory military service under Ethiopia's communist regime, Yenenesh attempts to send for them, but the Ethiopian government refuses to grant the boys permission to leave the country. Gradually, as the Ethiopian regime collapses, Yenenesh manages to reunite the family in the Kenyan camp. In 1993, with her third husband and now five children, Yenenesh arrives in Adelaide, under the Australian government's official refugee intake program.[51] To date, the tale is hardly that of Noyes's "ideal freedom of the disembodied wanderer" and certainly that of "the brute reality of the refugee,"[52] or, to return to Chambers (though in a different geographical context and from a different standpoint of legality), Yenenesh could represent "the figure of today's (illegal) migrant who carries within herself the complex inheritance of a *colonial* past, crossed with the longstanding historical processes that make the modern world the site of perpetual mobility and migration."[53]

In the years that follow, however, the brute reality of life for Yenenesh softens somewhat. Through her voluntary efforts for Adelaide's Refugee Association, together with the organic growth of the restaurant as a community hub, it seems that Yenenesh converts her life story from a narrative of displacement to one of reciprocal hospitality. In gratitude, and in the spirit of inclusivity, the "good" refugee offers loyalty and services not only to other refugees and immigrants in the new home but also to those of the host nation.[54] However, this is not a version of the nomad's arriving home at last that I want to adopt, that is, without complicating its intimations of myth-making and national self-congratulation. In my earlier account of the restaurant, as well as pointing to the relentless hours and hard work required to run this small business, I have written in some detail on how Yenenesh's embodied memories of taste and smell, intersecting with cosmopolitan sensibilities and insistence on collective reenactments of commensality rituals, together allow her at least limited forms of agency[55] ("without [these forms] being outside the field in which . . . [discipline] is exercised").[56] Within constraints then, there are glimpses of possibility for self-transformation from refugee to cosmopolitan, from guest to host.[57]

For this chapter, however, our central focus is the next generation. In 1993, Yenenesh's youngest son, Zed, aged fifteen, arrives in Adelaide with the rest of his family. There he completes his secondary education before moving into the hospitality industry where he meets his wife-to-be, Mel. In contrast to Zed, Mel is from an

Anglo-Celtic Australian background with parents and all but one grandparent (who arrived from Scotland as a two-year-old) born in Australia. She describes herself as from a "regular family in the suburbs," middle class, with her father an accountant and her mother in part-time employment. Growing up in the 1980s and 1990s, Mel remembers her family as an emotionally close one, with not much contact with other cultures ("I'm Aussie . . . we're all Aussies," she says). Meanwhile her mother, as a good Aussie cook ritually produces iconic suburban meals of spaghetti, casseroles, roasted lamb for the family, and Mel, in her turn, works after school in Western-style food chains—Pizza Hut, the Cheesecake Factory—and later, in various hotel restaurants. Following a period of school-based work experience at a convention center restaurant, Mel secures employment there, waiting on tables. It was here that she meets Zed. Remembering this moment in her life as a cultural epiphany of sorts, Mel says this was when "everything opened up," "meeting people from other cultures," attending (with Zed) a fundamentalist Christian church in the city where there were "lots of Asian students." On the culinary front, she claims, Zed taught her much about other cultures, for example, the use of a fork and spoon to eat spaghetti bolognaise ("He refused to take me out until I learnt that"), and during their court-ing days they tried different ethnic restaurants—Italian, Indian, Thai. After all, she muses, "[a]nything new is exciting."

So far, this seems to be more a story of a culinary coming of age rather than one of nomadism, at least from Mel's perspective as a young, white, Anglo-Australian woman. It is also a typical one. In recounting Australia's cultural history from the 1950s onward, urban Anglo-Australian baby boomers (children born in the decade or so immediately after the Second World War)[58] tend to construct their own food biographies as a narrative of progress from bland British-inherited cooking to mul-ticultural eating—to the cornucopia of tastes that postwar migration and beyond is supposed to have produced (even though migration as the only cause of this multiculinary spectacle is debatable).[59] Nevertheless, in John Newton's words, the second half of the twentieth century might be characterized as a period of radical transformation in Australian food and foodscapes—a transformation from "Ozfood" to "wogfood."[60] While white, middle-class British-descended Australia remains at the point of society's power dynamics (or so the story goes), the nomads, in turn, as exotics—from Central and Southern Europe, and later from Asia—come to us, bearing culinary gifts. Certainly, it seems that Mel's account might fit this analysis of dichotomy of the sedentary and the nomadic, especially along gendered lines: for a portrait of movement imagine her husband Zed, as a black African refugee, suffer-ing the effects of war and displacement throughout his childhood but, as an adult in his new home, using traditional cultural capital meshed with hospitality training to transform his identity to food industry professional with cosmopolitan sensibilities; imagine Mel herself, as a white Aussie woman, keeper of home and hearth, settled in the town of her birth (a former British colonial outpost), and raising her children according to their hybrid inheritance. They eat not only Ethiopian dishes such as siga wett, a spicy beef stew, and injera, a flatbread, cooked for the restaurant by Yenenesh their grandmother, but also injest, as third-generation Aussies, the culinary legacy of their other (white) grandmother. And taking pride of place in Mel's own repertoire of family meals is spaghetti bolognaise—a favorite dish to cook, to eat, and to remember, and in turn, to pass on . . . and about which more will be said later.

However, the binary of moving and settled in the above is not so convincing, and in narratives here the distinction between these terms often becomes muddied. The story, of course, is more complicated than these brief hints of differential gendered, racial, and mainstream class positioning allow. There is both movement and stasis in both of these biographies, whether actual or imagined. Here, we pull together threads from our earlier discussion: Braidotti's declaration that "[n]ot all nomads are world travellers, some of the greatest trips can take place without physically moving from one's habitat";[61] my own reflections on ingested nomadism as, in effect, a way of leaving home—at least, in imagination through the vehicles of memory, the senses, and the corporeality of palatal taste; Aldea's drawing on Braidotti to remind us that "the change from a sedentary to a nomadic order affects the subjectivity and identity not only of those who move, but of all the inhabitants of an area."[62] So, while reflecting on this earlier discussion, we could speculate there is some porosity of boundary between moving and settled, especially if we don't insist on taking these categories literally, and instead allow for the virtual world with its sensorial interfaces and its imagined movement through space and time.

Living then within the confines of a modern global city, Mel's exposure to people on the move and to difference—in languages, cultural traditions, religions, food—would seem inevitable. Through marrying into Adelaide's Ethiopian community, however, this exposure is intensified. With the exception of a period when Mel and Zed moved interstate before returning to Adelaide to take up management of the restaurant on Yenenesh's retirement, Mel might not have travelled physically far from home, but the cultural shifts required of her were of seismic proportions. Haunting this imagined nomadism is the trope of Africa, its references everywhere in daily Australian life—in Mel and Zed's children's skin color, in family meals that were dictated by the restaurant's leftovers, in the tightly-knit intimacy of a small diasporic community determined to preserve its traditions, and in the longue durée of ghostly generations and practices from that Africa of elsewhere. From the day Mel is taken by Zed to meet his mother (remembered by Mel as an "interview" . . . "it was an approval thing and without . . . [his mother's formal approval, Zed] wouldn't have gone ahead [with the marriage]"), Mel's life experience, in effect, became another country, the negotiation of its strangeness, compared to familiar Aussie landscapes, at that time, both exhilarating and challenging.

To emphasise the culinary dimensions of this imagined nomadism through "another country" we return to food cultures as a potential bridge between past and present, between here and elsewhere, between different groups of people "eating together." Earlier I argue that food is possibly a means to slip under the radar of difference—a back route of exchange to avoid the effects of ethnic or national gatekeeping. Kelvin Low, reflecting on examples of mixed Singaporean families' negotiating multiethnic eating, expresses the resilience and flexibility of food cultures for this task:

> [C]ulinary boundaries are more porous than ethnic boundaries . . ., where individuals think in ethnically bounded terms and simultaneously cook in hybridised ways. . . . At best, state heritage-making relies on simplistic ethnic categories whereas foodways as lived experiences importantly reflect otherwise.[63]

At the same time, Low continues, sometimes state and individual imperatives are in conjunction: boundary making through culinary practices is rendered meaningful by individuals and the state in concerted efforts to maintain ethnic identity."[64] Hence, it could be argued a form of "strategic essentialism" (however disputed this particular theorization might be)[65] is practiced in the interest of cultural maintenance at Addis Ababa Café. And, by literally marrying into the Addis Ababa family, Mel moves into Zed's nomadic history and across landscapes of imagined Africa to find a sense of belonging outside, and contrary to, her own mainstream positioning.

Remembering Ang's discussion of ambivalence in relation to hybridity—the precariousness (and rewards) of living in the interstices of competing cultures[66]—we return to another imaginary that persistently threads through Mel's culinary biography. As well as hauntings of Africa, there are those of Aussies, thrown more sharply into relief by the intimate presence of the stranger in their midst. Aussie families, Aussie identities, Aussie cooking, ingested tastes of Aussie food . . . these are signposts of national belonging to cling to when Mel's doubts creep in, such as: "I don't cook here in the restaurant . . . I'm only a kitchen hand. I can't live up to Yenenesh's reputation [for cooking Ethiopian food]"; "People look at the kids and say "Are you their mother?'"; "[My daughter] doesn't want to eat Ethiopian [food] and doesn't want to be in the restaurant." At such moments, Aussie comfort food—scrambled egg for breakfast, pastas for other meals, especially a large bowl of spaghetti bolognaise made by Mel to last several days, signal a different kind of travel. Taste and memory become the vehicles for journeying to that "other" country, not to Africa as exotic but to the familiar of an idealized, "regular," European-inflected past. So here (according to one of this chapter's opening quotations), we are reminded of "the way memory works . . . what we do with it, and what it does with us."

Nevertheless, a retreat to spaghetti bolognaise as quintessentially Aussie cuisine might seem somewhat puzzling. To what extent can a dish that is clearly Italian in origin claim to be a classic Australian one? Is it possible that its tastes, smells, and textures together gesture not only to an identity grounded in elsewhere but also to an identity inscribed with the changing gastronomic cultures of Australian suburbs? Writing of this dish as an example of "Australianization," Barbara Santich traces its history "as an exotic speciality, presented by sophisticated Sydney restaurants" in the 1930s to the reproduction of its recipe (with the addition of a spoonful of Worcestershire sauce as a familiar British ingredient) for home cooking in a national women's magazine in the 1950s. During that same decade, known for its increasing industrialization of Australian food, Heinz and Nestlé produced the dish's canned versions.[67] Santich concludes that "the [current] everyday spag bol might still be a long way from the classic Italian *Tagliatelle al ragù bolognese* but it has settled into a [meat-heavy] formula approved and appreciated by most Australians."[68]

I've elaborated on this example of much loved "spag bol" for the multiple resonances it offers my argument. As I've written elsewhere, in relation to Australia's appropriation of the fusion dish laksa (a dish originating from the intermarriage of Chinese traders with local women in the port cities of the Malacca, Singapore, and George Town), cuisines are not fixed, and display elements of mobility and plasticity.[69] After all, according to Lily Kong, cuisines are "dynamic phenomena" that "evolve and interact."[70] So it seems that, in Mel's account, the borrowing continues: not only does she savor the excitement of "anything new" in extending her range of palatal taste but even her nostalgia for a familiar dish of childhood has its own borrowed history. The irony, of course, is that Zed, who has been raised to eat traditional Ethiopian food with his fingers (using pieces of injera to scoop up spicy stews) is the person who insisted that his Anglo-Australian wife learn the etiquette of using correct cutlery to eat a European-based pasta dish.

Spaghetti bolognese, forks and spoons—injera, siga wett, and fingers—these images of intersecting cultures take us beyond cuisines and their practices to question the fixity of culinary imaginaries, imaginaries such as Africa and Aussie. While we might acknowledge the comforts of holding to myth for a sense of clear-cut loyalties and meanings of belonging, the unravelling of these imaginaries in fragments of personal storytelling indicates a far more textured account than one of essentialized identities and bordered territories. While Zed, for example, for cultural as well as business reasons, adheres to his mother's philosophy and political practice of serving only traditional Ethiopian food in the restaurant, his culinary knowledge clearly extends beyond tastes of Africa. In fact, when Mel was questioned about negotiation of their differing food cultures within the relationship, she replied, "[It's not so difficult.] Zed is pretty Westernized and has been here a long time."

Leaving aside Zed's length of time in Australia to become Westernized, perhaps the critical point to note here is that he and Mel not only draw on their respective childhood cultures of home cooking—however different for each these remembered and re-transmitted cultures might be—but they also draw on those "different-from-childhood" culinary imaginaries that together they encounter in adulthood. While working in various positions in the hospitality industry prior to taking on the management of Addis Ababa Café and since then, Zed and Mel absorb meanings of professionalism—its philosophies and practices. At the convention center, for example, both gain experience, admittedly though in varying ways, in providing stylish "bistro meals in a classy riverside space" to consumers in search of high-end or more casual dining experiences.[71]

With Mel waiting on restaurant tables and Zed tackling the tasks of restaurant management, both are exposed to a form of culinary cosmopolitanism—to an internationally-based cuisine, in this case one popularly known as Mod Oz.[72] Five-spice duck breast, snapper with feta and aioli, crispy pork belly, roma tomatoes and buffalo mozzarella, spiced tofu with miso dressing—these are only a few of the Adelaide Convention Center restaurant's current menu offerings. However, as a business that advertises its goal is to showcase modern South Australian ingredients in contexts of global culinary trends, there is no reason to doubt that this restaurant has had, from its establishment in 1987, a continuing history of fashionable international-style cooking.[73]

This is not to argue that exposure to upmarket restaurant cooking styles alone guarantees the development of cosmopolitan sensibilities and cross-cultural empathies. Nevertheless, as Donna Gabaccia says, eating the food of "others" is a start, at least, to recognition and acceptance of cultural and culinary difference: "The marketplace, and its consumer culture, may be a slim thread on which to build cross-cultural understanding. But . . . it is better to have it than not."[74] Hospitality workers seeing close at hand "how the other half eats" during service provision is certainly one of those slim threads, and hardly high on the list of a government's policy priorities compared to the need to guarantee food security and resource sustainability. On the other hand, workers' everyday activity on the floor of a restaurant does allow a degree of virtual boundary-crossing in food culture knowledge and a degree of recognition of the ways the nomadic order shapes gastronomic cultures—the diverse menus, tastes, styles: available. Nevertheless, the table of commensality is set primarily for valued customers, and the staff's opportunity to savor in a leisurely fashion the piquancy of five-spice duck is probably limited.

So although it is tempting to celebrate Zed as the authentic refugee who, in reaching the new home, draws on his inherited cultural capital in an entrepreneurial fashion to establish himself as a restaurant owner-manager, the story is obviously more complicated than that.[75] As well, Mel simply cannot be designated as the nurturing Aussie mother reproducing the dishes of her own childhood for her mixed-race children to counterbalance the need to protect the imagined tastes of Africa for a family's livelihood and a diasporic community's cultural survival. Instead a (mildly) disruptive tale has emerged, in keeping with Braidotti's claim that "the subversion of set conventions . . . defines the nomadic state, not the literal act of traveling."[76] So where are the subversive elements—if any—in my narrative of culinary nomadism meets global mixed race? What are the ambiguous traces in accounts of Africa meets Aussie, beyond mythic renderings of nation and nomadism—where are the cracks in myth's smooth surfaces—its "blissful clarity"[77]?

FRAGMENTS, SUBVERSIONS . . .

To date, the pervasive public image of the happy fusion family, drawing on the diverse ingredients, skills, and cooking styles of its members' mixed histories for producing daily meals, is one that is not easy to dispel.[78] Fusion implies that, by household agreement, some kind of culinary equal marriage is achieved. The reality, however, is much more contradictory, with relations of intimacy and their foodways shaped within complex, and seemingly inevitable, asymmetries. With Mel's entry into the Ethiopian community, for example, is it not the case that a middle-class white Australian woman from a position of mainstream privilege might be seen as marrying down as well as out in class, race, and gender terms? Alternatively, is this chapter's focus really a story of two migrations—one from Ethiopia and Kenya in the 1990s and one of previous generations from Scotland in the early twentieth century—however different and asymmetrical the reasons for departure, their routes, and eventual destinations might be? And pushing the limits of these migration stories, if we were to construct a narrative of social uneasiness when a white woman marries into an exotic (code for black) ethnic community (rather than from the perspectives of her male partner embracing an ambivalent position in the ethnic mainstream), is there a reversal, in hospitality terms, of who is the host, who is the guest at the table of culinary nomadism?[79]

Once again, there are too many vexing questions here for discussion in a single chapter, so we'll limit the focus to further flashes of Braidotti's subversions—intriguing moments for unpicking and challenging dominant mappings of migrational and nomadic pathways. Crucial among these is the persistence of spice and its secrets. In my earlier account of the restaurant, journalists' reviews of menu dishes and of Yenenesh's skills as an intuitive cook are wreathed in aromas of spices. The spice paste that forms the basis for flavoring Yenenesh's sauces, and hence the distinctive dishes she prepares, becomes a powerful motif. Spice pervades her cooking and her personal project of cultural maintenance. To prepare the paste, Yenenesh calls on organic memory, sensory landscapes of taste and smell, practices of trial and error, and knowledge of food cultures of local ethnic communities for substituting hard-to-find ingredients: "I'm thinking, I buy something, I mix it. Still no. And then I try the other thing. I go to buy from Gaganis [Middle Eastern wholesaler], I go to buy from the India shop, I go to Asia shop. I will try so many things." In this way spice is emblematic of grounded cosmopolitanism, with Yenenesh, as matriarch of the community, holding the power of spice in her hands. Hers are "hands that remember"[80] but also ones with secrets not to be given away lightly. Even after retirement, Yenenesh clings to her identity as spice-maker, as the only spice-maker.

In the restaurant, it seemed, Mel could be only a bit player to Yenenesh's performance of dazzling expertise. On the other hand, while spices and their inherited secrets might have been symptomatic of ingested nomadism in the microcosmic world of Addis Ababa Café, suburban Aussie homes had their own stories of travel, taste, aroma, and memory, especially if meanings of Aussie were stretched somewhat. Mel and Zed's kitchen proved no exception. Instead of this space transformed to "other," a space of not-Ethiopian food or of competing "other"—Aussie versus Africa—there was a case to be made for this kitchen as a sensorial interface—a meeting point, as we recall, of diverse sensory knowledges, their negotiation, and of "the production of something 'new' in their stead."[81] In this interface, tastes and aromas of traditional Ethiopian cooking in the form of restaurant leftovers mingled with the pungent smell of roasted lamb, an iconic Australian Sunday lunch dish;[82] historically borrowed flavors of spaghetti bolognese, naturalized, met acquired cosmopolitan sensibilities expressed through its mundane tools—a fork and spoon; eating out stretched beyond the restaurant that supplied one's liveli-hood to the taste of other exotic cuisines; a mélange of flavors and aromas signalled the ingestion of varying identities—home cook, kitchen hand, restaurant manager for Mel; refugee, kitchen observer (in the style of Giard's childhood absorption of "doing cooking"),[83] hotel and restaurant manager for Zed. It is obvious this sensorial interface was busy and messy with meaning, often competing, sometimes disruptive. Rather than arguing for a kitchen where meals, dishes, and ingredients neatly fused their assorted histories, in the sensorial interface there were separa-tions, tensions, ambiguities that stretched both meanings of Australian and African beyond their mythic associations. In this way, mundane practices of everyday meal provision were textured with subversive meanings.

Ang has long argued that complexity, not-quite-fitting, and ambivalence can be turned to productive ends. Writing of the tangle of interrelationships that are "*con-stitutive* of contemporary social life," Ang says:

> [R]ather than seeing hybridity as a synonym for an easy multicultural harmony . . . I want to suggest that the concept of hybridity should be mobilized to address and analyse the fundamental *uneasiness* in our global condition of togetherness-in-difference. . . . In short, hybridity is not only about fusion and synthesis, but also about friction and tension, about ambivalence and incommensurability, about the contestations and interrogations that go hand in hand with the heterogeneity, diversity and multiplicity we have to deal with as we live together-in-difference.[84]

As I noted earlier, Ang primarily is referring to different cultures living in close geo-graphic proximity, with this necessitating their negotiation of the inevitable "friction and tension . . . ambivalence and incommensurability" as well as seizing possibilities for "fusion and synthesis." Of course, if we transfer this "heterogeneity, diversity, and multiplicity" to a single kitchen as a sensorial interface, the ingestions of meaning and the nomadic foodways intimated become even more complex and, of course, more en-tangled and intimate. Aussie and Africa, in fact, may transmogrify into something else, challenging clear-cut national boundaries and hinting of more porous ones, grounded in everyday multiethnic, even cosmopolitan, sensibilities, as Gabaccia suggests.[85]

Nevertheless, before we become too comfortable with the idea of existing in a flex-ible and fluid state of cosmopolitanism, with practices of mixing across and beyond national boundaries, we should not forget Ang's warning about "the fundamental *un-easiness* in our global condition of togetherness-in-difference." It is this ""uneasiness" that makes us alert to the pitfalls of assuming "an easy multicultural harmony" and serves as a reminder that the tensions of "togetherness-in-difference" need constant negotiation. One of these "uneasy" moments occurs when I ask Mel about the school her children attend, specifically its ethnic demographic. She replies, "At school, there's a mixture of kids. Two of the other kids there are half-caste." Mel's use of the category "half-caste" is curious here. Firstly, the term is deemed to be an offensive one, outlawed as politically incorrect for its assumptions of genetic impurity of mixed-blood offspring. The obverse, of course, is that in Australia as a colonial settler society, its racialized hierarchies persisting in the present, white races are deemed pure and superior. The purity/impurity discourse is particularly resonant in the history of subjugation of Australia's indigenous peoples. As late as the 1970s, government "protective" legislation was directed toward breeding the "black" out of generations of mixed-race indigenous children through enforced removal of these children from their "black" families to institutionalized forms of "white" foster-caring.[86]

So, perhaps Mel's use of this term calls on traces of race memory, inherited from white parents, grandparents, teachers? However (and this is my second point), it is interesting she does not refer to her own children as "half-caste" but simply to "other kids" in this regard. The obvious explanation is that the term is employed here, perhaps ineptly, simply to mean different? Another explanation is that Mel, even though a mother of mixed-race children herself, uses the language of half-caste as a means of distancing herself: she calls on the discourse of the white majority to declare other children as "other," yet not to categorize her own in this way. In almost the same breath, however, Mel announces the "mix" is a fortunate one, and in blending the two cultures, she says, the family has "the best of both worlds." While uneasiness persists, there are ways of placating it, ways toward comfort, after all—and these are the familiar tactics of the everyday.[87]

Leaving aside those questions of endemic discrimination against indigenous populations in Australia and, sometimes, of well-meaning attempts to assuage white guilt,[88] a third route for thinking through the language of half-caste is, perhaps, as mixed-race, even post-race.[89] Given patterns of global movement, displacement, and diaspora, mixed populations, particularly within the spaces of global cities, might seem unremarkable, after all. Mica Nava, writing of London and the normalization of mixed-race, says:

> "Mixed-raceness" has become more and more ordinary and exists alongside the contemporary plurality of urban British physiognomies. Multiple national origins and languages are the norm in London schools. "Otherness" is no longer very different or remarkable. Nor . . . is merger or "fusion"—ie inter-racial and inter-cultural sexual partnerships and offspring. Difference these days is becoming as normal in the bed room as it is on the streets.[90]

If this seems somewhat optimistic, even utopian, Nava hastens to reassure readers that she is not denying evidence of continuing racism or xenophobia in British cities during the twentieth century and beyond, noting, for example, the recent "shameful spate of hostility towards Muslims and asylum seekers." Nevertheless, she claims that there has also been:

> a counter-tendency, with the allure of difference, with aspirations to be cosmopolitan, to go abroad, to be hospitable to foreigners. On the whole this mood or structure of feeling has constituted an alternative culture of modernity.[91]

And it is these desires for adventure, feelings of empathy, perhaps, more intuitive than rational, perhaps more grounded in the appetites of the body and deep in the gut than modernity's narratives of social and scientific progress allow, that invites us to think of cosmopolitanism differently—cosmopolitan as, in Nava's terms, "visceral," and in Mel's, "[a]nything new is exciting."

At this point, neither of the chosen fragments—spice, taste, and aroma as entree to commensality's porosity or reworking the grammar of half-caste as global mixed race—strike us as particularly subversive. And yet both might seem to trouble dominant ways of thinking—to serve as interventions in racist conceptions of the exotic nurturing black woman and the less than pure child of mixed blood. Bhabha, criticizing binaries of either-or choices of identification, argues instead for a "third space" as a position of enunciation:

> [I]f the act of cultural translation (both as representation and as reproduction) denies the essentialism of a priori given or original culture, then we can see all forms of culture are continually in a process of hybridity. But for me the importance of hybridity is not to be able to trace two original moments from which the third emerges, rather hybridity to me is the "third space" which enables other positions to emerge. This third space displaces the histories that constitute it, and sets up new structures of authority, new political initiatives, which are inadequately understood through received wisdom.[92]

I have quoted Bhabha at length since his "third space" sets up useful resonances, echoes of which also might be found in my argument to date. Expressed this way, "third space" connects with this chapter's earlier explication of "sensorial interface" as "a 'meeting point' of different kinds of sensory knowledge . . . and possibly, the production of something 'new' in their stead."[93] To be fair to Bhabha though, here I would need to emphasize once more the act of displacement in meaning that occurs, rather than simple incorporation of elements.

Perhaps even more important for my argument, however, is Bhabha's "all forms of culture are continually in a process of hybridity." Just as mixed identities have, in Nava's terms, become ordinary, in fact the norm, in twenty-first century global cities, so, too, are mixed cuisines. To rephrase Bhabha, "all cuisines are continually in a process of hybridity." Ingested nomadism then becomes the province of all, with particular examples of nomadic cuisine difficult to identify beyond the universality of this truism, and beyond embedded examples of everyday ingestions governed by meanings of mobility, memory, and social and cultural positioning. In this way, Massey's British pensioner, with fish and chips purchased from the Chinese takeout, becomes the modern take on culinary nomadism (and its inequities), after all.

LOVE SONGS TO GLOBAL CITIES, GLOBAL SELVES

Love songs to global cities (and "to our mongrel selves")[94] are not unusual in the literature, whether they take the form of Jean-Claude Izzo's sensual embrace of Marseille's food, seascapes, and communities of "exiles" ("I felt like going and losing myself in Marseilles. . . . My city") or Mica Nava's assurance that, in "this new London," normalization of difference has the possibility of producing "an alternative culture of modernity."[95] Meanwhile, walking the streets of Naples, Chambers relishes the traces of "multilateral modernity," although always under threat, he claims, from repression, historical amnesia, and national gatekeeping ("Each and every culture would have to let go, unlearn itself, and become a little less narcissistic"[96]). It seems that in cities of "exiles," "mongrel selves," and "other" modernities, Massey's figure of the British pensioner continues to haunt and to discomfort.

Nevertheless, a focus on the detail of the everyday sometimes allows different narratives to emerge. In this chapter, tracing the minutiae of food and cultural exchange within relations of intimacy suggests more textured possibilities than bald categorizations of movement versus stasis, of freedom versus constraint, of essentialized versus fluid identities or of closed versus open borders. Here, in this analysis, nomadism as a concept becomes slippery yet useful in its complexities, and culinary or ingested nomadism even more so. Following threads we have un-ravelled here, it seems that the demands of eating together—both in global cities like Marseille, London, and Naples, and, microcosmically, within mixed personal relationships—might be onerous. Darmon and Warde (2016, 707), in fact, com-pare the culinary cultures of mixed households to the food work of tourists seeking to expand their palatal range, to become more cosmopolitan. However, for cross-national couples, continue Darmon and Warde:

> [T]he need to establish joint routines and a shared diet imposes heavier demands [than for tourists]. The tensions involved in negotiating between desires and embodied feel-ings include experiences of disgust, saturation, exasperation and trepidation. In devising strategies to cope, cross-national couples have much to teach about processes of change.[97]

How much of the "strategies to cope" in dealing with the stranger at the gates involves Chambers's "letting go" and "unlearning" oneself remains the critical ques-tion. And likewise, one can only speculate on possibilities for moving toward "the wider, worldly, and more fragile constellation of a multilateral modernity."[98] At the very least, however, forms of ingested nomadism appear to offer interstitial, senso-rial spaces for "fashion[ing] a diasporic modernity and feel[ing] at home . . . in the world."[99] In other words, in a very literal sense, everyday mixed spaces in the local (spaces within households, on the streets, and within cities), are resonant, if ambiva-lent, sites of cosmopolitan identity. As well, these sites include imagined possibilities for travel, and eating, beyond their boundaries.

BIBLIOGRAPHY

Adelaide Convention Centre. Accessed 20 September, 2017. http://www.eventconnect.com/venue/finder/1889/adelaide-convention-centre/.

Aldea, Eva. "Nomads and Migrants: Deleuze, Braidotti and the European Union in 2014." *Open Democracy*, 10 September, 2014. Accessed 19 September, 2016. https://www.open

democracy.net/can-europe-make-it/eva-aldea/nomads-and-migrants-deleuze-braidotti-and
-european-union-in-2014.

Ali, Suki. *Mixed Race, Post-Race: Gender, New Ethnicities and Cultural Practices*. Oxford: Berg, 2003.

Ang, Ien. *On Not Speaking Chinese: Living between Asia and the West*. London: Routledge, 2001.

Bhabha, Homi. "Cultural Diversity and Cultural Differences." In *The Post-Colonial Studies Reader*, edited by Bill Ashcroft, Gareth Griffiths, and Helen Tiffin, 206–9. London: Routledge, 1995.

Barthes, Roland. *Mythologies*. London: Paladin, 1973.

Braidotti, Rosi. *Nomadic Subjects: Embodiment and Sexual Difference in Contemporary Feminist Theory*. New York: Columbia University Press, 1994.

Chambers, Iain. *Mediterranean Crossings: The Politics of Interrupted Modernity*. Durham, NC: Duke University Press, 2008.

———. "Another Map, Another History, Another Modernity." *California Italian Studies* 1, no. 1 (2010): 1–14.

D'Andrea, Anthony. "Neo-Nomadism: A Theory of Post-Identitarian Mobility in the Global Age." *Mobilities* 1, no. 1 (2006): 95–119.

Darmon, Isabelle, and Alan Warde. "Senses and Sensibilities; Stabilising and Changing Tastes in Cross-National Couples." *Food, Culture and Society* 19, no. 4 (2016): 705–22.

de Certeau, Michel. *The Practice of Everyday Life*. Berkeley: University of California Press, 1984.

Deleuze, Gilles, and Felix Guattari. *A Thousand Plateaus: Capitalism and Schizophrenia*. Minneapolis: University of Minnesota Press, 1987.

Derrida, Jacques. *On Cosmopolitanism and Forgiveness*. London: Routledge, 2001.

Durmelat, Sylvie. "Tasting Displacement: Couscous and Culinary Citizenship in Maghrebi-French Diasporic Cinema." *Food and Foodways* 23, nos. 1–2 (2015): 104–26.

Duruz, Jean. 1999. "Food as Nostalgia: Eating the Fifties and Sixties." *Australian Historical Studies* 30, no. 113 (1999): 231–50.

———. "Eating at the Borders: Culinary Journeys." *Environment and Planning D: Society and Space* 23, no. 1 (2005): 51–69.

———. "From Malacca to Adelaide: Fragments towards a Biography of Cooking, Yearning and *Laksa*." In *Food and Foodways in Asia: Resource, Tradition and Cooking*, edited by Sidney C. H. Cheung and Tan Chee-Beng, 183–200. London: Routledge, 2007.

———. "Tastes of Hybrid Belonging: Following the Laksa Trail in Katong, Singapore." *Continuum* 25, no. 5 (2011): 605–18.

———. "Tastes of the 'Mongrel City': Geographies of Memory, Spice, Hospitality and Forgiveness." *Cultural Studies Review* 19, no. 1 (2013): 73–98.

———. 2018. "Trucking in Tastes and Smells: Adelaide's Street Food and the Politics of Urban 'Vibrancy.'" In *Senses in Cities: Experiences of Urban Settings*, edited by Kelvin E. Y. Low and Devorah Kalekin-Fishman, 169–84. London: Routledge, 2018.

Duruz, Jean and Gaik Cheng Khoo. *Eating Together: Food, Space and Identity in Malaysia and Singapore*. Lanham, MD: Rowman and Littlefield, 2015.

Frankenberg, Ruth. *White Women, Race Matters: The Social Construction of Whiteness*. Minneapolis: University of Minnesota Press, 1993.

Gabaccia, Donna. *We Are What We Eat: Ethnic Food and the Making of Americans*. Cambridge, MA: Harvard University Press, 1998.

Giard, Luce. "The Nourishing Arts." In *The Practice of Everyday life Volume 2: Living and Cooking*, by Michel de Certeau, Luce Giard, and Pierre Mayol, 153–69. Minneapolis: University of Minnesota Press, 1998.

Guttentag, Daniel. "Airbnb: Disruptive Innovation and the Rise of the Informal Tourism Accommodation Sector." *Current Issues in Tourism,* 2 September 2013. Accessed 26 August, 2014. http://dx.doi.org/10.1080/13683500.2013.827159.

Harvey, David. *The Condition of Postmodernity: An Enquiry into the Origins of Cultural Change.* Oxford: Basil Blackwell, 1989.

Hernandez, Michael, and David Sutton. 2005. "Hands that Remember: An Ethnographic Approach to Everyday Cooking." *Expedition* 45, no. 2 (2005): 30–37.

Huggins, Jackie. "Government Has Not Met Its International Human Rights Standards." Speech delivered to the United Nations Permanent Forum on Indigenous Issues in New York, 20 May 2016. Accessed 29 September 2017. http://www.sbs.com.au/nitv/nitv-news/article/2016/05/20/jackie-huggins-un-government-has-not-met-its-international-human-rights-standards.

Hugo, Graeme. *Background Paper for Africa Australians: A Review of Human Rights and Social Inclusion Issues.* Sydney: Australian Human Rights Commission, 2009. Accessed 22 September 2017. https://www.humanrights.gov.au/sites/default/files/content/africanaus/papers/africanaus_papr_hugo.pdf.

Iyer, Pico. "Where Worlds Collide: In Los Angeles International Airport, the Future Touches Down." *Harpers*, August 1995, 51–57. Accessed 21 September 2017. https://harpers.org/archive/1995/08/where-worlds-collide/.

Izzo, Jean-Claude. *Garlic, Mint and Sweet Basil: Essays on Marseilles, Mediterranean Cuisine and Noir Fiction.* New York: Europa, 2013.

King-O'Riain, Rebecca C., Small, Stephen, Mahtani, Minelle, Song, Miri, and Spickard, Paul, eds. *Global Mixed Race.* New York: NYU Press, 2014.

Kong, Lily. "From Sushi in Singapore to Laksa in London: Globalising Foodways and the Production of Economy and Identity." In *Food, Foodways and Foodscapes: Culture, Community and Consumption in Post-Colonial Singapore*, eds. Lily Kong and Vineeta Sinha, 207–41. Singapore: World Scientific, 2016.

Lively, Penelope. *Ammonites and Leaping Fish: A Life in Time.* London: Penguin, 2013.

Low, Kelvin E. Y. 2016. "Tasting Memories, Cooking Heritage: A Sensuous Invitation to Remember." In *Food, Foodways and Foodscapes: Culture, Community and Consumption in Post-Colonial Singapore*, edited by Lily Kong and Vineeta Sinha, 61–82. Singapore: World Scientific, 2016.

Low, Kelvin E. Y., and Devorah Kalekin-Fishman. "Afterword: Towards Transnational Sensescapes." In *Everyday Life in Asia; Social Perspectives on the Senses*, edited by Devorah Kalekin-Fishman and Kelvin E. Y. Low, 195–203. Farnham, Surrey UK: Ashgate, 2010.

MacFarlane, Kit and Jean Duruz. "Technologies of Nostalgia: Vegetarians and Vegans at Addis Ababa Café." In *Eat, Cook, Grow: Mixing Human-Computer Interactions with Human-Food Interactions*, edited by Jaz Hee-Jeong Choi, Marcus Foth, and Greg Hearn, 33–49. Cambridge, MA: MIT Press, 2014.

Mackay, Hugh. *Generations: Baby Boomers, Their Parents and Their Children.* Sydney: Macmillan, 1997.

Massey, Doreen. *Space, Place and Gender.* Cambridge UK: Polity, 1994.

May, Jon, and Nigel Thrift. 2001. "Introduction." In *Timespace: Geographies of Temporality*, edited by Jon May and Nigel Thrift, 1–46. New York: Routledge, 2001.

Mehta, Brinda J. "Culinary Diasporas: Identity and the Language of Food in Gisele Pineau's *Un Papillon dans Le Cite* and *L'Exil selon Julia.*" *International Journal of Francophone Studies* 8, no. 1 (2005): 23–50.

Mintz, Sidney W. *Tasting Food, Tasting Freedom: Excursions into Eating, Culture, and the Past.* Boston: Beacon, 1996.

Morley, David. *Home Territories.* London: Routledge, 2000.

Morris, Madeleine. "High-Rise Residents Fight Short-Stay Economy over 'Pop-Up Brothels,' All-Night Parties." *ABC News*, 7 January, 2016. Accessed 22 February, 2016. http://www .abc.net.au/news/2016-01-06/high-rise-residents-fight-back-against-short-stays/7071042.

Nava, Mica. *Visceral Cosmopolitanism: Gender, Culture and the Normalisation of Difference.* London: Bloomsbury, 2007.

———. 2010. "Visceral Cosmopolitanism: The Specificity of Race and Miscegenation in UK." *Politics and Culture* 3, 10 August 2010. Accessed 29 August 2017. https://politics andculture.org/2010/08/10/mica-nava-visceral-cosmopolitanism-the-specifici-2/.

Newton, John. *Wogfood—An Oral History with Recipes.* Sydney: Random House, 1996.

Noyes, John. "Nomadism, Nomadology, Postcolonialism: By Way of Introduction." *Interventions* 6, no. 2 (2004): 159–68.

Potts, Rolf. *Vagabonding: An Uncommon Guide to the Art of Long-Term World Travel.* New York: Random House, 2003.

Ram, Kalpena. "Listening to the Call of the Dance: Re-Thinking Authenticity and 'Essentialism.'" *Australian Journal of Anthropology* 11, no. 3 (2000): 358–64.

Ray, Krishnendu. *The Ethnic Restaurateur.* London: Bloomsbury, 2016.

Rbar@Regattas. Accessed 30 November, 2017. https://www.regattas.com.au/.

Rutherford, Jonathan. "The Third Space: Interview with Homi Bhabha." In Johnathan Rutherford, *Identity, Community, Culture, Difference*, ed. Jonathan Rutherford, 207–21. London: Lawrence & Wishart, 1990.

Sandercock, Leonie. *Cosmopolis II: Mongrel Cities in the 21st Century.* London: Continuum, 2003.

Santich, Barbara. *Bold Palates: Australia's Gastronomic Heritage.* Kent Town SA: Wakefield, 2012.

Small, Stephen, and Rebecca C. King-O'Riain. "Global Mixed Race: An Introduction." In *Global Mixed Race*, edited by Rebecca C. King-O'Riain, Stephen Small, Minelle Mahtani, Miri Song, and Paul Spickard, vii–xxii. New York: NYU Press, 2014.

Symons, Michael. *The Shared Table: Ideas for Australian Cuisine.* Canberra; Australian Government Publishing Service, 1993.

Wa, Veronica Mac Sau. "Southeast Asian Chinese Food in Tea Café and Noodle Shops in Hong Kong." In *Chinese Food and Foodways in Southeast Asia and Beyond*, edited by Tan Chee-Beng, 218–35. Singapore: NUS Press, 2011.

Ward, Johnny. "Five Reasons to Become a Digital Nomad." *One Step 4ward*, published online 4 December 2014. Accessed 18 September 2017. https://onestep4ward.com /digital -nomadism-5-reasons-to-become-a-digital-nomad/.

Wilson, Ronald Darling. *Bringing Them Home: Report of the National Inquiry into the Separation of Aboriginal and Torres Strait Islander Children from their Families.* Sydney: Human Rights and Equal Opportunity Commission, 1997.

Wong, Hong Suen. "A Taste of the Past: Historically Themed Restaurants and Social Memory in Singapore." In *Food and Foodways in Asia: Resource, Tradition and Cooking*, edited by Sidney C. H. Cheung and Tan Chee-Beng, 115–28. London: Routledge, 2007.

Wong, Julie Carrie. "Most Wanted: San Francisco Flyers Name and Shame Airbnb Hosts." *The Guardian*, 22 July 2016.

10

The Traveling Priest

Food for the Spirit and Food for the Body

Luciano Maffi

At the age of thirty, Don Marchelli, a young priest from Pavia, started traveling once yearly throughout Northern Italy, combining tourism with spiritual objectives. The priest described Italy in a period following its unification, between 1865 and 1876. His reports contain a variety of information regarding territories, cities, arts, churches, infrastructures, hotels, and restaurants.

He took his meals in cafés, restaurants, hotels, and train stations, and noted the details of all the dishes consumed.

The information he collected enables us to describe the economic and social growth of Italy, in particular of the middle class, which had commenced traveling for both business and tourism.

It is, however, necessary to make certain considerations before analyzing the data in detail in order to contextualize them within the broader historical setting. In the decades following Italy's unification, the young nation's society was in turmoil and undergoing profound infrastructural, urban, and technological change. The main cities of Northern Italy, for example, were radically transformed. On the other hand, no model of economic growth enabling the increase of individual incomes, and thus innovation in the enjoyment of leisure time, had yet been established.[1]

In the early post-unification decades, the phenomenon of tourism had not yet assumed the economic relevance for the country's development that it was to have later. Tourism was still an elitist phenomenon, though the beginnings of constructive ferment in the area of tourism was already apparent in some areas, especially the areas of the lakes (Lake Garda, Lake Como) and the spa towns.[2]

However, to fully understand the development of tourism in Northern Italy in the second half of the nineteenth century, we must consider the role played by infrastructures. The great transformation that took place to both land and sea transport after the introduction of the steam engine, as well as the construction of increasingly extensive and widespread infrastructural networks (above all railways) is referred to as the "transport revolution." The post-unity governments had to provide the country with the requirements for economic development, breaking down the borders that separated the pre-unification states. To do this, investments were made to modernize infrastructures by strengthening the road and rail networks that, prior to unification, had been present almost exclusively in the northern states. In general, the construction of infrastructures influenced the growth of all the existing forms of tourism, from spa, seaside, and mountain tourism.

In addition to the infrastructures, it is essential to consider the main productive sectors of the Italian peninsula, as well as the political and economic stability and the income available to tourists, as fundamental factors for the development of the tourism sector. The situation was highly complex and, alongside elements that indicated development in the industrial manufacturing sector, many elements of backwardness remained, especially in the countryside.

DON LUIGI MARCHELLI AND
HIS TRAVELS IN THE PENINSULA

The protagonist of this article is Don Luigi Marchelli (1837–1909), a priest from Pavia who traveled through Northern and Central Italy for a little more than a decade, from 1865 to 1876.

He left eleven journals reporting his experiences on these trips (one a year, except in 1870, when he made two). These are now preserved in the Diocesan Historical Archive of Pavia.[3] In the early years, the priest traveled with his father Giovanni and his brother Antonio, also a priest. At the time of his first trip Don Luigi was twenty-eight, and he was thirty-nine years old by the last. The trips all took place in the months of August or September.

These documents are useful for a series of different reasons, not only from a historical-linguistic and literary point of view but also from an historical-artistic point of view. In fact, the journals' descriptions of cities, churches, and museums make them a useful source for social history as they are rich in information that indicates how the infrastructures were changing and, therefore, people's movements (especially train journeys). They also indicate the expansion in the size of towns and the growing urbanization of the cities over those years as a consequence of the overall population increase and the development of the secondary sector and commercial activities, especially in the northern cities. In addition, we can find valuable information on meals, accommodation facilities, and guidebooks available to tourists. From a more strictly historical-economic and historical-tourism point of view, the travel reports are a source of incomparable value, since the priest recorded all his expenses at the end of each journal. All these aspects allow us to understand the costs of both travel and food, confirming that at the time tourism in Italy was very expensive.

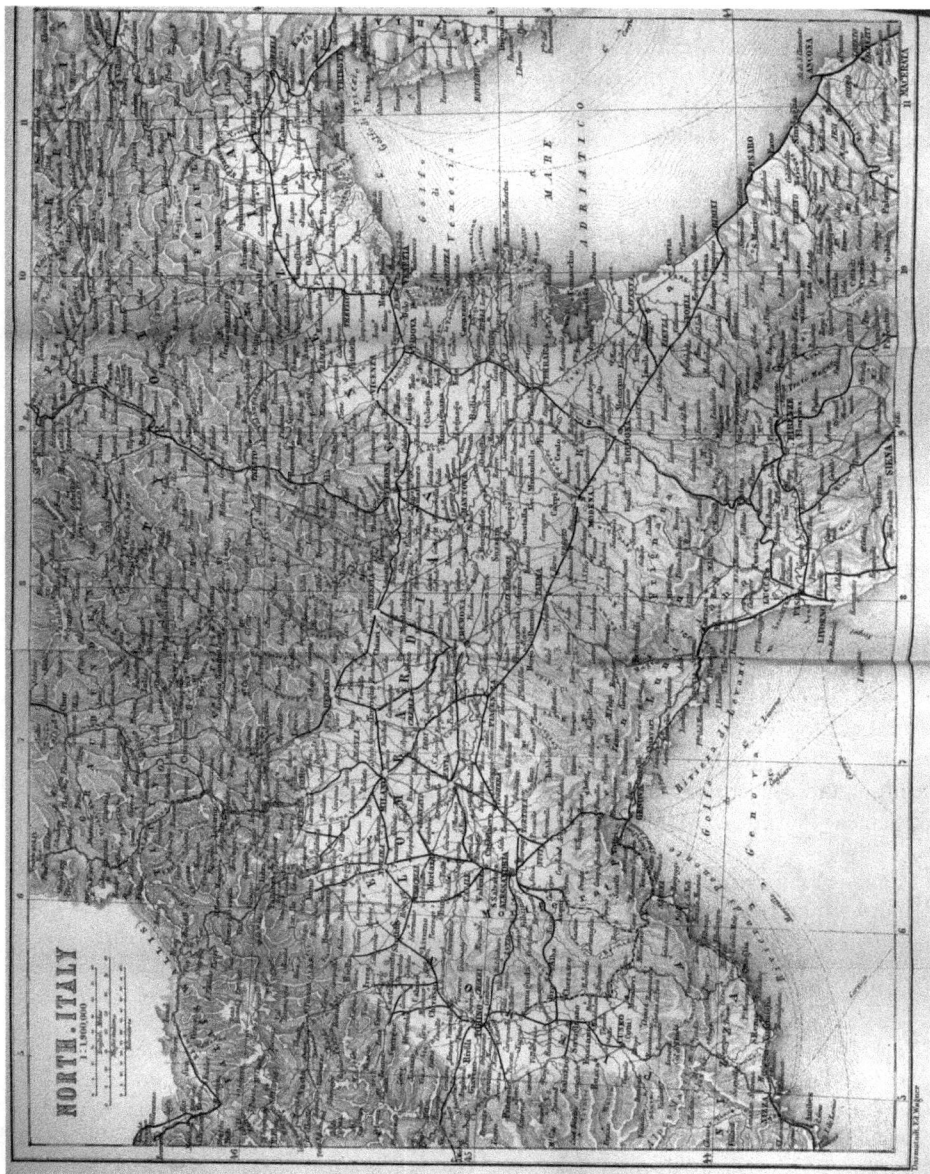

Figure 10.1. Cities visited by Don Marchelli during his travels.

Don Luigi Marchelli was a cultural tourist, to use a contemporary categorization, primarily interested in palazzi, museums, churches, and exhibitions, but also showing an interest in scenery and both natural and man-made sights. Moreover, he was attentive to his food and drink; he loved to enjoy a cup of black coffee or soda in the cafés and to listen to the bands providing musical entertainment in the public gardens and squares. He was a curious man, interested in the world around him, in art, Italian culture, and food; furthermore, in the few days of tourism he enjoyed each year, he could afford to spend an amount of money on leisure activities that was not affordable for the majority of the population at the time.

Luigi Marchelli was born January 19, 1837, in Pavia, from a family of modest conditions: his father Giovanni was a shoemaker and his mother, Angela Ratti, a seamstress. Like his elder brother Antonio, he entered the priesthood. He was ordained March 16, 1861, a significant date as the following day the Unification of Italy was proclaimed.

Don Marchelli also undertook his pastoral activity in Pavia[4] during the years of his travels; the priest celebrated mass in the church of Santa Teresa and in the Oratory of the Canossians. He also worked in the bishop's curia and probably lived with his family, as we learn from his 1874 journal. In 1876, he became the diocese registrar and archivist, a post he would maintain until his death. The trips reported in his journals belong to his youth and, we could say, to a formative phase of his life. The journey thus becomes an experience of learning and growth.

MEALS WHILE TRAVELING

From reading Don Marchelli's travel reports, he appreciated innovation, both as regards the transformations occurring in the cities, to which he paid particular attention, and concerning transport, especially trains and steamships. His description of Venice's Piazza San Marco in the evening (1870) is highly evocative:

> I retraced my steps and went to Piazza di San Marco, where I stayed until 10 pm to listen to the band of a Grenadiers regiment and to enjoy the view of the illuminations, especially those of the shops below the arcades with their beautiful lighting that enhanced the goldsmiths' showcases, enveloped in grandiose crystal and overflowing with sparkling gold and silver, the bazars full of bric-a-brac and all kinds of novelties, a bookshops and stationery shop, and the cafés. To make the most of this magnificent sight, from which I could not drag myself away, I walked up and down under the arcades several times, mixing with a busy and cheerful crowd and occasionally making my way to the middle of the Piazza to hear the band playing in the glow of a gas tree, radiant with the light from another thirty small flames.

The journals inform us of the traveler's eating habits and "quality of life." In addition to his breakfast, which was never abundant, the priest consumed only one meal daily, almost always in the hotel where he was staying and at different times, in the afternoon or in the evening:[5] this last aspect would be very unusual nowadays but it shows how meals could be consumed and served through most of the day in nineteenth-century hotels.[6] The priest's one daily meal was, however, abundant and almost always combined a soup with one or more dishes of meat or fish, a side dish, a dessert, and wine. From the journals and the receipts that the priest meticulously preserved, we can see the content of his many dinners. He ate in the restaurants of the hotels where he was staying, or in inns and restaurants outside the hotel.

Don Marchelli stayed in good quality premises, many of which were mentioned by the Baedeker guide of 1868 for Northern Italy, such as the Hotel Roma in Turin, the Italia in Varallo, the Cappello in Cremona, the Svizzero in Savona, and the Tre Garofani in Vicenza. He also frequented the Hôtel de Rome in Florence, in Piazza Santa Maria Novella, indicated by the guide as a first-class hotel, the Aquila Nera e Pace in Bologna, the Biscione in Milan, the Croce Verde in Mantova, the San Marco in Modena, and the Hotel Italia in Parma. This choice of accommodation indicates that the priest was careful in his use of tourist services, as the Baedeker was mainly aimed at travelers through Northern Europe who were accustomed to a high-quality tourist offer. Moreover, his journals demonstrate that a network of infrastructural and tourist services was forming in Italy in the second half of the nineteenth century.[7]

Below are some examples taken from the journals listing his dinners, as well as some considerations on the customary diet of the times in Lombardy, the geographical area to which Don Marchelli belonged.

In 1868, he traveled to Milan, Bergamo, Brescia, and Cremona, with his father and brother. On August 26, in Bergamo, on the city's patronal feast day he ate "rice and cabbage soup, beef with potatoes, stewed veal and fruit and cheese with table wine." On August 28, in Cremona, "a fairly good rice and cabbage vegetable soup, fried fish, roast fish, cheese and fruit and a liter of wine."

On the trip to Genoa and Savona in 1869, on August 30 at the Trattoria del Commercio in Genoa: "soup, frying of brains, stewed veal, fruit, bread and a liter of wine." On August 31 at the Albergo Svizzero in Savona: "Soup. Fine pasta shaped like lentils. Deep-fried brain. Boiled fish with roasted potatoes. Veal stew. Pigeon with buttered salsify. Sweet dish. Dessert with cheese, fruit and sweets. A liter of wine and bread." September 1: "minestrone, deep-fried brain, boiled fish (sea bream), and milk pudding, fruit and 2. cups of coffee."

Monday, September 4, 1871, in Varese, at the Albergo del Gambero at 4:30 pm they ate "cold salami, mixed-fry, minestrone, roast with salad, cheese, sweets and fruit and wine." On September 5, they dined at about 4:00 pm in the same hotel and ate "mixed-fry, minestrone, pigeon in tomato sauce, fruit pudding, cheese, fruit and wine."

In 1874, he traveled alone and on August 10 at the Albergo del Biscione in Milan he ate "minestrone–sautéed mushrooms–meatballs in gelatin–sweet pudding–half a liter of wine and bread." In the same hotel, on August 11: "mix of deep-fried brain and offal–soused carp–half a liter of wine and bread." The following day: "risotto in bonetto, kid with potatoes (excellent), spiced stracchino cheese, half a liter of wine and bread."

On August 11, 1875, he was at the Albergo del Commercio in Genoa, where he had stayed on the previous two journeys. He dined at Trattoria del Commercio, but he was a good deal less satisfied with his meal this time: "The food was reasonably tasty, but much less so than the other times." On this visit he ate: "fairly pleasant pasta and vegetable soup, very tasty boiled veal, stewed fish and juleped pears. The bread was however tasteless and the wine was not very good, of which I drank little." On August 13, on a day when he was abstaining from meat, he had, in the same restaurant: "minestrone, fried fish, fish stew and gorgonzola cheese."

As shown by his summaries of the meals consumed, there are few of what we consider typical regional dishes. However, there is variety with regards to both the soups and broths and especially the meat and fish dishes. Moreover, there are many dishes that would be unusual for us now, such as deep-fried brain and pigeon cooked in various ways. Bread and wine are never lacking. The wines are both red and white, but the type is never indicated; all were probably generic table wines.

It is noticeable that no pasta dishes appear among the meals consumed, while soup is always present and cooked in various ways, with or without rice.[8] We should also note that the priest observed the religious precepts of abstaining from meat on days of fasting, eating mainly soups, fish, and cheese.

Don Marchelli's journals, therefore, permit us to analyze some characteristics of the food available for travelers in that period; obviously, his point of view is rather particular as he was traveling on vacation. His normal meals were probably different, but what his writings report is still indicative of the meals available in the city hotels as well as providing information about the upper middle class. The nineteenth century was also important for changes in food consumption and the foodstuffs used for nutrition. The social and economic changes described above began to change habits that had previously been deeply rooted in Lombardy: a great gap had existed in the past between what the wealthiest classes ate and the food consumed by the majority of the population that belonged to poverty or subsistence categories. We know that in the nineteenth century the meals of the Italian elite would include soups, meats, fish, vegetables, cheeses, fruit, sweets, and wines within the same meal. Foreign travelers reported the wide range of dishes featuring in the dinners of the aristocracy and bourgeoisie as well as those served in hotels: a varied, lavish diet that clearly set the social classes apart.[9] Don Marchelli's journals always indicate the different methods of cooking meat and fish: roasted, boiled, stewed. Alongside beef and veal, game birds are frequently present. The offal of all the animals is also cooked and consumed.

In the mid-nineteenth century in Italy foodstuffs were either "generic" and consumed by the masses, or luxury goods.[10] Consumption, in fact, depended on the economic activity in which people were involved, but in addition to purely economic data, it also enables us to understand the culture and traditions as well as social and psychological aspects.

As Sergio Zaninelli writes when discussing Milan in the nineteenth century: "Wheat, corn and millet for bread, wheat for pastas and desserts, corn for polenta, rice for soup—one of the basic dishes on the table of all the population's social classes—they were essential and recurring products in the diet."[11] Many food products were obtained from these cereals and these made up the typical diet of the Milanese in the nineteenth century. The consumption of meat, whose nutritional values were known to satisfy the needs of the demanding work performed in a society in which industrialization was underway, was generally limited.[12] On the other hand, wine was common with an abundant per capita consumption.[13]

Continuing with other food products, Sergio Zaninelli (1974) observes that following wine in order of importance was of a group of foods that were clustered by considering their use according to the customs of the local cuisine. There were substances that were used when preparing the basic dishes, such as fats, substances that completed and enriched the basic diet (for those who could afford it) such as milk and its derivatives, and eggs. Finally, there were substances that were rarely consumed, such as sugar and coffee.

As far as fats were concerned, lard was widespread among the less affluent classes. In Milan, oil was considered a luxury and therefore scarcely used. Butter appeared in the diet in a similar way to meat: "The law of agricultural production governs the flow of supply of these two foodstuffs: epizootics, a poor harvest, exceptionally high exports play an equally important part in consumption" (Zaninelli, 1974).

Milk was a common commodity, but difficult to measure, as it was sold directly by producers who came to the city from the countryside. With regards to cheese, Zaninelli finds a substantial difference between the cheese used by the wealthy classes and those of the less well-off classes: in particular, grana cheese and gorgonzola were the prerogative of the wealthiest members of society.

These considerations are important and help us to understand the great difference that existed in the mid-nineteenth century between the food consumed by the well-off and that of the less well-off, but also to comprehend how the economic and social dynamism of the period was producing significant changes in this regard.

MEALTIMES: BREAKFAST AND DINNER

We mentioned earlier that Don Marchelli consumed only one large meal daily. This particular aspect makes it possible to reflect on the changing habits regarding eating times in nineteenth-century Italy: following first the English, and then the French model, the main mealtime of the day shifted to later in the afternoon. This change in custom occurred in the highest social classes, and above all in the cities rather than rural areas.

Alessandro Barbero writes: "Between the end of the eighteenth and the beginning of the nineteenth century there was a tendency in high society to move dinner time to later in the day. It appears likely that this innovation began in England, where high society already preferred to eat later than on the continent."[14] Among the main consequences of delaying dinner, was the disappearance of lunch and the appearance of a hearty breakfast. In Italy, this habit began to spread from the first half of the nineteenth century and then became established in the second half. However, dinner was not consumed in the evening, as in Paris and London. Barbero observes how Alessandro Manzoni usually dined at 5:00 pm and how Stendhal, when living in Milan, could preserve his Parisian habits. Outside the large cities, people dined earlier; for example, in Pavia, Don Marchelli's city, at the home of Bassini, the president of the chamber of commerce, dinner was served at 3:00 pm.[15]

Don Marchelli's mealtimes followed this trend: he generally dined in the afternoon between 2:00 pm and 6:00 pm (see Table 10.1). These times shifted to the evening or early afternoon as required by the necessities of his travels, especially when he had to take a train or was arriving at a destination in the evening. Thus, in Vicenza, on August 29, 1870, he ate at 8:30 pm; in Verona, on September 1, 1870, at 9:00 pm; in Como, on September 30, 1870, at 8:00 pm. He consumed his meals much later in Milan in 1874: on August 11 at 10:30 pm and on August 12 at 9:30 pm. The only dinner eaten before 2:00 pm was the one served in Novara on September 18, 1867, because on that occasion the priest had to take the mail train to reach Varallo Sesia. The fact that dinner could always be consumed in the afternoon and in the evening enables us to understand how hotels were developing in post-unification Italy.[16]

The shift toward a later dinnertime in England and France led to the introduction of the *déjeuner à la fourchette*, a hearty breakfast. From Don Marchelli's travels this habit was also widespread in Italy in the second half of the nineteenth century. While traveling, the priest sometimes began the day with black coffee, drunk between 6:00 and 8:00 am, but he had breakfast later. The time for breakfast could vary considerably between 9:00 am and 12:00 pm, often due to the journeys the priest had scheduled. Generally, the priest drank chocolate, but he might also have other foods for breakfast, such as *barbagliata*,[17] coffee with milk, soda and sugared almonds, Cedro lemon water with cakes, seasoned bread or lemon-ice with pastries. As can be seen, these high-energy foods were all sweets. In two cases, he also ate fruit: in Verona in 1870 he had grapes, in Genoa in 1875 he had peaches, both times taken for consumption during a train journey. Only in one case did he have a "continental" breakfast following a long walk up to the Sacro Monte in Varese in 1871, when in the company of his brother, he ate cutlets, roast meat, cheese, and bread for breakfast.

THE CONVIVIAL PLEASURE OF CAFÉS

In addition to food, another element featuring in a tourist's "life quality" is the chance to enjoy leisure and recreational activities. For Don Marchelli this focused on his enjoyment of the cafés he frequented, going every day and sometimes several times a day. He almost always visited the café in the morning and at night, but sometimes also at other times of the day. He usually drank black coffee, often soda and hot chocolate. More rarely he drank beer, coffee and milk, coffee with rum,

Table 10.1. Don Luigi Marchelli's Dinners

Place	Date	Menu	Time	Cost in Italian Lire
Genoa, Trattoria del Commercio	4 September 1865	good soup and three good dishes	17	5.70
	5 September 1865	soup and two dishes including a large and very fine fish	18.30	6.12
	6 September 1865	soup and three dishes	15.30	5.55
	7 September 1865	bread, soup, beef, breaded cutlet and roast pigeon with salad	16	6.84
Novara, Albergo Italia	18 September 1867	abstaining from meat, this Wednesday being an Ember day (soup, two dishes, dessert and a liter of wine)	13.30	7.85
Varallo Sesia, Albergo Italia	19 September 1867	menu not specified	15.30	4.65
Novara, Albergo Italia	20 September 1867	soup, boiled meat, ribs, trout, bread, white wine	15.30	7.95
Milan, Albergo del Beltramolo	21 September 1867	abstaining from meat	16	7.50
Bergamo, Albergo del Cappello d'Oro	25 August 1868	a wretched pasta soup because overcooked, two dishes, namely mixed-fry, veal stew with potatoes and some fruit, with table wine	14.30	4.55
Brescia, Albergo del Cappello	26 August 1868	rice and cabbage soup, beef with potatoes and veal stew and fruit and cheese with table wine	14	6.35
Cremona, Albergo del Cappello	27 August 1868	rice and cabbage soup, two dishes, and fruit and two small bottles of wine	16	10.30
Genoa, Trattoria del Commercio	28 August 1868	fairly good rice and cabbage vegetable soup, fried fish, roast fish, cheese and fruit and a liter of wine	14	5.35
	30 August 1869	soup, deep-fried brain, veal stew, fruit, bread and a liter of wine	16.30	4
Savona, Albergo Svizzero	31 August 1869	soup. Fine pasta shaped like lentils. Deep-fried brain. Boiled fish with roasted potatoes. Veal stew. Pigeon with buttered salsify. Sweet dish. Dessert with cheese, fruit and sweets. A liter of wine and bread	16	9

(continued)

Table 10.1. *Continued*

Place	Date	Menu	Time	Cost in Italian Lire
Genoa, Trattoria del Commercio	1 September 1869	minestrone, deep-fried brain, boiled fish (seabream), and milk pudding fruit and 2. cups of coffee	15	6
Vicenza, Albergo dei Tre Garofani	29 August 1870	rice and celery soup, deep-fried brain, breaded cutlets, fruit and wine	20.30	2.52
Venezia, Albergo del Pellegrino	30 August 1870	rice, roast fish, grilled veal, fruit, ½ bottle of wine, bread	15	3.50
	31 August 1870	rice, beef, Veny-style liver, bread, ½ bottle of wine, fruit, grapes	17	3.50
Verona, All'Albergo della Posta	1 September 1870	*menu not specified*	21	5.25 (with accommodation too)
Como, Albergo Como	30 September 1870	*menu not specified*	20	7.30 (with accommodation too)
Varese, Albergo del Gambero	4 September 1871	cold salami, mixed-fry, minestrone, roast with salad, cheese, sweets and fruit and wine	16.30	4.70
Varese, Albergo del Gambero	5 September 1871	mixed-fry, minestrone, pigeon in tomato sauce, fruit pudding, cheese, fruit and wine	16	5.80
Milan, Osteria Beltramoli	4 September 1872	*menu not specified*	17.30	2.15
Firenze, Albergo Roma	5 September 1872	*menu not specified*	time not specified	4.20
Bologna, Albergo dell'Aquila Nera	6 September 1872	abstaining from meat, I had to content myself with foods that were rather unpleasant both as regards preparation and taste	15	2.50

Table 10.1. Continued

Place	Date	Menu	Time	Cost in Italian Lire
Milan, Albergo del Commercio (commonly called Beltramolli)	10 September 1873	*menu not specified*	16	2.45
Bellano, hotel not specified	11 September 1873	*menu not specified*	15.30	2.44
Milan, Albergo del Commercio (commonly called Beltramolli)	12 September 1873	abstaining from meat	19	2.92
Milan, Albergo del Biscione	10 August 1874	minestrone—sautéed mushrooms—meatballs in gelatin—sweet pudding—half a liter of good red wine and bread	18	2.95
	11 August 1874	mix of deep-fried brain and offal—soused carp—half a liter of wine and bread	22.30	2.15
	12 August 1874	Risotto 'in bonetto,' kid with potatoes (excellent), spiced stracchino cheese, half a liter of wine and bread	21.30	2.10
Genoa, Trattoria del Commercio	11 August 1875	fairly pleasant pasta and vegetable soup, very tasty boiled veal, stewed fish and juleped pears. The bread was however tasteless and the wine was not very good	14	2.25
	13 August 1875	Friday fast: minestrone, fried fish, fish stew and gorgonzola cheese	14	1.95
Mantova, Albergo della Croce Verde	4 September 1876	soup, two dishes including steamed beef, and bad cheese and fruit and half a liter of reasonable wine	20	3.40
	5 September 1876	soup, two dishes and fruit, and ½ liter of wine	14	3
Parma, Albergo Italia	6 September 1876	soup, meat with mushrooms and tomato, gorgonzola and ½ liter of table wine	15	2.50

Source: Archivio storico diocesano di Pavia, *Manoscritti* VIII, 2, L. Marchelli, Viaggi—*Appunti*. Processed by authors.

lemonade, barbagliata and sugared almonds. Drinking coffee was, therefore, a part of the priest's vacation. He almost always chose cafés in the city center as these were places where people went to socialize and exchange ideas;[18] however, when making an out-of-town excursion, he would also visit cafés in more isolated places (e.g., Pegli and Bellano).

The priest was also a man of habit: in Milan, a city he visited every year, he always went to the same café, the "cioccolattiere" Brunetti, in Contrada San Raffaele.[19] This café also frequently served him as a stop-off where the priest could deposit his bag, as we read in the notes on his 1871 trip: "we went to Brunetti's (who lost his wife a month ago) to leave our bag and umbrella and we had breakfast."[20] At Brunetti's he almost always drank black coffee, rarely soda, and once, in 1874, a beer. In 1876, he had breakfast with "lemon-ice and 4. sweet pastries."

On his trips to Genoa, too, he stuck to his habits: in 1865 he went to the Caffè della Concordia, defined as "magnificent,"[21] to the Caffè della Borsa and the Caffè Nazionale on Piazza Nuova.[22] In Pegli, after visiting the park of Villa Pallavicino, he went with his relatives "to the Caffè di Pegli and took some refreshments, cheered by the somersaults and chatter of Pegli's sturdy young boys, to whom we threw some coins." In 1869, again in Genoa, he returned to the Caffè della Borsa; on the same trip, in Savona, he went to the Caffè Svizzero.[23]

Sometimes he drank or bought something at the station cafés: three coffees in 1866 in Alessandria; in 1872 he bought sugared almonds at the Venice station and drank a lemonade in that of Bergamo; in 1874 "half a pound of peaches" at Arona station; in 1875 a chocolate and soda at the station café in Pisa and another soda at the station in Tortona that left him with a very bad impression: "I entered the Restaurant della Stazione and had a soda in the garden, but I was not satisfied because they made me wait a long time; there was a group of rowdy people at the table, and as I was leaving after paying, I had the impression that the owner made some disparaging comment about me."

Thus, Don Marchelli visited cafés at various times of the day, after breakfast. During the afternoon excursions when visiting towns, he stopped in the cafés and had either black coffee (once coffee with rum) or more often soda. He often returned to the cafés in the evening, before returning to the hotel, for a coffee, soda, or beer.

FOOD EXPENSES WHEN TRAVELING

Don Marchelli's journals are an interesting historical-economic source. As already mentioned, at the end of the description of each trip, they contain a detailed account of the costs incurred, directly indicating the expenses of a vacation in the main cities of Northern Italy in the 1860s and 1870s. The historiographical questions to which the journals provide an answer are above all linked to the cost of travel (and food expenses) in proportion to the wages and the cost of living in that period.[24]

From the analysis of the publications of the second half of the nineteenth century and from the studies of contemporary historiography, it emerges that farmworkers (at the time the vast majority of the workforce employed) earned between 0.80 and 1.50 lire a day.[25] In the agricultural sector, only farm owners and tenants could afford to take a vacation, but there is no direct information on the revenues, income, and tourism habits of these categories. In a society in which most of the workers were employed in agriculture, tourism was an elitist practice and destined for the privileged few. However, farmworkers were paid partly with a wage and partly in foodstuffs and accommodation.

The analysis, therefore, excludes the well-off who had income from land and real estate, including entrepreneurs, be they industrialists or traders.

For other employment areas, Giovanni Vigo's study on education and economic development in Italy in the nineteenth century provides information on the salaries of teachers,[26] which ranged from 1 lira to 2 lire per day. Equally important is the information relating to construction workers that can be obtained from the studies of Giuseppe Aleati, relating to sources in the Lombardy area, and Giuseppe Felloni, related to the area of Genoa.[27] In this case, we are talking about wages ranging from 0.80 to 3 lire a day depending on the job and the place.

There is also much data on the salaries of civil servants,[28] though here the situation is more complex because the category includes a broad range of job positions, ranging from ushers to the highest public officials within a pyramidal hierarchy that was obviously reflected in earnings. As can be seen from the paper written by Giuseppe Felloni concerning the Kingdom of Sardinia, salaries ranged considerably and had a pyramidal structure; in 1859, for example, most of the salaries (65.20 percent) ranged between 200 and 1,600 lire a year, but at the top of this pyramid some individuals would earn a salary above 20,000 lire a year.[29] Similar assessments can be found in Ugo Tucci's essay on salaries in the Kingdom of Lombardy–Venetia.[30] This brief overview underlines the fact that only those at the top of the pyramid had enough economic resources available to undertake a trip for purposes of tourism.

The information collected by Pietro Rota relates to the years 1847, 1859, 1866, and 1874, and thus overlaps with the last two years of Don Marchelli's travels: quarry workers (marble, building stone, soapstone) in 1866 could earn a daily wage ranging from a maximum of 2.50 lire to a minimum of 1.15 lire. In 1874, the highest wages had increased to 5 lire, the lowest had remained at 1.15 lire.[31]

In the textile industry (workers employed in the spinning of linen and hemp, the spinning and weaving of cotton and wool, and the reeling and twisting of silk) wages varied according to the area of Lombardy and the specific duties of the worker. However, the daily wages in 1866 ranged from a maximum of 3 lire to a minimum of 0.90, while in 1874 the top wages were 3.20 lire and the lowest 1 lira. Here, too, in an industry dominated by the presence of women workers, female wages were much lower: in 1866 their highest recorded wages were 1.20 lire and the lowest 0.40, remaining unvaried in 1874.[32]

Luciano Maffi

Pietro Rota gathered information on numerous other fields of production, each including various professional categories: dyeing and printing of fabrics, leather tanning, manufacture of bricks, cutting and processing of stone, foundries, blast furnaces, forges, mechanical plants, woodworking, typography, bookbinding, manufacture of gas appliances, weapons, carriages, glass, wax, combs, paper, hats, beer, room painters, shoemakers, tailors, seamstresses, embroiderers, hairdressers, pastry chefs, workers in confectioneries, cafés, bakeries, and butchers. From the analysis of the data concerning all these labor categories, it emerges that in 1874 the highest monthly wages were those of tailors (producing men's coats and suits) that might earn up to 12 lire a day, second (but far behind) were glass workers with 6 lire, then wood carvers with 5.50 lire, workers manufacturing carriages with 5.50 lire, workers manufacturing cylinders in iron-working forges with 5 lire, and printers with 5 lire. Among the lowest wages (excluding women, children, errand boys, and apprentices) were those of porters in the leather-tanning factories with 1.20 lire, bricklayers with 1.20 lire, workers in cast-iron foundries with 1.20 lire, workers in blast furnaces with 1.20 lire, carpenters with 1.50 lire, paper-manufacturing workers with 1.30 lire, and finally bookbinders with 1 lira.[33]

In the early decades of post-unification, traveling for tourism was, therefore, an activity reserved for a small group of people. In just a few days (from three to five per year) Don Marchelli spent the equivalent of two to four months' salary for most of the labor categories. A trip for recreational and cultural purposes was, therefore, the prerogative of wealthy people who had income from capital, property, and businesses: a small minority of society at that time.[34]

An important part of the trip expenses was spent on accommodation and food. As a comparison with current parameters it is interesting to note that meals were proportionately more expensive than accommodation: remember that Don Marchelli only had one dinner a day and it was abundant. In proportion to the salaries of all the categories shown, the refreshments that the priest had at various times during the day at the cafés were also expensive. The cost of a cup of black coffee varied according to the place and the year, from a minimum of 16 cents in Bergamo in 1868 to 20 cents in Milan in 1874. The chocolate, that he often had for breakfast, ranged from 23.50 cents to Genoa in 1865 to a maximum of 28.50 in Milan in 1868. Barbagliata cost 35 cents. The cost of a soda ranged from 20 cents in Bergamo in 1868 to 30 cents in Pisa in 1875. The chocolate bars that the priest bought for trips by steamer cost 40 cents; the lemonade 30 and beer 20 cents. Pastries were very expensive and unaffordable for many; for example, in 1874 Don Marchelli bought two hundred grams of small sugared almonds and a small panettone for 2.35 lire in a Milan pastry shop on Corso Vittorio Emanuele.

The cost of dinner also varied depending on the place and the amount of food eaten, ranging from a minimum of 1.95 lire in Genoa in 1875 to a maximum of 4.50 lire in Savona in 1869. In any case, the high cost compared to the salaries of most people in active employment in post-unification Italy is evident.

Table 10.2. Places where Don Luigi Marchelli has breakfast or consumes beverages during his travels

Place	Date	Café	Refreshment	Time	Cost in Italian Lira
Genoa	4 September 1865	Caffè della Concordia	breakfast: one chocolate and two cups of cold coffee and milk	11.30	2
	5 September 1865	Caffè della Borsa	3 cups of black coffee	evening	0.50
		Caffè Nazionale	three black coffees	6.30/7	0.50
		Caffè della Borsa	breakfast: three cups of chocolate	10.30	0.70
Pegli	5 September 1865	Caffè of Pegli	two sodas	17	1
Genoa	5 September 1865	Caffè della Borsa	three black coffees	evening	0.50
	6 September 1865	Caffè della Borsa	three black coffees	6.30/7	0.50
		Caffè della Borsa	breakfast (three cups of chocolate). Two bottles of soda	10.30	1.20
		Caffè della Borsa	Three sodas	evening	0.60
	7 September 1865	Caffè della Borsa	breakfast (three cups of chocolate). Three bottles of soda	10.30/11	1.40
		greengrocer	fruit, grapes and peaches.	afternoon	0.60
		Caffè della Borsa	three black coffees	afternoon	0.50
Milan	21 August 1866	café not specified	breakfast: two cups of chocolate and one of barbagliata	11	0.88
		Caffè della Stazione	two bottles of water	12.30	0.40
Torino	22 August 1866	café not specified	breakfast three cups of chocolate	11.30	0.75
Torino	23 August 1866	Caffè della Giammaica	breakfast	11	0.75
			not specified		
Torino	24 August 1866	café not specified	breakfast	11	0.75
			not specified		
Alessandria	24 August 1866	Caffè della Stazione	three black coffees	20.30	0.45
Milan	18 September 1867	Cioccolattiere Brunetti	breakfast	9.30	0.80
			3. cups chocolate		
Novara	18 September 1867	Albergo Italia	three black coffees	14	0.75
Varallo Sesia	19 September 1867	Albergo Italia	breakfast not described	11	3.30
Arona	20 September 1867	Caffè della Stazione	breakfast not described	8.30	1.40

Table 10.2. *Continued*

Place	Date	Café	Refreshment	Time	Cost in Italian Lira
Novara	20 September 1867	*café not specified*	three black coffees	afternoon towards evening	0.75
Milan	21 September 1867	Cioccolattiere Brunetti	breakfast (3 cups of chocolate)	9	0.75
Milan		Cioccolattiere Brunetti	three black coffees with rum	afternoon	0.45
Milan	25 August 1868	Cioccolattiere Brunetti	breakfast (3 cups of chocolate)	10	0.85
Bergamo	25 August 1868	Caffè in Piazza Baroni	two sodas	afternoon towards evening	0.40
Bergamo	26 August 1868	*café not specified*	breakfast (3 cups of chocolate)	9	1.25
Bergamo		Café near Albergo del Cappello d'Oro	two sodas	afternoon towards evening	0.40
Bergamo	27 August 1868	Café near Albergo del Cappello d'Oro	three black coffees	6.30	0.48
Brescia	27 August 1868	Café near Albergo del Cappello	breakfast (3 cups of chocolate)	9.30	1
		Café near Albergo del Cappello	two sodas	afternoon towards evening	0.40
Cremona	28 August 1868	Caffè in Piazza Duomo	breakfast (3 cups of chocolate)	10	0.75
		Caffè in Piazza Duomo	3 sodas	evening	0.60
Genoa	30 August 1869	Caffè della Borsa	2 black coffees	evening	0.32
Genoa	31 August 1869	Caffè della Borsa	breakfast (2 cups of chocolate)	8.30	0.43
Savona	31 August 1869	Caffè Svizzero	1 bottle of soda and 2 black coffees	afternoon towards evening	0.80
Genoa	1 September 1869	Caffè della Borsa	breakfast: 2 *barbagliate*	9.30	0.48
Genoa	1 September 1869	Albergo del Commercio	2 black coffees	17	—
Milan	29 August 1870	Cioccolattiere Brunetti	breakfast: cup of chocolate	10	0.35
Padova	1 September 1870	Hotel near the Saint's Sanctuary	meal	12	2.60
Padova	1 September 1870	Caffè della Stazione	sweets	14.30	0.15
Verona	2 September 1870	Station	grapes	10.15	0.15
Milan	2 September 1870	Cioccolattiere Brunetti	black coffee	17.30	0.15
Milan	30 September 1870	Cioccolattiere Brunetti	breakfast	9	0.50

Table 10.2. Continued

Place	Date	Café	Refreshment	Time	Cost in Italian Lira
Como	30 September 1870	Caffé on lakeside	2 black coffees	evening	0.40
Milan	4 September 1871	Cioccolattiere Brunetti	breakfast (2 cups of chocolate)	9.30	0.50
	5 September 1871	Cioccolattiere Brunetti	bottle of soda	13	0.30
Varese, Sacro Monte	5 September 1871	Albergo del Sacro Monte	breakfast (cutlets, roast, cheese and 2 bottles of white wine with bread)	10	3.90
Varese, Roberello	5 September 1871	Café called Sacro Monte	bitter beer and lemon soda	12	0.70
Milan	6 September 1871	Cioccolattiere Brunetti	breakfast (2 cups of chocolate)	9.45	0.50
	6 September 1871	Cioccolattiere Brunetti	two sodas	17	0.40
Milan	4 September 1872	Cioccolattiere Brunetti	breakfast: *barbagliata*	10.30	0.35
Milan	4 September 1872	Cioccolattiere Brunetti	sodas	afternoon	0.40
Firenze	5 September 1872	Caffé near piazza Duomo	soda	evening	0.25
Bologna	6 September 1872	Café in the main street	soda	evening	0.25
Venezia	6 September 1872	Caffé in Piazza San Marco	breakfast: lemon squash with 5. sugared almonds	9	0.50
Venezia	6 September 1872	Caffé in Piazza San Marco	sugared almonds	10	0.50
Bergamo	6 September 1872	Caffé della Stazione	lemon squash	15	0.30
Milan	10 September 1873	Cioccolattiere Brunetti	breakfast: cup of chocolate	10.30	0.30
Milan	10 September 1873	Cioccolattiere Brunetti	soda	afternoon	0.20
Milan	10 September 1873	Cioccolattiere Brunetti	black coffee	21.30	0.20
Milan	11 September 1873	Cioccolattiere Brunetti	black coffee	22	0.20
Milan	12 September 1873	*café not specified*	breakfast: flavored bread	Early morning	0.16
Lodi	12 September 1873	*café not specified*	soda	Morning	0.25
Vigevano	12 September 1873	*café not specified*	soda	afternoon	0.25
Milan	12 September 1873	Cioccolattiere Brunetti	black coffee	21.30	0.20
Milan	13 September 1873	Cioccolattiere Brunetti	black coffee	8	0.20
Milan	10 August 1874	Cioccolattiere Brunetti	breakfast: cup of chocolate	8.30	0.30
Milan	10 August 1874	Cioccolattiere Brunetti	beer	21.30	0.20
Lago Maggiore	11 August 1874	S. Bernardino steamship	bar of chocolate	12	0.40
Arona	11 August 1874	Station	peaches (half pound)	19,30	0.30
Milan	12 August 1874	Cioccolattiere Brunetti	bar of chocolate for the journey	Early morning	0.40
Carate	12 August 1874	*café not specified*	soda	12	0.25

(continued)

Table 10.2. *Continued*

Place	Date	Café	Refreshment	Time	Cost in Italian Lira
Lecco	12 August 1874	Café near the Station	soda	16.30	0.20
Milan	12 August 1874	Cioccolattiere Brunetti	black coffee	22.30	0.20
Milan	13 August 1874	Pasticceria in Corso Vittorio Emanuele	200 grams of small sugared almonds and a small panettone, partly to take home	7	2.35
Milan	10 August 1875	Cioccolattiere Brunetti	lemon soda	afternoon	0.20
Pavia	11 August 1875	At home	black coffee	6	—
Genoa	11 August 1875	café not specified	soda	evening	0.30
Pisa	12 August 1875	Caffè della Stazione	breakfast: chocolate	morning	0.22
Pisa	12 August 1875	Caffè della Stazione	soda	15.30	0.30
Genoa	13 August 1875	Salita San Francesco da Paola	breakfast: 1 kg of peaches	8	0.25
Genoa	13 August 1875	café not specified	soda	evening	0.25
Genoa	14 August 1875	Unspecified pastry shop	Sweets and bread	morning	1.75
Tortona	14 August 1875	Restaurant della Stazione	soda	19.15	0.25
Milan	4 September 1876	Cioccolattiere Brunetti	breakfast: lemon-ice with 4 pastries	13	0.50
Mantova	5 September 1876	Café under the porticoes in Piazza del Mercato	breakfast: lemon-ice with 4 pastries	11.30	0.45
Modena	6 September 1876	Albergo di S. Marco	breakfast: a cutlet with one bottle of white wine	9	1.35
Piacenza	7 September 1876	Caffè in Piazza della Cattedrale	breakfast: Cedro lemon water with pastries	9.45	0.30
Milan	7 September 1876	Pastry shop in the Umberto subway	pastries	18	1.45

Source: Archivio storico diocesano of Pavia, *Manoscritti* VIII, 2, L. Marchelli, *Viaggi—Appunti.* Processed by authors.

A TASTE FOR ART

Don Marchelli's journals provide a continual testimony for his appreciation and interest in art. A fundamental aid for the cultural tourist is the guidebook for the places visited. The pioneering of modern tourist communication, facilitated by guidebooks, commenced in the nineteenth century. This travel aid was an essential aspect of the sector's development. There had been travel literature in previous centuries, but it did not aim to indicate, orientate, and inform as guidebooks later did. The style of the latter was dry and succinct, very different from the travel literature that narrated journeys while conveying the idea of travel as a learning experience.

Among the first and most famous international guidebooks appearing in that period and dealing with Northern Italy, were Murray's: *Handbook for Travellers in Northern Italy: Embracing the Continental States of Sardinia, Lombardy and Venice, Parma and Piacenza, Modena, Lucca, and Tuscany as Far as the Val d'Arno*,[35] and Baedeker's *Northern Italy, as far as Leghorn, Florence and Ancona, and the island of Corsica*.[36] These guidebooks contained descriptions of tourist locations and monuments; moreover, they provided practical information for the traveler: art, architecture, nature, traditions, food, means of transport, and accommodation possibilities, all with relative costs.

Don Marchelli used this kind of material on his travels; in fact, the priest procured the guidebooks of the places he was visiting, as witnessed in his journals. Some details are noted in his journal relating to Turin in 1866. On the first day of vacation, in Milan, the priest writes: "purchased the Sonzogno Guide to Turin for L. 3."[37] In relation to his trip to Novara in 1867, we read: "from a bookseller located in Piazza del Duomo [. . .] we bought the Guide to the Sanctuary of Varallo." In Milan, in 1868, just before leaving for Bergamo: "we also went to Sonzogno to look for a guidebook containing the topographic map of Bergamo, but not having found it, we started walking although it was raining to the Railway Station." In 1870, the priest wished to make "the Circular journey of Milan-Turin-Genoa-Alessandria-Piacenza-Milan"; once in Milan, and having failed to find a convenient timetable for this type of trip, he changed his mind and decided to "take a trip to Venice, considering that being alone, the expense would not have been too much greater." The next action was, therefore, to buy from "Sonzogno a Guide to Venice."

Despite having the printed guidebook in hand, during his travels, Don Marchelli often chose to be accompanied by a local guide who would show him the city. The guides proffered their services to tourists at the station or on the streets and often proposed itineraries to local sights. The priest's opinions on such guided tours were generally favorable, although there are a few cases where his judgment is clearly negative.

The priest's reports on expenditure indicate that these guides earned a reasonable daily income. In 1865, the priest, together with his family, visited the Villa Pallavicini of Pegli with a guide; in fact, he wrote: "led by a good guide we started the tour that lasted about two hours," this person was paid 3.50 lire. In Turin, in 1866, a guide accompanied them to visit several of the city's monuments: "After reaching Piazza Castello we met a guide who offered to accompany us to visit the king's palace, the royal armory and other precious monuments in Turin." This guide spent most of the day with them, presenting several monuments and museums; he received 6 lire. As for the excursion to the Sacro Monte in Varallo Sesia in 1867, Don Marchelli wrote: "A guide to climb the mountain was sought and we started walking a little after 7 am"; this guide was given 4 lire. The following day, in Arona, they took "as a guide a poor man of the place," first to visit the parish church and then to climb the mountain to see the statue of San Carlo; they paid him 2 lire.

In Brescia, in 1868, they were very happy with the guide who accompanied them around the city in the morning, partly because he asked for, what they considered, a very honest fee: they also requested his services for the afternoon. In 1872, in Florence, the priest found a guide to visit Palazzo Vecchio, the Uffizi, and Palazzo Pitti; the guide, with whom he remained for a few hours, was paid 7.50 lire.

In 1873, Don Marchelli stopped at Bellano during his trip to Lake Como. Here, after visiting the church, he was accompanied by a guide to visit the gorge: "Later we employed a guide and went to see the famous Orrido di Bellano formed by the river Pioverna and which you reach by passing through an enclosed space then ascending a steep ladder, made of wood." In this case, the priest merely tipped their guide.

Don Marchelli often rose very early and visited the cities in the early morning. The most unusual aspect for us is that many of the monuments were open at five or six o'clock, especially the churches. Moreover, he found guides on the streets available to accompany him at that early hour. This was the case in Pisa in 1875: "At 5½ I finally arrived in Pisa, where at the exit of the station, I immediately met a person who offered his services as a guide, an offer that I willingly accepted."

This chapter analyzes in great detail all the expenses recorded in Don Marchelli's journals pertaining to food and accommodation during his numerous trips that took place in just over a decade, between 1865 and 1876.

Comparing these expenses with the wages and overall economic situation of Italian society after unification, well indicated by the available literature (we mention, among others, the studies of Aleati, Felloni, Vigo, and Zaninelli), it was possible to understand which sections of the population could afford to travel for pleasure and to enjoy the artistic, historical, and sometimes natural features offered by the Italian tourist sites, as well as to enjoy a certain comfort while staying in the country's principal cities.

It is thus clear that tourism in that period was an elitist option, although it is possible already to identify hints of what would become one of Italy's main resources: from solutions that could only be afforded by a very restricted part of society, to others that were also within reach of the middle or, at least, the upper middle classes, within which the priest considered here, and the relatives who sometimes traveled with him, can be placed.

At the same time, we also wanted to add to the predominantly socioeconomic nature of this study, a perspective that might suggest considerations on the sociocultural aspects that emerge to some extent from Don Marchelli's journals. We attempt to reveal this aspect by analyzing the meals taken by the traveler and, consequently, the offer available to the proto-tourists (to borrow the terminology of Giuseppe

Rocca) who could afford to partake of it. The publication and dissemination of printed guidebooks fall wholly within the area of business arising from pleasure trips: the famous Italian publication, *Sonzogno*, that the priest from Pavia sometimes bought, was part of a range of guidebooks available throughout Europe in a sector dominated by the Baedeker and the Murray guidebooks.

BIBLIOGRAPHY

Aleati, Giuseppe, ed., "Le retribuzioni dei lavoratori edili in Milano, Pavia e nei rispettivi territori dal 1819 al 1890," *Archivio economico dell'unificazione italiana* 11, no. 1 (1961).

Arcari, Maria Paola, "La variazione dei salari agricoli in Italia dalla fondazione del Regno al 1933," *Annali di Statistica* 36, (1936).

Arnaboldi, Gazzaniga Bernardo, *Monografia del circondario di Pavia. Premiata al concorso indetto dalla Giunta per la inchiesta agraria sedente in Roma* (Pavia: G. Marelli, 1880).

Baedeker, Karl, *Northern Italy, as far as Leghorn, Florence and Ancona, and the island of Corsica* (Koblenz: Baedeker; London: Williams & Norgate; Paris: Haar & Steinert, 1868).

Banti, Alberto Mario, *Storia della borghesia italiana. L'età liberale (1861–1922)* (Roma: Donzelli, 1996).

Barbero, Alessandro, *A che ora si mangia? Approssimazioni storico-linguistiche all'orario dei pasti (secoli XVIII-XXI)* (Macerata: Quodlibet, 2017).

Bardelli, Daniele, "Fra storia e geografia: il pellegrinaggio turistico alle origini della nazione. Il caso del Touring Club Italiano," in *L'identità nazionale. Miti e paradigmi storiografici ottocenteschi (atti del seminario Cavallino-Lecce, 30–31 ottobre 2003)*, eds. Quondam Amedeo and Rizzo Gino (Roma: Bulzoni, 2005), 167–97.

———, *L'Italia viaggia. Il Touring club, la nazione e la modernità (1894-1927)* (Roma: Bulzoni, 2004).

Battilani, Patrizia, and Strangio, Donatella, eds., *Il turismo e le città tra XVIII e XXI secolo. Italia e Spagna a confronto* (Milano: FrancoAngeli, 2007).

Battilani, Patrizia, *Vacanze di pochi vacanze di tutti. L'evoluzione del turismo europeo* (Bologna: il Mulino, 2001).

Bechelloni, Giovanni, ed., *Identità italiana e modernizzazione. Percorsi controversi (1861–1990)* (Roma: Il Campo, 1991).

Betri, Maria Luisa, "L'alimentazione popolare nell'Italia dell'Ottocento," in *Storia d'Italia. Annali 13. L'alimentazione*, eds. Alberto Capatti, Alberto De Bernardi, and Angelo Varni (Torino: Einaudi, 1998), 7–22.

Bodio, Luigi, "Sulla statistica dei salari. Risultati sommari di una indagine iniziata sulla alimentazione delle classi operaie," *Annali di Statistica* 7, (1883).

Boyer, Marc, *Il turismo, dal Grand Tour ai viaggi organizzati* (Torino: Electa-Gallimard, 1997).

Bussedi, Giovanni Maria, *Diario 1864–1869*, ed. Volpi Mirko (Milano: Cisalpino, 2013).

Calcagno, Giorgio, ed., *L'identità degli italiani* (Roma-Bari: Laterza, 1998).

Cardona, Maria Clelia, *La storia della villeggiatura: dall'epoca romana al Novecento* (Roma: Edizioni Abete, 1994).

Colli, Andrea, and Amatori, Franco, eds., *Impresa e Industria in Italia. Dall'Unità ad oggi* (Venezia: Marsilio, 1999).

De Maddalena, Aldo, ed., "I prezzi dei generi commestibili e dei prodotti agricoli sul mercato di Milano dal 1800 al 1890," *Archivio economico dell'unificazione italiana* 5, no. 3 (1957).

————, *Prezzi e mercedi a Milano dal 1701 al 1860* (Milano: Banca Commerciale Italiana, 1974).

Di Vincenzo, Riccardo, *Milano al caffè. Tra Settecento e Novecento* (Milano: Hoepli, 2011).

Felloni, Giuseppe, ed., "Le retribuzioni dei lavoratori edili a Genova dal 1815 al 1890," in *Archivio economico dell'unificazione italiana* 12, no. 3 (1963).

Felloni, Giuseppe, ed., "Stipendi e pensioni dei pubblici impiegati negli stati sabaudi dal 1825 al 1859," *Archivio economico dell'unificazione italiana* 10, no. 2 (1960).

Geronimo, Giuliana, "Storia e storie dell'imprenditoria alberghiera milanese," in *Storia del turismo. Le imprese*, ed. Patrizia Battilani (Milano: FrancoAngeli, 2011), 71–97.

Guderzo, Giulio, "1859: Pavia, Italia, Europa," *Bollettino della Società Pavese di Storia Patria* 110 (2010): 201–21.

Guderzo, Giulio, *Amore di Pavia* (Milano: Edizioni Unicopli, 2011).

Leonardi, Andrea, "Dal 'Grand Hotel' alle stazioni di sport invernali: le trasformazioni del turismo alpino italiano," in *La evolución de la industria turística en España e Italia*, eds. Barciela López Carlos, Manera Erbina Carlos Pablo, Molina de Dios Ramón, and Di Vittorio Antonio (Palma de Mallorca: Institut Balear d'Economia, 2011), 609–69.

Leonardi, Andrea, "Turismo e sviluppo in area alpina. Una lettura storico-economica delle trasformazioni intervenute tra Ottocento e Novecento," *Annale di Storia del Turismo* 6 (2007): 53–82.

Maffi, Luciano, *Turismo dell'Ottocento. I viaggi in Italia di un prete pavese* (Milano: Cisalpino, 2015).

Mosca, Monica, *Il turismo degli affari a Milano negli anni della prima industrializzazione (1871–1914)*, in *Temi di storia economica del turismo lombardo (XIX–XX secolo)*, ed. Carera Aldo (Milano: Vita e Pensiero, 2002), 109–36.

Nuovissima guida illustrata della città di Torino e de' suoi dintorni (Milano: Sonzogno, 1859).

Paloscia, Franco, *Storia del turismo nell'economia italiana* (Roma: Petruzzi, 1994).

Repossi, Cesare, "La cultura letteraria a Pavia dalla Restaurazione alla metà del Novecento," in *Storia di Pavia*, ed. Emilio Gabba (Pavia: Banca del Monte di Lombardia, 2000), 489–537.

Rocca, Giuseppe, *Dal prototurismo al turismo globale. Momenti, percorsi di ricerca, casi di studio* (Torino: Giappichelli, 2013).

Romani, Mario, *Storia economica d'Italia nel secolo XIX* (Bologna: il Mulino, 1982).

Rota, Pietro, "Salari degli operai addetti ad alcune delle principali industrie della Lombardia negli anni 1847, 1859, 1866, 1874," *Annali di Statistica* 14, (1885).

Saglio, Pietro, *Condizioni agricole della provincia di Pavia e mezzi per migliorarle: monografia* (Voghera: Tipografia sociale, 1879).

————, *Monografia agraria del circondario di Voghera* (Stradella: G. Perea, 1881).

Stefano, Somogyi, "L'alimentazione nell'Italia unita," in *Storia d'Italia*, eds. Ruggiero Romano and Corrado Vivanti, (Turin: Einaudi, 1972–1976), 5: 839–87.

Tesoro, Marina, "Politica e amministrazione nell'Età liberale," in Gabba, *Storia di Pavia*, 85–121.

Teti, Vito, *Il colore del cibo. Geografia, mito e realtà dell'alimentazione mediterranea* (Roma: Meltemi, 2007).

Tucci, Ugo, ed., "Stipendi e pensioni dei pubblici impiegati nel Regno Lombardo-Veneto dal 1824 al 1866," *Archivio economico dell'unificazione italiana* 10, no. 4 (1960).

Vigo, Giovanni, *Istruzione e sviluppo economico in Italia nel secolo XIX* (Torino: ILTE, 1971).

Zamagni, Vera, "L'evoluzione dei consumi fra tradizione e innovazione," in *L'alimentazione*, eds. Capatti Alberto, De Bernardi Alberto, and Varni Angelo (Torino: Einaudi, 1998), 151–205.

Zaninelli, Sergio, *I consumi a Milano nell'Ottocento* (Roma: Edindustria, 1974).

Zanini, Andrea, *Un secolo di turismo in Liguria. Dinamiche, percorsi, attori* (Milano: FrancoAngeli, 2012).

11

From Anthropology to History

Jean-Pierre Williot

This book offers many points of view that, on the face of it, direct us as much toward the observation of nomadisms as toward that of food practices. Crossing the two could mean researching the ways of eating of nomadic peoples, the nutritional adaptations created by traveling even though a person is not actually a nomad, and the design of food products intended for multiple economic circulations. This book is not concerned with sedentary eating habits. When we started our purpose, nomadic food was the only goal.

Firstly, it explores the vast territory, or more exactly, territories of nomadism within the complexity of their boundaries. Indeed, with all its routes, movements, and paths, what other concept can display so much geographical fluidity, so many unlikely interconnections, and so many blurred frontiers?

The various chapters report on a rather unusual portrait gallery of nomads as well as travelers who borrow forms of mobility from nomads. Senegalese, Italians, Mongols, Bedouins, astronauts, Corsican hikers, Siberian herdsmen, and an Australian consumer all find themselves brought together in one homogeneous study. How do their peregrinations, their unusual situations, or their journeys oblige them to eat and drink differently from within the limited perimeter of a fixed place of eating? Some make return trips between Africa and Europe, and another winds his way across the Italian peninsula searching for new recipes in a spirit of discovery. Some travel vast distances in hostile environments that require environmental adaptation strategies, while others find the expression of freedom and shared identity in a consumption that can no longer be globalized. One person describes herself in her individuality, which is plural rather than singular and straddles many continents. The interplay of globalized trade balances is also touched on to show how Italian products have become just as much the economic as cultural symbols of an "Italianness" that is scattered all over the planet. Still others substitute the conquest of paths and tracks during leisure time walking activities for the walking that indigenous people are forced to do. For some it is the mixing of so-called traditional uses with the lures of supposed modernity that guide their food choices in an area that covers several time zones. And it is not just to the far reaches of the planet where care and forethought are essential as far as food is concerned. Astronauts take their food along with them like Polish noblemen and women used to take along vinegar powder among their travel provisions. Anybody who travels in space must plan a specific supply of food, but it could also be said that the person who travels must know how to get fresh supplies. All these witnesses have one thing in common, across time and space, in that they move around and their food changes with them. But they are not nomads whose journeys are made necessary in order to meet their food needs. They are rather semi-nomads or irregular sedentaries. Their movement is a creator of culinary opportunities or needs for eating, and the appropriation and change that they are making of these is shifting the "nomadic" attribute to the side of food and drink rather than it being the description of their human condition.

The heart of the book is in this food circulation approach. A group of such varied texts that feature cases whose circumstances, contexts, and positions can appear to be extremely heterogeneous from one point of the globe to another, could have come from a publication of miscellany in an ethnographic and anthropological journal.

Our approach is different. The book is primarily the product of a voluntary coming-together of anthropologists and historians in order to examine a common theme. It aims to suggest that the journey in its numerous forms supports diverse mobilities and is an essential vector for commensality and the interpenetration of tastes thereby contributing to the spreading of a "food nomadism" whose interpretations are many and varied. They can be social through the encounter of other lifestyles, they are most certainly economic on account of the products and markets which find new dynamics, and they also seek out technical developments in order to meet diverse demands. Above all, however, a depth of time can be discerned in the transmission of the nomads' practices to the contemporary construction of new nomadisms.

It seems obvious today to accept that transnational mobility is an essential means for cultures to meet and mix, and it covers various aspects. Tourist mobility is continually increasing due to the scope and range of air, road, sea, and railway networks. Migratory mobility's issues are based on geopolitical instability or the search for work that impel people to cross borders whatever the cost. The geographical scales are many, and thus produce very varied experiences. The traveler who in Europe is content with crossing the immediate national border remains in a world that is quite familiar to them. However, this does not rule out discovery, whether chance or intentionally created to develop markets. A person who endures jet lag to get to another continent becomes immersed in a world that can be, perhaps literally, poles apart from their normal habits and routines. So there seems to be a profusion of new things, and the circulations that arise from these journeys have often decisive effects on food registers. The tourist who experiences less well-known products during their journey associates the new flavors with their trip. The migrant who changes countries can import their culinary knowledge, adopt the ways of eating of the place that is home to their new sedentary lifestyle, or mix one with another in food recomposition. Everybody's identities change as a result of these many appropriations that are triggered by spatial mobilities. From the embracing and incorporation of new things to the passing on of ways of life, a shift is taking place between the innovation mechanism and the assertion of a heritage. Often-exclusive regionalist or nationalist approaches that assert that food heritagization is the mainstay of very solid, old, and protected national cultures, omit this historical interchange-encouraging substratum. Spatial mobilities play a central role here, and this can be evoked to suggest shared heritages. Food nomadism illustrates the mechanism of innovation.

The texts in this book have, in the end, directed the initial aim in several directions as a result of the freedom of writing enjoyed by its contributors. They show how food cultures linked to nomadic practices in globalization mix and mingle. One could, for example, by taking the chapter on Siberia and that on Senegalese migrants, find some resemblance between the two extremes. On the one hand, a northern area displays nomadic food habits that are inherent to a specific lifestyle, but which are now intermixed with other food demands that are so strong that they are changing the nutritional structure of the indigenous people. The nomads of Siberia were already food nomads, being the perfect embodiment of food nomadism as they were detached from the dietary principles of societies exterior to them. However, their nomadism has been changed by its encounter with another movement, that of the meeting of cultures in which the attraction of the new and its related practices has been a vector of change. Adaptation to the environment has continued with the assimilation of these new features and forms of food or products have thus been abandoned. Fundamental needs that beforehand had been satisfied by local resources now have to be satisfied by other means. The change of lifestyle and the exchange of a nomadic way of eating for the adoption of food forms that have come from the outside world has upset previous balances. Products of sedentarization are catching up with and changing nomadic practices, and as part of this, food portability has become a market issue that the Siberian nomads, with their use of different resources, used to be expert in. Similarly, the packaging of food products to be used over a long period on their journeys is a permanent feature. The design of food adapted to the constraints of space flight is only an application, with innovative technologies, of earlier methods of food conservation. However, those dishes that are designed for astronauts incorporate other specifications concerning ingestion, nutritional intake, and satisfaction; all features that were more intuitive and less scientific in former times.

Far away from Siberia another region shows the situation of Senegalese migrants, who are also making use of a succession of adaptations. They have learnt the effects of a food nomadism created by the many cultures that make contact with each other in the areas that have become familiar to them. In their food heritages certain products were standard, with millet seed, thiof fish, baobab fruit juice, and leaves of the niebe bean traveling with them. They have become the bearers of a food nomadism by giving rise to the creation of new businesses. The products that they needed for their customary sedentary cooking have had to move with them in order to maintain the ways of life that are consistent with their food practices. By changing places, Senegalese migrants have created new demands, which, thanks to them, have entered the urban food space. Thus peanut butter, peanut flour, palm oil, and spices have reached French plates in Bordeaux and in other cities with a large migrant population. These new cuisines give the feeling of innovation and are actually creating fusion recipes that are the product of food cultures that have been deliberately preserved, of products that circulate to respond to tastes, and of adaptations to local contexts. Senegalese practices have therefore been doubly nomadic through travel and the assimilation elsewhere of products whose exoticism only stems from an autocentric Western point of view. The newness of yassa chicken with mussels is hitting the Aquitaine region today, but it is only one example of the re-ses and changes that the circulation of products could show in many countries over a long period of time. Paella and pizza no longer have anything in common with the area in which they originated. They, too, have traveled and have changed in the process.

At the center of these culinary reconstructions appear specific places, and these areas of connection in the middle of flows and movements appear to be conducive to exchanges. The Gironde capital of Bordeaux, which is Chantal Crenn's field of study in this book, is historically an innovation convergence location. When cargoes of Colombian products piled up on the quaysides of the port in the eighteenth century, the same movement of the appropriation of newness created forms of food nomadism. One of the most interesting points of her presentation is the highlighting of how much places of transit are also platforms of exchanges as they provide the dynamics for the circulation of products. Ports are special spaces, but other places also contribute, with the airport, for example, also being a special space because of the movements that it intersects.

It should be briefly emphasized that another area of circulation and exchange has been able to play a similar role. The railway station took on the role as a kind of town or city identity card for those who alighted there, and as such replaced the central urban square where the coaching inn functioned as a crossroads. Food nomadisms also occurred within the station as in the nineteenth century this entrance to the town corresponded to the discovery of the unknown. The station became more familiar when the flow, and especially the diversity, of travelers increased, with, for example, visiting tourists, commuting workers on their daily migrations, farmers going to sell produce at market, and soldiers from the local garrison. The station, which was also a place of departure, became the heart of spatial mobilities. Whether these were small-scale, between nearby towns and cities, or whether they were at the start of long-distance journeys, such as English people leaving for the Riviera or soldiers leaving for the front, the time that people spent at the station meant that it was useful for shops and other businesses to be set up there. For a long time the station was closed to the outside world as access was only authorized to rail travelers—a situation that existed in France until the twentieth century—and only holders of concessions within the station area could attract customers. The port intermingled migrations, the inn established a particular area's cuisine, and the station would produce the interaction of both of these features. The non-places that are presented as the separation points between old and new practices lead us to reconsider whereabouts the hubs of food nomadism are located—ports, railway stations, airports, and, more commonly, retail outlets. Ultimately, what brings Siberian nomads and Senegalese migrants together is that they are both receivers and diffusers of innovative food choices.

It is a similar form of the re-creation of a specific space that other nomads, such as the Bedouins observed and described by Nier Avieli, are looking for in their appropriation of McDonald's restaurants. This is a superimposed nomadism that has arisen from the consideration of these restaurants as spaces of freedom, particularly for women. Freely coming here to encounter modern forms of Western food provides the opportunity for understanding the food nomadism of a multinational industrialized culture. The nomad becomes sedentary, but their food is nomadic.

Several other texts, like those of Jane Duruz and Luciano Maffi, restrict themselves more strictly to the undertaking of the journey, which is presented as a form of nomadism as soon as the actors go in search of their food. They are the opportunity for chance or, at times, deliberately sought-after discoveries. The experience of the journey is fundamental to the appropriation of fresh perspectives on food as it offers a whole mix of flavors and tastes. Some food-related emotions, however, do not originate in one's own journey. The evocation of recipes or the ploys used to attract consumer demand are sometimes the result of the suggestive power of an advertisement or a marketing strategy. When a certain product brand develops operations to promote the Japanese bento or Indian tandoori, the nomadism is virtual, but it appeals to the eater's wishes and wants. Successive nomadic cuisines that have become established in countries other than their countries of origin have enhanced this ability to change one's food choices. The delocalization of tastes here again forms part of a very long history of which street cuisines are quite a powerful reflection. Although they are only outlined in this book, they correspond to what can be pictured as an Ethiopian café in Adelaide or the amazement of a Florentine priest looking for the dishes of another city in Italy. They have created one of the most powerful economic food phenomena that there is, which is described by Stefano Magagnoli and Giovanni Ceccarelli when they examine the transition of Italian home cooking; the Italian migrants' nostalgia for which has resulted in the reconstruction of a cuisine that has traveled far. "Italian-sounding" has become one of the most significant banners of a food nomadism that has been recomposed on symbolic bases. If the eater is not mobile, at least they can think they are since they are consuming—on the face of it—dishes that have been given a remote seal of approval by a mental universe.

Obviously, modern food cultures are those of an increasing mobility. They are becoming nomadic through the increase in movements and an increased knowledge of the world, but they are also nomadic as a result of the increasing globalization of trade flows. Transported to the transnational level by air, sea, or instant internet flows, food cultures no longer seem to have frontiers. Food nomadism condemns heritage-related retrenchment and campaigning, which are able, at best, to defend economic interests, and at worst, to aim to embody models. The cultural traveler described by Luciano Maffi was already in this mindset of freeing himself from any constraint when he set off to discover eateries that were far away from home but so near in geographical terms. Curiosity and an interest in exchanging motivated him, and he was not so far removed from the peregrinations that food tourism is reconfiguring today on different scales. Whereas the Italian priest was like the aristocrat of the Grand Tour, the average tourist today assimilates parts of other cultures through their cuisine.

The food nomadism that could now be associated with a limitless quest for ever-renewing culinary experiences offers other multiscale perceptions when restored to its place in the diversity of experiences. Whereas the Corsican shepherd's movements around the island's paths depended on what work he was doing and, in doing so, he adapted himself to his environment, the hiker who was observed by Philippe Pesteil, and who follows the same tracks, tries to protect himself from his environment. He creates his own food nomadism by organizing his vital equipment with care and forethought. Prepacked and prepared food must be suitable for his physical effort as he would not know how to make do with what he could find in his immediate environment. He therefore makes use of any technical method, from freeze-dried products to the modern portable wineskin, to ensure the ease of his food supply. He ultimately is not too far removed from the cosmonaut who will certainly not find any food unless he takes it with him. Both of them create a product nomadism to support their loss of sedentariness, but they make precise choices when it comes to deciding exactly what food product they need. While walking on the same paths, the shepherd was in a very different situation to that of the hiker, and was also very aware of the constraints imposed by his movements, while his mobility was only a very short interval between moments of stability.

Sandrine Ruhlmann gives another example of this by recalling that the motivations for the movements of Mongolian pastoral herdsmen are many, complex, and diverse. The driving of the herd or flock has nothing to do with visits that are required by the many rules of social behavior. Carrying goods to a town does not have the same meaning as going back loaded with supplies from the town. Making visits to the shaman does not have the same implication as journeying across grandiose landscapes. Nomadism for them is functional but it is not food-related, and, if it is, it originates in habits and customs that nomadic life has created by knowing how to adapt tools, utensils, crockery, and cooking methods.

Three proposals are put forward in this book through the different situations that it brings together. It firstly asserts that the increase in the number of places of exchange causes the convergence of food practices, and that this can occur at varying scales of meeting points, such as station buffets, motorway service stations, and airport hubs, each of which can be a strategically important business hub. Is this new? Not necessarily so when one considers the organization of commercial flows in towns and cities. Throughout history, the planning of towns has opened up roads where eating places have been attached and where the best trade routes have been indicated through the durability and continuity of these eateries. One just has to consider the regular street trading pitches of street vendors, who have known for centuries where their customers will come from.

Several of the authors' contributions then identify which forms of mobility generate most food movements, but on reading them, one hesitates between two viewpoints. Is it the migrations related to work and international tourism, which are certainly diverse and with their comings and goings account for the largest number of trips? Or is it not rather at the scale of small groups or even that of the individual actor that the addition of personal discoveries better reveal what can attract, circulate, and be the subject of food transfer or of a change of consumer habits?

Finally, it must be mentioned how much the intuitive analysis of a market has been able to bring about innovation in practices. These innovations explain why today food nomadism appears to us as a confirmed fact of our contemporary globalized societies. The depth of time must not be evaded, for if foods travel they are primarily an offer responding to an identified need, which is the need to find something to eat outside the home. This demand is not new. Street food has been declared a major innovation, but in fact it is part of age-old practice and tradition. The inventive and finely-tuned ability of street sellers to gain the attention of passers-by, well before convenience foods met mobility needs and food trucks sold their wares in profitable locations, has long been proof of this. What about the importance of the street sellers in nineteenth-century London? When the oyster seller used to shout out, "Penny a lot! Oysters! Penny a lot!" he was part of the street scene selling nomadic food for economic reasons based on his perception of people's mobility, though this was certainly on a smaller scale. A quarter of the oysters sold in London in the mid-nineteenth century were sold by these costermongers!

This book aims to show that there is a history of economic and behavioral shifts from mobile cooking to mobile ways of eating. For all that, the practices of "real" nomads have not been fully assimilated by sedentary people simply because they are increasingly mobile. Habits that have been changed by travel are the real and most effective promotional support of other culinary cultures, and in that is created food nomadism. Commercial sales strategies for food that can be a simple means of subsistence, means of provision, or a quick chance to satisfy hunger have understood the importance of this by making available eating patterns that offer new tastes in line with growing need. From street food to nomadic attitudes, it is the mobility link that is apparent in a given and multiplying space.

Notes

CHAPTER 1. FROM NOUN (THE FOOD OF THE NOMADS) TO ADJECTIVE (NOMADIC EATING)

1. Rasse and Debos, 2006: 7.
2. Bernus, 1986: 43.
3. Attali, 1990: 10.
4. Quoted by Ingrid Sénepart, 2011: 32.
5. Charlier, 103.
6. Bourgeot, 2009.
7. Bernus, 1986: 141.
8. Deleuze and Guattari, 472.
9. Deleuze and Guattari, 473.
10. Stepanoff, 2013: 8.
11. Claudot-Hawad, 2002: 79.
12. Golovnev, 2013: 96.
13. Bianquis, 2000.
14. Golovnev, 2013: 70.
15. Claudot-Hawad, 2002: 57.
16. Golovnev, 126.
17. Golovnev, 127.
18. Boulay 2008: 2.
19. Boulay 2008: 2.
20. Ruhlmann 2009.
21. Frey, 1993.
22. Bernus, 1990: 41.
23. Amselle, 2011.
24. Poulain, 1997.
25. Barthes, 1961: 978.

26. Barthes, 1961: 985.
27. Barthes, 1961: 986.
28. www.e-marketing.com, 2002.
29. www.e-marketing.com, 2002.

CHAPTER 2. MONGOLIAN NOMADIC
HERDERS ARE SEDENTARY EATERS

1. Figures from the website of the National Statistics Office of Mongolia (http://www
.en.nso.mn/index.php) in 2014.
2. Troy Sternberg, 2008.
3. This convergence on the goat species—single-species herding—leads to overgrazing
crises. Climatic crises or disasters (*zud*) unfortunately seem to be the only regulation of livestock overpopulation. See Blanc et al. (2013) and Devienne (2013) concerning the herding
system's evolution, land-pasture management, herd mobility reduction, access to circuits de-
regulation and overgrazing crisis augmentation in the Mongolian environment. See Reading
et al. (2006) regarding pastoral uses, rangelands managements, and biodiversity conservation
measures. See Lkhagvadorj et al. (2013) on the consequences of economic and climate changes
on the pastoral nomadism. Finally, see Fernández-Giménez et al. (2012) for the study of gov-
ernance, adaptive capacity, and resilience confronted with climatic and economic changes, and
Fernández-Giménez et al. (2015) to comprehend the role of formal community-based natural
resource management in responding and adapting to the climatic disasters (*zud*), mobility and
wintry hay storage being the most important strategies to limit livestock losses.
4. Ruhlmann, 2015 and 2019.
5. I devoted an article to the pot as an evolving and adaptive toll, allowing to adopt new
cooking modes (fried, steam) by adding new cooking elements (animal or vegetable fat for frying)
or new attributes on or in the pot (perforated steaming plate or stages), see Ruhlmann, 2015.
6. Chabros and Dulam, 1990: 32; Ruhlmann, 2019: 17.
7. Testart, 1982a and 1982b.
8. Ruhlmann, 2018.
9. Testart, 1982a, 1982b, and 1988.
10. Ingold, 1983: 555.
11. Mintz, 1985. See also Mintz and Schlettwein-Gsell, 2001.
12. The Mongolian sheep is a local type of the fat-tailed, coarse-wool sheep that is said to
derive from the Tibetan sheep. It is a smaller type than the fat-crumped Kyrgyz sheep. Other
sheep breeds have been imported into Mongolia and crossbred with the local species. See Accolas and Deffontaines, 1975: 36–47.
13. Verdier, 1966; Ruhlmann, 2019: 7.
14. Ruhlmann, 2019: 45.
15. Sobal and Nelson, 2003.
16. Fischler, 2011.
17. This argument seems to be valid in other cultures, as Mary Douglas stated about the
English food system (1972: 66).
18. Ruhlmann, 2019: 121–129.
19. Hamayon, 1970; Ruhlmann, 2019: 92–94.
20. Chabros and Dulam, 1990: 11; Ruhlmann, 2019: 29–30.
21. The same for the goat and marmot, concerning the technical details of stew cooking in
their skin once the skeleton has been removed, see Ruhlmann 2019: 73.

22. Empson, 2011 and 2012.
23. Ruhlmann, 2019: 109–112.

CHAPTER 3. MCDONALD'S IN THE DESERT: BEDOUINS, FAST-FOOD, AND MODERNITY IN SOUTHERN ISRAEL

1. Yiftachel, 2009.
2. McKee, 2014: 1180. In the past there existed an image of the Negev Bedouins as loyal and pro-Israeli, mainly due to the support they sometimes extended to pre-state Jewish settlements in the desert and their service as combat soldiers and trackers in the Israeli military. The growing gap between the Bedouins and the state, and the failed promises of civil rights and equality in exchange for loyalty, led to increasing political and religious polarization that very much eroded this perception among Israeli Jews (Mckee 2014).
3. Ritzer, 1993.
4. Ritzer 1994: 154.
5. Toynbee, 2000: 191.
6. Watson, 1997a.
7. Yan, 1997.
8. Wu, 1997.
9. Watson, 1997b.
10. *Golden Arches East* book jacket blurb, 2nd edition.
11. Caldwell (2004) on McDonald's in Moscow; Rarick, Falk, and Barczyk (2012) on McDonald's in the Philippines; Beng-Huat (2012) in Singapore; Brembec (2005) in Sweden; and Debouzy (2006) in France, to name but a few.
12. Azaryahu, 1999.
13. Azaryahu, 2000: 62, my emphasis.
14. Ram, 2004.
15. Ulin, 1995.
16. Since 1998, McDonald's Israel offers charcoal-grilled burgers. Other local features include kosher franchises, freshly chopped salad, McKebab, and McFalafel, as well as the largest McRoyal in the world (325 grams).
17. See https://www.ynet.co.il/articles/0,7340,L-3947423,00.html for 2010 prices (sampled September 2018).
18. https://www.mcdonalds.co.il/%D7%93%D7%A8%D7%95%D7%A9%D7%99%D7%9D/%D7%9B%D7%9C%D7%9C%D7%99, sampled September 2018.
19. https://www.mcdonalds.com/us/en-us/careers.html, sampled September 2018.
20. Rothschild and Darr, 2005.
21. For example, Fischer and Shavit, 1995.
22. Samman, 2010; Toninato, 2018
23. Fabian, 2014: 32.
24. Atwood, 1996: 114.
25. Jakubowska, 1992: 98.
26. http://www.hebrewsongs.com/song-shirahavabedui.htm, sampled September 2018. For a similar take on Jordanian Bedouins, see Massad, 2001.
27. Jakubowska, 1992: 98.
28. Ritzer, 2011: 220.
29. Yan, 2010: 203.

30. Yan, 2010: 220.
31. Ritzer, 2011.
32. Yan, 2010.
33. http://www.beer-sheva.muni.il/City/OnTheCity/Pages/b7-Misparim.aspx, sampled September 2018.
34. Turner, 1969.
35. Yiftachel, 2009: 244.
36. https://news.walla.co.il/item/2654997, sampled September 2018.
37. Illouz and Nick, 2003.
38. Illouz and Nick, 2003: 221.
39. Illouz and Nick, 2003: 223.

CHAPTER 4. NOMADISM IN THE FOOD CULTURE OF THE YAKUTS AND THE INDIGENOUS PEOPLES OF YAKUTIA

1. Deleuze, G., and Guattari, F. Rizhome *A Thousand Plateaus: Capitalism and Schizophrenia—An Online Almanac*, Vostok Press, 2005: 672.
2. Deleuze and Guattari, 2005: 183.
3. Deleuze and Guattari,1986: 183.
4. Deleuze and Guattari, 2005: 183.
5. Deleuze and Guattari, 2005: 184.
6. Deleuze and Guattari, 2005: 185.
7. Deleuze and Guattari 2005: 185.
8. Deleuze and Guattari, 2005: 186.
9. Deleuze and Guattari, 2005: 187.
10. Deleuze and Guattari, 2005: 672.
11. Somers-Hall, Henry. "Deleuze's philosophical heritage: Unity, difference, and onto-theology." *The Cambridge companion to Deleuze*. Daniel Smith and Henry Somers-Hall (eds.). Cambridge: Cambridge University Press, 2012, 337–56.
12. Robbek, M. E. *Traditsionnaya pisha evenov* (Traditional Food of the Evens). Novosibirsk: Nauka Press, 2007, 164.
13. Robbek, M. E., 2007: 164.
14. Seroshevsky, V. L. *Yakuty* (the Yakuts), Vol. 1. St. Petersburg: 1896: 117–38.
15. Robbek, V. A., and Robbek, M. E. (2004). *Evensko-Russkiy Slovar-Evedy-nuchidi tore-ruk* (Evenki-Russian Dictionary). Novosibirsk, Nauka Press: 623.
16. *Yakutsko-russkiy slovar* (Yakut-Russian Dictionary). Sovietskaya Entsiklopedia Press. Moscow, 1972: 191.

CHAPTER 5. CIRCULATING FOOD PRACTICES AND FOOD REPRESENTATIONS ON SENEGALESE INHABITANTS OF BORDEAUX AND DAKAR

1. Here, this does not mean legal status but rather a description used in the process of differentiation/identification in social relationships, providing a symbolic framework for routine actions and carrying representations of self and other.

2. Other than ethnic affiliations, the reasons for the retirees' moves fluctuate: in the case of familial stability, seasonal migrations determine a time loop between Dakar and the village of origin (winter) and Bordeaux (summer); in the case of family crisis, significant marital instability, illness, and administrative reasons, these retirees undertake longer or shorter journeys geographically or temporally. In all these cases, being mobile enables the positive preservation of their identity as aging immigrant men and women.

3. In the French republican model, migrant eating habits occupy the unique position of being at the same time irreducible and a mark of integration.

4. Their wives are younger than they are and for the most part still work in Bordeaux as janitors and personal care assistants. Thus, the husbands generally leave by themselves to live out their old age intermittently in Senegal.

5. Martiniello, Puig, and Suzanne, 2009, "Créations," 7–11.

6. In the return trip between Dakar and Bordeaux, within the framework of globalization, they must be cosmopolitan but avoid being turned away at the ethnic border by the members of the family who remain in Senegal or by the family in France and in order to be respected as elders.

7. Augé, 1992, *Non-Places*. The airport is a "non-place" par excellence; a supermodern territory. One walks around there alone, silently, in transit, anonymously, waiting for a connecting flight. However, the functionality of these non-places is similar to practices arising from those observed in places conducive to sociability. Marc Augé therefore allows us to think about localization and mobility together in our supermodern societies.

8. Tarrius, 2019, "Territoires circulatoires et étapes urbaines des transmigrant(e)s," 63–70.

9. Corbeau and Poulain, 2002, *Penser l'alimentation*.

10. Dolphijn, 2004, *Foodscapes*, and Appaduraï, 2015, *Après le colonialisme*.

11. Warnier, 1998.

12. Lestage, 2008, "De la circulation des nourritures."

13. Abbots, 2015, "Approaches."

14. Retirement pensions in Senegal, when they exist, are very low compared to those of Senegalese retirees from France. One hundred euros every trimester compared to an average of 900 euros per month.

15. They have to break the habit of stocking up that is facilitated by bimonthly purchases from superstores and by using freezers to store the previously prepared dishes made by their wives over the weekend.

16. Normally *cee bu jen* for lunch can be substituted with fried green beans/chicken for an important guest. Ever since colonization, "French dishes" have remained symbolically highly regarded.

17. Living alone or with the extended family entails feeding at least a dozen people every day.

18. By cutting his portion of the shared bowl of *cee bu jen* or rice and fish by two-thirds.

19. Crenn et Hassoun, 2014.

20. The middle class is characterized by "small prosperity." This allows a shop owner to buy him or herself a 1500 CFA hamburger from time to time, depending on how business was that week.

21. Getting back up after a meal "sitting on the ground around" a bowl constitutes a painful and humiliating physical ordeal for these "young-old men" who do not wish to be "helped," and even more so because of the physical pain earned from thirty or forty years of repetitive work on the assembly line, which makes itself felt again strongly still gives them back pain.

22. They may provide lodging for the nephews and nieces in their homes in exchange for services such as cooking or running a small restaurant, and provide financial aid for their studies.

23. In Dakar, the term *talibé* is used to describe young boys who live under the tutelage of a marabout (master of a Koranic school belonging to an association). Some retirees from Bordeaux work personally to feed these children begging in the streets, which would, according to them, be disdained by many members of Senegalese society.

24. There are businesses that specialize in the sale of alcohol that are most often owned by Catholics, and where Muslims come to drink discreetly.

25. A brotherhood that is reinforced when connecting flights are canceled, delayed, or pushed back two or three days and they end up living together at a hotel (sharing collection of information for the next flights, meals eaten together, acknowledging racism lived by the Senegalese).

26. At other times in their lives, when they were working, McDonald's incarnated modernity and America, like the Ford factory cafeteria, which, according to them, allowed them to "eat French-style."

27. Desjeux, 2002: 25.

28. This is a stick made from trees that have many healthy properties and mystic virtues and that protect its user from the evil eye. The soccou (*matt xewë*) is highly prized by migrants.

29. Visiting the elders in Senegal allows them to become their spokesperson in Bordeaux and to remind the French family of the respect that their age is due.

30. Augé, 2002: 131.

CHAPTER 6. SPACE-FOOD: FOOD IN MOBILE TECHNOLOGICAL ENVIRONMENTS OF LATE HIGH-MODERNITY

1. Levi, 2006: 162.
2. Lane and Feeback, 2002: 797.
3. Ulrich Herbert, 2007: 10.
4. James C. Scott, 1994: 4.
5. Latour, 1983.
6. Rosa, 2013: 21.
7. Von Hermann, 2016; Keller, 2005.
8. Gertel, 2002.
9. Scholz, 1995: 20.
10. Streck, 2002: 1.
11. Korff, 1985: 344.
12. McCurdy, 2007: 10.
13. Spreen, 2014: 42.
14. NASA, TN D-7720: 9.
15. NASA, SP–202: Jones.
16. Spreen, 2014: 54.
17. NRC, 1963: 3.
18. NRC, 1963: 7–8.
19. Ross-Nazzal, 2007: 220.
20. Perchonok and Bourland, 2002: 915.

21. NRC, 1963: 4–10.
22. NASA, TN D7720: 13.
23. Ross-Nazzal, 2006.
24. Cf. Ross-Nazzal, 2007.
25. NRC, 1963: 4–10.
26. NRC, 1963: 17; Belasco 2006: 230.
27. NRC, 1963: 14.
28. NRC, 1963: 4.
29. NASA, PK 65-81: 6.
30. NASA, CTG – GT3 1965: 45.
31. NASA, CTG – GT3 1965: 47. For a more detailed account of this episode, see Levi 2010: 6–11.
32. NASA, SP–202: Humphreys.
33. NASA, TN D-7720: 10.
34. NASA, TN D-7720: 33.
35. NASA, SP–202: Humphreys.
36. Levi, 2010: 7.
37. McCurdy, 2007: 8.
38. WaPo, October 10, 1968.
39. Montanari, 2006: 99.
40. Cf. Tolksdorf, 2017.
41. Kerwin and Seddon, 2002: 921.
42. Perchonok and Bourland, 2002: 914.
43. Kerwin and Seddon, 2002: 921.
44. NBC, 1965: S1E4.
45. Humphreys, 2014: 114.
46. Ross-Nazzal, 2006.
47. Sanders, 2018.
48. Kerwin and Seddon, 2002: 922.
49. LAT, July 26, 1971; Reser, 2017.
50. NYT, October 21, 1962.
51. Levi, 2008: 14.
52. NASA, SP-202: Smith.
53. Guideposts, October 1970.
54. NASA, SP-202: Smith.
55. NASA, SP-202: Smith.
56. For a detailed history of airline (and space) food, see Foss, 2016.
57. NASA, SP-202: Treadwell.
58. NASA, TN D-7720: 1.
59. NASA, SP-202: Smith.
60. NASA, SP-202: Smith.
61. LAT, July 17, 1969.
62. NYT, June 29, 1969.
63. LAT, July 17, 1969.
64. Fekl, 1974: 263.
65. Ross-Nazzal, 2006.
66. NASA, 8/2004.

67. Ross-Nazzal, 2006.
68. Chaikin, 2007: 59; Herbert, 2007: 20.
69. NYT, April 4, 1976.
70. Cawley, 2017.
71. Mumford, 1970: 300.
72. Mumford, 1970: 308–10.
73. Spreen, 2014: 41.
74. Sachs, 1994: 197.
75. Sachs, 1994: 200.
76. Bourland and Vogt, 2010: 22.
77. NYT, January 16, 1985.
78. Belasco, 2006: 12.
79. Fellner and Riedl, 2009.
80. NASA, 8/2004.
81. Pikaar et al., 2018.
82. Miggelbrink et al., 2013: 14.

CHAPTER 7. EATING ON CORSICA'S GR FOOTPATHS AND TRAILS: CHOOSING BETWEEN HI-TECH AND TRADITION

1. As part of the drafting of Act II of the Loi Montagne (mountain law), Corsica's Commission des Affaires Economiques de l'Assemblée Nationale (the national assembly's economic affairs committee) adopted the amendments proposed by the territorial majority to the Corsican parliamentarians on September 27, 2017, thus recognizing Corsica as a mountain island.

2. Pesteil, 2016: 293–30.

3. On this temporary accommodation, see Weiss M.-C., *Les bergeries traditionnelles de Corse*, Ajaccio, Albiana (2019).

4. Bread *intintu* (soaked) with olive oil and the onion are symbols of the frugal, convivial meal of a bygone age.

5. See Pesteil, 2008.

6. We will discuss the Restonica trail, whose slogan is: "Venez courir sur le mythique GR20" ("Come and run on the legendary GR20").

7. As a tribute, the Punta Rossa (2,247 m), which is located in the Cinto mountain range and overhangs the legendary Cirque de la Solitude (or Cascettoni, or more precisely E Ghjove Turchine), was renamed Pic von Cube.

8. *Corse*, 1979.

9. See, among others, M. Fabrikant, 2012.

10. The appetite for seasonal vegetables, especially refreshing and inexpensive tomatoes in the summer, led to the emergence in the 1970s of the name *pumataghji* (tomato eaters or *tomatards* in French) to describe the tourist walkers, who were instantly recognizable by their backpacks and their reluctance to spend money. This disparaging label has survived to this day and denotes, by extension, a type of tourism that is thought not to benefit Corsica and even less so Corsicans. Reflecting an insular view of a certain type of tourism, of physical appearance, of presentation of self, and of a relationship with money, this observation would seem to merit further analysis.

11. It is not possible to list all the events now staged in each region of the island. Mention should be made, however, of the Napoleon Trail in Ajaccio, with its three trails (10, 23, 43 km) attracting 1,200 participants in 2018. Moreover, some trails are multievent courses (running, swimming, cycling, etc.), such as the Corsica Raid adventure, and some are team events, such as the Corsica Coast Race, held annually from October 20–28. On the continent, there is the famous Tour du Mont Blanc, which is now restricted to 10,000 selected runners, Saintélyon, which attracts 17,000 participants, and the Grand Trail of the Templiers dans les Causses (76.9 km).

12. The calorific expenditure for an adult male weighing about 70 kilograms carrying a bag of 6 kilograms is 500 kilocalorie/hour (although this can rise to 800 kcal). For a walk of seven hours per stage, therefore, his expenditure would be 3,500 kilocalories plus the basic daily amount of 1,800 kilocalories. Dinner and breakfast should replenish the glycogen supply to ensure a good start. Fast sugars, which metabolize quickly (25 to 30 minutes), should be consumed while walking so as to maintain reserves, to avoid creating too many triglycerides, and to have a good glycogen reserve to provide for the first ninety minutes of exertion (role of the evening meal and breakfast). Lunch can be light if food intake has been regular but can include slow sugars, which metabolize more slowly (90 to 120 minutes), and leguminous plants. Dinner must restore reserves. Proteins are essential for muscle maintenance and for taking over for the carbohydrates if exertion is prolonged. Protein intake should not be excessive because it contributes to weakening the body. Since water consumption is especially important in summer, individuals should not wait until they feel thirsty before they have a drink. Individual quantities should be around two liters per stage, and fluid intake should continue after the walking or running activity has finished. Any exertion that is out of the norm should be preceded by a medium- and long-term preparatory stage. In addition to tailored physical training, this should include a hypotoxic diet (gluten-free and low in dairy products, fat and animal proteins) comprising raw foods and using gentle, normocaloric cooking methods.

13. Bragard, 2009.

14. Camelbaks are water pouches worn on the back. Their capacity varies depending on the sport or trip in question.

15. This technology is based on biocide, which in this case means the silver ions associated with chlorine. The tablets can be used with the addition of a filter if the water is cloudy.

16. BCAA stands for branched-chain amino acids. They generally comprise three amino acids: leucine, isoleucine, and valine. They work to produce proteins and participate in endurance and recovery capital.

17. This dimension is very important. Internet users say they weigh their backpacks by the gram and aim to do without anything that is superfluous. There is an ongoing debate about the useful, minimum, essential, and maximum weights. Options range between 20 kilograms for the brave and 10 kilograms for the "smart." Some hikers opt for a porter service that ensures their bag is taken to every stage. The range of backpacks varies from hiking versions that are suitable for a walk lasting a few hours (15–20 l), to those designed for solo expeditions (110 l).

18. The glycogen reserve is on average one and a half hours for sustained effort.

19. Having to stop is time-consuming for a competitor. Generally, the product will be consumed while walking, but this will depend on the hiker's physical condition at the time of refuelling. In addition to the trials of the trail itself, competitors need to decide whether to eat when stationary, walking, or running. Chewing dried fruit (bananas, for example) is a more delicate operation at high speed because of respiratory increase, among other things.

20. Even in these circumstances, where it might be supposed that contraindications would be heeded, old habits can die hard. Many runners will consume cola-based drinks, coffee, and bananas, which are not recommended by nutritionists.

21. The interviews we conducted highlighted the gap that exists between the two types of race. The short trail is designed as a relatively short burst of energy, where the best runners sprint for most of the race. The long trail is another world entirely. Preparation is essential, with a controlled daily food intake and daily training, involving running for several hours a day to establish "a solid foundation" that is built up over several years.

22. This recipe came from a trail runner who told us he was a fan of a pre-run breakfast of crushed banana and yogurt.

23. When a competitor is forced to withdraw from a race, it is usually more to do with an energy intake problem than the physical effort itself or any pain, injuries, or falls. One trail runner told us that he was in constant search of the right food, which can vary from one race to the next:

> Sometimes products are really good but then they're no good when it comes to the next trail . . . maybe it's me getting the start wrong, I start off too fast . . . I don't know . . . you can make numerous mistakes, you're on the wrong rhythm at some point, you follow the guy next to you, you fall into the wrong rhythm and that sets you back a bit, then it's all about precision, all along it's about precision . . . if you eat well, regularly, you'll get to the end, that's not a problem, there's no problem with the diet . . . the trail's like the twenty-four hours of Le Mans race, you have to regulate yourself . . . it's not obvious, even an experienced runner can get it wrong."

It should be noted that the mechanical metaphor of the body as a machine consuming fuel (food) or as a piece of precision mechanics that can easily malfunction and which needs to be looked after was often used, both in the interviews we conducted and in the blogs.

24. Bottles are forbidden on the main long-distance trails in Corsica. Refreshment stations distribute eco-cups, and participants are provided with their own personal cups. There is currently a move to exclude plastic from mountain races altogether.

25. See, for example, www.expemag.com, which offers a table of calories according to foods.

26. These confessions as well as accounts of tragic events help to reinforce the legend. The history of the GR20 is peppered with deaths, from the seven walkers who died of hypothermia in May 1983 to the seven hikers crushed by rockfall in the Cirque de la Solitude in June 2015. There are also many tales of the mountain rescue services having to be called out to help the injured.

27. Le Breton, 2000.

28. Pesteil, 2013: 83–99.

29. The marketing focus on the authenticity of Corsica, its people, and its produce not only reflects a concern for truth and the desire to escape from a "fake" world, it also implicitly responds to doubts over what could in reality just be a sham.

30. European policies on mountain territories are converging for the development of an integrated tourism. As an illustration, see, for two distinct contexts, G. Lacquement, 2011, 497–520 and F. Fourneau, 2011, 575–87.

31. Héritier, 2008.

32. Pesteil, 2010: 116–36.

33. On contempt for the tourist and the "tourist as merchandise" concept, see Urbain, 2002.

34. Pesteil, 2012: 263–83.

35. Balandier, 1994.

36. Le Monde, 2017.

37. "We cannot help but be impressed by the way ultra-trailers, the champions of an antinormative discourse, have reproduced transformations that have impacted other spaces such as those of work and school since the 1980s. This situation challenges us, in particular, because it results in a new synthesis between deeply contradictory values, which include sporting hierarchy and relationship horizontality, hyperconnectivity and withdrawal from the world and organic diets and the consumption of gels and chemical powders. This DIY identity is nevertheless barely discussed in the ultra-trail world, where it is seemingly self-evident" (translated from French).

38. This is a company and think tank that presents itself as a "marketing agency for the sport of tomorrow."

39. An allusion to the Tarahumaras, a Mexican ethnic group from the state of Chihuahua.

40. On walking as an extender of time and a philosophical act, see Gros, 2011, Flammarion, and as a remedy for an accelerating and alienated daily life, see Sansot, 2000.

41. Michel, 2012: 26–35.

42. Convergence noted by Lhérété, 2012.

43. Many interviewees stressed the importance of the presence of women in both hiking and trail runs, which they believe symbolizes the "progressive" and barrierless nature of these disciplines.

44. Baudrillard, 1979: 113.

45. While hiking and trail running cannot be considered a "risky" or "serious sport" in the Routier and Soulé sense of mountaineering, parachute jumping, and climbing, this dimension is not totally absent from these practices and remains present in the minds of participants. See Routier, 2010.

46. Bragard, 2016.

47. Pecaud, 2005.

CHAPTER 8. ITALIAN-SOUNDING:
A WORLD CARRIER OF A TRAVELING *CUISINE*

This chapter is based on joint research using a common methodology, but sections 1–6 are the work of Stefano Magagnoli and sections 7–8 of Giovanni Ceccarelli. Section 9 was written by both authors.

1. Francesco Panella, *Brooklyn Man. La guida insolita alla cucina di New York* (Rome: Newton Compton, 2014).

2. *Little Big Italy*, Nove, https://it.dplay.com/nove/little-big-italy/ (accessed: 9 July 2018).]

3. The first series featured New York, Manhattan, Paris, Boston, San Francisco, London, Seville, and Berlin.

4. See Antonio Gibelli and Fabio Caffarena, "Le lettere degli emigranti," and Vito Teti, "Emigrazione, alimentazione, culture popolari," in *Storia dell'emigrazione italiana*, vol. I, *Partenze*, eds. Piero Bevilacqua, Andreina De Clementi, Emilio Franzina (Rome: Donzelli, 2001), 563–74 and 575–97.

5. On "the flavor of the homeland," see Victor Ego Ducrot, *Los sabores de la patria. Las intrigas de la historia argentina contadas desde la mesa y la cocina* (Buenos Aires: Grupo Editorial Norma, 2009).

Notes

6. The idea of using the concept of an island was inspired by reading Fernand Braudel, *Civiltà and imperi del Mediterraneo nell'età di Filippo II*, third edition (Torino: Einaudi, 1986; ⁰ed. orig.: *La Mediterranée et le Monde méditerranéen à l'époque de Philippe II*, Paris: Librairie Armand Colin, 1949), 145 ss.

7. Divergent evolution occurs when two or more populations with a common ancestor develop different characteristics. It can lead to different varieties of the same species adapted to their enviornmental conditions or if it is sufficenty long-lasting to the birth of a new species. See Valeria Balboni, *Evolution ed evoluzionismo* (Milano: Alpha Test, 2002), 53 ss.

8. Bob Dylan, "Like a Rolling Stone," in *Highway 61 Revisited*, 1965.

9. Piero Valdiserra, *Spaghetti alla Bolognese: l'altra faccia del tipico* (Bologna: Edizioni Edi House, 2016).

10. Accounts of how the dish spread outside Italy appear in Patrizia Battilani and Giuliana Bertagnoni, *Il restyling di una vecchia icona pop: la storia transnazionale degli Spaghetti alla bolognese*, conference paper presented at VII AISU Congress, *Food and the City* (Padua 3–5 September 2015).

11. Félix Lope de Vega, "Fuente Ovejuna," in Id., *Teatro* (Firenze: Sansoni, 1963), 173 ss.

12. Ettore Boiardi, for example, emigrated to the United States at the beginning of the twentieth century and became a popular chef in high demand. Boiardi's chief claim to fame was his range of canned Italian food, including the well-known Chef Boy-ar-dee Ravioli, sold under the slogan "Enjoy Ravioli as truly Italian as the Tower of Pisa"; Anna Boiardi and Stephanie Lyness, *Delicious Memories. Recipes and Stories from the Chef Boyardee Family* (Hong Kong: Stewart, Tabori & Chang, 2011).

13. Paola Corti, "Emigrazione e consuetudini alimentari. L'esperienza di una catena migratoria," in *Storia d'Italia, Annali*, 13, *L'alimentazione*, eds. Alberto Capatti, Alberto De Bernardi and Angelo Varni (Torino: Einaudi, 1998), 715.

14. John Dickie, *Delizia! The Epic History of the Italians and Their Food* (New York: Free Press, 2008). The film *Big Night* (Stanley Tucci and Campbell Scott, 1996) shows two brothers from Abruzzo trying to serve "real" Italian food in a New Jersey restaurant in the 1950s. Their brave attempts are unsuccessful, but a neighboring restaurant run by Pascale from Sicily meets with success by offering checked tablecloths, candles in wine flasks, and meatballs and spaghetti.

15. Franco La Cecla, *La pasta e la pizza* (Bologna: il Mulino, 1998), 104.

16. La Cecla, 104.

17. La Cecla, 55.

18. Peppino Ortoleva, "La tradizione e l'abbondanza. Riflessioni sulla cucina degli Italiani d'America," *Altreitalie*, no. 7 (January–June 1992).

19. Frederick J. Turner, "The Significance of the Frontier in American History," *Annual Report of the American Historical Association (1893)*: 197–227.

20. Blas Matamori, *La ciudad del Tango (Tango histórico y sociedad)* (Buenos Aires: Editorial Galerna, 1969).

21. Fabio Parasecoli, *Al Dente. Storia del cibo in Italia* (Gorizia: Leg edizioni, 2015), 247 ss. (or. ed. *Al Dente. A History of Food in Italy*, London: Reaktion Books, 2014).

22. Krishnendu Ray, *The Ethnic Restaurateur* (New York: Bloomsbury USA Academic, 2016).

23. See Stefano Magagnoli, "The Italian Way of Eating Round the World: Italian-Sounding, Counterfeit, and Original Products," in Kazunobu Ikeya (ed.), *The Spread of Food Cultures in Asia*, Osaka, National Museum of Ethnology (Senri Ethnological Studies 100), 2019, pp. 173–95.

24. La Cecla, 72.

25. Pierre Bourdieu, *La Distinzione. Critica sociale del gusto* (Bologna: il Mulino, 1983) (or. ed. *La Distinction. Critique sociale du jugement*, Paris: Les éditions de Minuit, 1979).

26. Vanni Codeluppi, "Evoluzione e caratteristiche del Made in Italy," in *Il Made in Italy. Natura, settori e problemi*, eds. Ampelio Bucci, Vanni Codeluppi, and Mauro Ferraresi (Roma: Carocci, 2011), 13.

27. Stefano Magagnoli, "Reputazione, *skill*, territorio," *Storia Economica*, no. 2 (2011): 247–74.

28. Mario Rigoni Stern, *Il sergente nella neve* (Torino: Einaudi, 1953), 9 [translation of question in Bergamo dialect: "Sergent Major, will we go home to our huts?"].

29. Stefano Magagnoli, "Eating Tradition. Typical Products, Distinction and the Myth of Memory," in *Consuming the World: Eating and Drinking in Culture, History and Environment*, eds. Michelle Mart, Daniel J. Philippon, special issue of *Global Environment—A Journal of Transdisciplinary History* 11, no. 1 (2018): 154–72.

30. La Cecla, 104.

31. *Lost*, Season 2, Ep. 18 "Dave" (2006) 00:03:24.

32. Jonathan Morris, "Making Italian Espresso, Making Espresso Italian," *Food and History* 8, no. 2 (2010): 155–83; Ken Albala, "*Italianità* in America: The Cultural Politics of Representing 'Authentic' Italian Cuisine in the U.S.," in *Representing Italy through Food*, eds. Peter Naccarato, Zachary Nowak, and Elgin K. Eckert (London: Bloomsbury Academic, 2017), 205–17.

33. Fabio Parasecoli, "Deconstructing Soup: Ferran Adrià's Culinary Challenges," *Gastronomica* 1, no. 1 (Winter 2001): 60–73; Gualtiero Marchesi, Carlo G. Valli, *Marchesi si nasce: questa è la mia storia* (Milano: Rizzoli, 2010); *I ristoranti d'Italia: 1978*, ed. Federico U. D'Amato (Roma: L'Espresso, 1978), s.v. "Gualtiero Marchesi."

34. Mauro Di Giandomenico, "La scienza, il cibo, il gusto," in *Educare al (buon) gusto. Tra sapore, piacere e sapere*, ed. Franco Bochicchio (Napoli: Giapeto, 2013), 43–44.

35. Alfredo Viazzi, *Cucina e nostalgia: A Gastronomic Memoir by the Master Italian Chef with More Than 130 Recipes* (New York: Random House, 1983); Albala, 212–13.

36. Nancy Jenkins, "Italians State the Case for Authentic Pasta," *New York Times*, May 9, 1984.

37. The cover and the cover story of *Time* magazine was devoted to the TV series shortly after it first aired; Richard Zoglin, "Video: Cool Cops, Hot Show," *Time*, September 16, 1985, http://content.time.com/ time/ subscriber/article/0,33009,959822-1,00.html.

38. Laura Lindenfeld and Fabio Parasecoli, *Feasting Our Eyes: Food Films and Cultural Identity in the United States* (New York: Columbia University Press, 2017) 33–35. Apparently, the first references to different rice varieties in US cookbooks dates to 1992; Albala, 213.

39. Kate Ahlborn and Louisine Frelinghuysen, "Sex and the City: A Product-Placement Roundup," *Vanity Fair*, May 30, 2008, https://www.vanityfair.com/ news/ 2008/05/sex-and-the-cit; Jane Arthurs, "Sex and the City and Consumer Culture: Remediating Postfeminist Drama," *Feminist Media Studies* 3, no. 1 (2003): 83–98; *Friends*, "The One Where Chandler Can't Remember Which Sister," season 3, ep. 11 (1997) 00:16:50.

40. Martha Frankel, "Stanley Tucci," *Cosmopolitan*, October 1996, 120; "Ciao Italia!" *Woman's Day*, October 3, 2000, 137–46, 162–73.

41. *Chef's Table*, "Massimo Bottura," season 1, ep. 1 (2015); *Chef's Table*, "Nancy Silverton," season 3, ep. 3 (2017); *Anthony Bourdain: No Reservations*, "Emilia Romagna," season 9, ep. 4 (2012). Aliza S. Wong, "Authenticity all'italiana: Food Discourses, Diasporas, and the

Limits of Cuisine in Contemporary Italy," in *Representing Italy through Food*, eds. Peter Naccarato, Zachary Nowak, and Elgin K. Eckert (London: Bloomsbury Academic, 2017), 39–40.

42. Morris, 181; Peter Naccarato, Zachary Nowak, and Elgin K. Eckert, "Afterword: Italy represented," in *Representing Italy through Food*, eds. Peter Naccarato, Zachary Nowak, and Elgin K. Eckert (London: Bloomsbury Academic, 2017), 263–65.

43. Joe Bastianich, *Restaurant Man* (New York: Penguin, 2012).

44. http://bandbhg.com/our_restaurants.cfm (ultimo accesso 22/8/2018), About B&B, Batali & Bastianich (B&B) Hospitality Group, accessed August 8, 2018, http://bandbhg.com/our_restaurants.cfm; Marco Tonelli, "Friuli Uniti d'America," *Spirito di Vino*, July, 2010, 58–62.

45. *Friends*, "The One after the Superbowl, Part 1," Season 2, ep. 12 (1996) 00:08:55; *MasterChef*, "Auditions #1," Season 1, ep. 1. (2010); *MasterChef Italia*, "Selezioni 1," Season 1, ep. 1. (2011).

46. *Barolo Boys. Storia di una rivoluzione*. Directed by Paolo Casalis, Tiziano Gaia. Bra: Stuffilm Creativeye, 2014.

47. Carlo Petrini, *Slow Food: The Case for Taste*, trans. William McCuaig (New York: Columbia University Press, 2004), 1–34; Geoff Andrews, *The Slow Food Story: Politics and Pleasure* (London: Pluto Press, 2008), 4–12.

48. Alan Tardi, "Postmodern Barolo. The War that Never Was," *Sommelier Journal*, July 15, 2012, 88–95. These tensions appear to be an unavoidable by-product of the interaction between local and global, slow and fast. Ginevra Adamoli, "The Slow Food Movement and Facebook: The Paradox of Advocating Slow Living through Fast Technology," in *Representing Italy through Food*, eds. Peter Naccarato, Zachary Nowak, and Elgin K. Eckert (London: Bloomsbury Academic, 2017), 55–73.

49. Grom and Guido Martinetti, *GROM Storia di un'amicizia, qualche gelato e molti fiori* (Milano: Bompiani, 2012), 93–147; Carlo Petrini, "Il vero gelato con latte di vacca d'alpeggio," *La Stampa Tutto Libri Tempo Libero*, July 6, 2003, 6.

50. Grom and Martinetti, 149–230; Marxiano Melotti, "Oltre la crisi. Il turismo culturale tra riscoperta delle radici e lentezza rappresentata," *La critica sociologica* 185 (Spring 2013): 60–63. For the anticipatory trend in the coffee retail industry see Morris, 178–80.

51. "Unilever Acquires GROM," Unilever, accessed August 22, 2018, https://www.unilever.com/news/press-releases/2015/Unilever-acquires-GROM.html.

52. Anna Sartorio, *Il Mercante di Utopie. La storia di Oscar Farinetti, l'inventore di Eataly* (Milano: Sperling & Kupfer, 2008); Stefano Magagnoli, *"Made in Eataly*. Identità e falsificazione," in *Contraffazione e cambiamento economico. Marche, imprese, consumatori*, ed. Marco Belfanti (Milano: EGEA, 2013), 71–97.

53. Michael Mario Albrecht, "'When You're Here, You're Family': Culinary Tourism and the Olive Garden Restaurant," *Tourist Studies* 11, no. 2 (2011): 99–113; *Carrabba's Italian Grill: Recipes from Around Our Family Table* (Hoboken, NJ: John Wiley and Sons, 2011); Fabio Parasecoli, "We are Family: Ethnic Food Marketing and the Consumption of Authenticity in Italian Themed Chain Restaurants," in *Making Italian America: Consumer Culture and the Production of Ethnic Identities*, ed. Simone Cinotto (New York: Fordham University Press, 2014), 244–55.

54. "Franchising," Rossopomodoro, accessed August 22, 2018, http://www.rossopomodoro.it/it/franchising/franchising. This and the following citations, originally in Italian, are translated by the authors.

55. Davide Girardelli, "Commodified Identities: The Myth of Italian Food in the United States," *Journal of Communication Inquiry* 28, no. 4 (Fall 2004): 307–24.

56. Parasecoli, 244–47. "I nostri valori," Rossopomodoro, accessed August 22, 2018, http://www.rossopomodoro.it/it/i-nostri-valori/i-nostri-valori.

57. "I nostri prodotti."

58. M. M. Albrecht, "'When You're Here,'" 204–05; F. Parasecoli, 254; "La storia di Rossopomodoro," Rossopomodoro, accessed August 22, 2018, http://web.rossopomodoro.it/italiano/page.aspx? content=0&domain=&root=684&lang=IT&docs=1.

59. Simone Cinotto, *The Italian American Table* (Urbana: University of Illinois Press, 2013), 4–5.

60. See Peter Naccarato, Zachary Nowak, and Elgin K. Eckert, "Editors' Introduction: Presenting Food, Representing Italy," in *Representing Italy through Food*, eds. Peter Naccarato, Zachary Nowak, and Elgin K. Eckert (London: Bloomsbury Academic, 2017), 6.

61. On this issue see Giovanni Ceccarelli, Alberto Grandi, and Stefano Magagnoli, "The Avatar: An Economic History Paradigm for Typical Products," in *Typicality in History. Tradition, Innovation, and Terroir / La typicité dans l'histoire. Tradition, innovation et terroir*, eds. Giovanni Ceccarelli, Alberto Grandi, and Stefano Magagnoli (Bruxelles: Peter Lang, 2013), 69–86.

62. Cinotto, 3–9.

63. Carol F. Helstosky, *Garlic and Oil: Food and Politics in Italy* (New York: Berg, 2006).

64. The fight carried out by the futurist movement against pasta and in support of rice is a good example. Marinetti, leader of the movement, writes passionate pages against pasta, the expression of a vile bourgeois routine. It was, actually, an endorsement he made to the autarchic policies of the fascist regime at reducing the imports of wheat; S. Magagnoli, "Le futurisme au service de la révolution. Artistes, politiciens, et une assiette de Spaghetti . . . , " paper presented at the *2nd International Conference on Food History and Cultures* Tours, May 26–27, 2016.

65. Agehananda Bharati, "The Hindu Renaissance and its Apologetic Patterns," *Journal of Asian Studies*, 29, no. 2 (February 1970): 267–87.

CHAPTER 9. IMAGINING CULINARY NOMADISM: FOOD EXCHANGES SHAPED BY GLOBAL MIXED RACE, DIASPORIC BELONGINGS, AND COSMOPOLITAN SENSIBILITES

1. Brinda Mehta, "Culinary Diasporas: Identity and the Language of Food in Gisele Pineau's *Un Papillon dans Le Cite* and *L'Exil selon Julia*," *International Journal of Francophone Studies* 8, no. 1 (2005): 31.

2. Penelope Lively, *Ammonites and Leaping Fish: A Life in Time* (London: Penguin, 2013), 4.

3. Anthony D'Andrea, "Neo-Nomadism: A Theory of Post-Identitarian Mobility in the Global Age," *Mobilities* 1, no. 1 (2006): 116.

4. Leonie Sandercock, *Cosmopolis II: Mongrel Cities in the 21st Century* (London: Continuum, 2003); Jean Duruz and Gaik Cheng Khoo, *Eating Together: Food, Space and Identity in Malaysia and Singapore* (Lanham, MD: Rowman & Littlefield, 2015).

5. Mehta, "Culinary Diasporas," 31.

6. David Morley, *Home Territories* (London: Routledge, 2000), 210.

7. See, for example, Rosi Braidotti, *Nomadic Subjects: Embodiment and Sexual Difference in Contemporary Feminist Theory* (New York: Columbia University, 1994); Gilles Deleuze and Felix Guattari, *A Thousand Plateaus: Capitalism and Schizophrenia* (Minneapolis: University of Minnesota Press, 1987).

8. Jean Duruz, "Tastes of the 'Mongrel City': Geographies of Memory, Spice, Hospitality and Forgiveness," *Cultural Studies Review* 19, no. 1 (2013): 73–98; Kit MacFarlane and Jean Duruz, "Technologies of Nostalgia: Vegetarians and Vegans at Addis Ababa Café," in *Eat, Cook, Grow: Mixing Human-Computer Interactions with Human-Food Interactions*, eds. Jaz Hee-Jeong Choi, Marcus Foth, and Greg Hearn (Cambridge, MA: MIT Press, 2014), 33–49.

9. Eva Aldea, "Nomads and Migrants: Deleuze, Braidotti and the European Union in 2014," *Open Democracy*, published online 10 September, 2014, https://www.opendemocracy .net/can-europe-make-it/eva-aldea/nomads-and-migrants-deleuze-braidotti-and-european -union-in-2014 (accessed 19 September, 2016); Iain Chambers, *Mediterranean Crossings: The Politics of Interrupted Modernity* (Durham, NC: Duke University Press, 2008), 6–7.

10. Ien Ang, *On Not Speaking Chinese: Living between Asia and the West* (London: Routledge, 2001), 193–201.

11. Rebecca C. King-O'Riain, Stephen Small, Minelle Mahtani, Miri Song, and Paul Spickard, eds., *Global Mixed Race* (New York: NYU Press, 2014).

12. John Noyes, "Nomadism, Nomadology, Postcolonialism: By Way of Introduction," *Interventions* 6, no. 2 (2004): 159.

13. Daniel Guttentag, "Airbnb: Disruptive Innovation and the Rise of the Informal Tourism Accommodation Sector," *Current Issues in Tourism,* published online 2 September, 2013, http://dx.doi.org/10.1080/13683500.2013.827159 (accessed 26 August 2014).

14. Julie Carrie Wong, "Most Wanted: San Francisco Flyers Name and Shame Airbnb Hosts," *The Guardian*, July 22, 2016; Madeleine Morris, "High-Rise Residents Fight Short-Stay Economy over 'Pop-Up Brothels,' All-Night Parties," *ABC News*, 7 January, 2016, http://www.abc.net.au/news/2016-01-06/high-rise-residents-fight-back-against-short -stays/7071042 (accessed 22 February, 2016).

15. D'Andrea, "Neo-Nomadism," 100 (original emphasis).

16. D'Andrea, "Neo-Nomadism," 97.

17. Rolf Potts, *Vagabonding: An Uncommon Guide to the Art of Long-Term World Travel* (New York: Random House, 2003), 5.

18. D'Andrea, "Neo-Nomadism," 98.

19. Johnny Ward, "Five Reasons to Become a Digital Nomad." *One Step 4ward*, published online 4 December, 2014, https://onestep4ward.com/digital-nomadism-5-reasons-to -become-a-digital-nomad/ (accessed 18 September 2017).

20. Potts, *Vagabonding*, 5, xi.

21. D'Andrea, "Neo-Nomadism," 116.

22. David Harvey, *The Condition of Postmodernity: An Enquiry into the Origins of Cultural Change* (Oxford: Basil Blackwell, 1989), 284–307; Jon May and Nigel Thrift, "Introduction," in *Timespace: Geographies of Temporality*, eds. Jon May and Nigel Thrift (New York: Routledge, 2001), 1–46; Doreen Massey, *Space, Place and Gender* (Cambridge UK: Polity, 1994), 149–50.

23. Pico Iyer, "Where Worlds Collide: In Los Angeles International Airport, the Future Touches Down," *Harpers*, August 1995, https://harpers.org/archive/1995/08/ where-worlds -collide/ (accessed 21 September 2017).

24. D'Andrea, "Neo-Nomadism," 116.

25. Iain Chambers, "Another Map, Another History, Another Modernity," *California Italian Studies* 1, no. 1 (2010): 10 (original emphasis).

26. Noyes, "Nomadism, Nomadology, Postcolonialism," 160.

27. Deleuze and Guattari, *A Thousand Plateaus.*

28. Braidotti, *Nomadic Subjects*, 5 (emphasis added).

29. Mehta, "Culinary Diasporas," 35–36.

30. Jean Duruz, "Trucking in Tastes and Smells: Adelaide's Street Food and the Politics of Urban 'Vibrancy,'" in *Senses in Cities: Experiences of Urban Settings*, eds. Kelvin E. Y. Low and Devorah Kalekin-Fishman (London: Routledge, 2018), 180; see also Kelvin E. Y. Low and Devorah Kalekin-Fishman, "Afterword: Towards Transnational Sensescapes," in *Everyday Life in Asia: Social Perspectives on the Senses*, eds. Devorah Kalekin-Fishman and Kelvin E. Y. Low (Farnham, Surrey UK: Ashgate, 2010), 200–1.

31. Wong Hong Suen, "A Taste of the Past: Historically Themed Restaurants and Social Memory in Singapore," in *Food and Foodways in Asia: Resource, Tradition and Cooking*, eds. Sidney C. H. Cheung and Tan Chee-Beng (London: Routledge, 2007), 121 (original emphasis).

32. Michel de Certeau, *The Practice of Everyday Life* (Berkeley: University of California Press, 1984), xiv–xxiv.

33. Deleuze and Guattari, *A Thousand Plateaus*, 414–15.

34. D'Andrea, "Neo-Nomadism," 117.

35. Aldea, "Nomads and Migrants."

36. Aldea, "Nomads and Migrants."

37. Ang, *On Not Speaking Chinese*, 193–201.

38. Ang, *On Not Speaking Chinese*, 201.

39. Aldea, "Nomads and Migrants."

40. Jean Duruz, "Eating at the Borders: Culinary Journeys," *Environment and Planning D: Society and Space* 23, no. 1 (2005): 59.

41. Kelvin E. Y. Low, "Tasting Memories, Cooking Heritage: A Sensuous Invitation to Remember," in *Food, Foodways and Foodscapes: Culture, Community and Consumption in Post-Colonial Singapore*, eds. Lily Kong and Vineeta Sinha (Singapore: World Scientific, 2016), 73.

42. Donna Gabaccia, *We Are What We Eat: Ethnic Food and the Making of Americans* (Cambridge, MA: Harvard University Press, 1998), 232.

43. Morley, *Home Territories*, 210.

44. Ang, *On Not Speaking Chinese*, 200 (original emphasis).

45. Stephen Small and Rebecca C. King-O'Riain, "Global Mixed Race: An Introduction," in *Global Mixed Race*, eds. Rebecca C. King-O'Riain, Stephen Small, Minelle Mahtani, Miri Song, and Paul Spickard (New York: NYU Press, 2014), vii.

46. Ruth Frankenberg, *White Women, Race Matters: The Social Construction of Whiteness* (Minneapolis: University of Minnesota Press, 1993).

47. Morley, *Home Territories*, 232–34.

48. Sidney W. Mintz, *Tasting Food, Tasting Freedom: Excursions into Eating, Culture, and the Past* (Boston: Beacon, 1996), 96.

49. All quotations attributed to Mel Wondimu are from an interview with her at Addis Ababa Café in December 2009 and reflect her family situation and food cultures at that particular time.

50. Duruz, "Tastes of the 'Mongrel City,'" 73–98; MacFarlane and Duruz, "Technologies of Nostalgia," 33–49.

51. Graeme Hugo, *Background Paper for Africa Australians: A Review of Human Rights and Social Inclusion Issues*, Australian Human Rights Commission, Sydney, 2009, 32–33, https://www.humanrights.gov.au/sites/default/files/content/africanaus/papers/africanaus_paper_hugo.pdf (accessed September, 22, 2017).

52. Noyes, "Nomadism," 160.

53. Chambers, "Another Map," 10 (original emphasis).

54. Biographical details (and occasional quotation) attributed to Yenenesh Gebre or to Zed Wondimu are from interviews conducted at Addis Ababa Café in August 2008 and December 2009, respectively.

55. Duruz, "Tastes of the 'Mongrel City,'" 73–98.

56. de Certeau, *The Practice of Everyday Life*, 96.

57. For issues of hospitality, see Jacques Derrida, *On Cosmopolitanism and Forgiveness* (London: Routledge, 2001).

58. Hugh Mackay, *Generations: Baby Boomers, Their Parents and Their Children* (Sydney: Macmillan, 1997).

59. Jean Duruz, "Food as Nostalgia: Eating the Fifties and Sixties," *Australian Historical Studies* 30, no. 113 (1999): 249–50; Michael Symons, *The Shared Table: Ideas for Australian Cuisine* (Canberra" Australian Government Publishing Service, 1993) 7–13.

60. John Newton, *Wogfood—An Oral History with Recipes* (Sydney: Random House, 1996) 3–4.

61. Braidotti, *Nomadic Subjects*, 5.

62. Aldea, "Nomads and Migrants."

63. Low, "Tasting Memories," 73–74.

64. Low, "Tasting Memories," 74.

65. Kalpena Ram, "Listening to the Call of the Dance: Re-Thinking Authenticity and 'Essentialism,'" *Australian Journal of Anthropology* 11, no. 3 (2000): 358–64.

66. Ang, *On Not Speaking Chinese*, 200.

67. Barbara Santich, *Bold Palates: Australia's Gastronomic Heritage* (Kent Town, SA: Wakefield, 2012), 301.

68. Santich, *Bold Palates*, 301. Note that I suspect Santich's statement applies more to Anglo-Australians and their food cultures and less to increasing numbers of Australians of Italian descent.

69. Jean Duruz, "From Malacca to Adelaide: Fragments towards a Biography of Cooking, Yearning and *Laksa*," in *Food and Foodways in Asia: Resource, Tradition and Cooking*, eds. Sidney C. H. Cheung and Tan Chee-Beng (London: Routledge, 2007), 183–200; Jean Duruz, "Tastes of Hybrid Belonging: Following the Laksa Trail in Katong, Singapore," *Continuum* 25, no. 5 (2011): 605–18; see also Veronica Mac Sau Wa, "Southeast Asian Chinese Food in Tea Café and Noodle Shops in Hong Kong," in *Chinese Food and Foodways in Southeast Asia and Beyond*, ed. Tan Chee-Beng (Singapore: NUS Press, 2011), 226.

70. Lily Kong (citing Henderson), "From Sushi in Singapore to Laksa in London: Globalising Foodways and the Production of Economy and Identity," in *Food, Foodways and Foodscapes: Culture, Community and Consumption in Post-Colonial Singapore*, eds. Lily Kong and Vineeta Sinha (Singapore: World Scientific, 2016), 230–31.

71. RBar @Regattas, www.regattas.com.au/ (accessed November 30, 2017).

72. Santich, *Bold Palates*, 24.

73. Adelaide Convention Centre, http://www.eventconnect.com/venue/ finder/1889/ adelaide-convention-centre/ (accessed September 20, 2017). See also https://www.icadelaide .com.au/dining/riverside-restaurant/ (accessed June 13, 2019).

74. Gabaccia, *We Are What We Eat*, 231.

75. Krishnendu Ray, *The Ethnic Restaurateur* (London: Bloomsbury, 2016), 11.

76. Braidotti, *Nomadic Subjects*, 5.

77. Roland Barthes, *Mythologies* (London: Paladin, 1973), 143.

78. Ang, *On Not Speaking Chinese*, 200.

79. Duruz, "Tastes of the 'Mongrel City,'" 91–92.

80. Michael Hernandez and David Sutton, "Hands that Remember: An Ethnographic Approach to Everyday Cooking," *Expedition* 45, no. 2 (2005): 31.

81. Duruz, "Trucking in Tastes," 180; Low and Kalekin-Fishman, "Afterword," 200–1.

82. Santich, *Bold Palates*, 180.

83. Luce Giard, "The Nourishing Arts," in *The Practice of Everyday life Volume 2: Living and Cooking*, by Michel de Certeau, Luce Giard, and Pierre Mayol (Minneapolis: University of Minnesota Press, 1998), 153.

84. Ang, *On Not Speaking Chinese*, 200 (original emphasis).

85. Gabaccia, *We Are What We Eat*, 231.

86. Ronald Darling Wilson, *Bringing Them Home: Report of the National Inquiry into the Separation of Aboriginal and Torres Strait Islander Children from their Families* (Sydney: Human Rights and Equal Opportunity Commission, 1997).

87. de Certeau, *The Practice of Everyday Life*, xvii–viii.

88. Jackie Huggins, "Government Has Not Met Its International Human Rights Standards," Speech delivered to the United Nations Permanent Forum on Indigenous Issues in New York, May 20, 2016, http://www.sbs.com.au/nitv/ nitv-news/article/2016/05/20/jackie-huggins-un-government-has-not-met-its-international-human-rights-standards (accessed 29 September, 2017).

89. Suki Ali, *Mixed Race, Post-Race: Gender, New Ethnicities and Cultural Practices* (Oxford: Berg, 2003).

90. Mica Nava, "Visceral Cosmopolitanism: The Specificity of Race and Miscegenation in UK." *Politics and Culture* 3, August 10, https://politicsandculture.org/2010/08/10/mica-nava-visceral-cosmopolitanism-the-specifici-2/ (accessed 29 August, 2017).

91. Nava, "Visceral Cosmopolitanism."

92. Bhabha cited in Jonathan Rutherford, 1990. "The Third Space: Interview with Homi Bhabha," in *Identity, Community, Culture, Difference*, ed. Jonathan Rutherford (London: Lawrence & Wishart, 1990), 211.

93. Duruz, "Trucking in Tastes," 180; Low and Kalekin-Fishman, "Afterword," 200–1.

94. Mica Nava, *Visceral Cosmopolitanism: Gender, Culture and the Normalisation of Difference* (London: Bloomsbury, 2007), 133.

95. Jean-Claude Izzo, *Garlic, Mint and Sweet Basil: Essays on Marseilles, Mediterranean Cuisine and Noir Fiction* (New York: Europa, 2013); Nava, "Visceral Cosmopolitanism."

96. Chambers, *Mediterranean Crossings*, 128.

97. Isabelle Darmon and Alan Warde, "Senses and Sensibilities; Stabilising and Changing Tastes in Cross-National Couples," *Food, Culture and Society* 19, no. 4 (2016): 708.

98. Chambers, *Mediterranean Crossings*, 129.

99. Sylvie Durmelat, "Tasting Displacement: Couscous and Culinary Citizenship in Maghrebi-French Diasporic Cinema," *Food and Foodways* 23, no. 1–2 (2015): 123.

CHAPTER 10. THE TRAVELING PRIEST: FOOD FOR THE SPIRIT AND FOOD FOR THE BODY

1. On the cultural, social, and economic changes underway in Italy see: Alberto Mario Banti, *Storia della borghesia italiana. L'età liberale (1861–1922)* (Roma: Donzelli, 1996);

Giovanni Bechelloni, ed., *Identità italiana e modernizzazione. Percorsi controversi (1861–1990)* (Roma: Il Campo, 1991); Giorgio Calcagno, ed., *L'identità degli italiani* (Roma-Bari: Laterza, 1998); Mario Romani, *Storia economica d'Italia nel secolo XIX* (Bologna: il Mulino, 1982); Andrea Colli and Franco Amatori, eds., *Impresa e Industria in Italia. Dall'Unità ad oggi* (Venezia: Marsilio, 1999); Vera Zamagni, "L'evoluzione dei consumi fra tradizione e innovazione," in *L'alimentazione*, eds. Alberto Capatti, Alberto De Bernardi, and Angelo Varni (Torino: Einaudi, 1998), 151–205; Sergio Zaninelli, *I consumi a Milano nell'Ottocento* (Roma: Edindustria, 1974).

2. On the evolution of tourism in Italy see the following studies: Patrizia Battilani, *Vacanze di pochi vacanze di tutti. L'evoluzione del turismo europeo* (Bologna: il Mulino, 2001); Franco Paloscia, *Storia del turismo nell'economia italiana* (Roma: Petruzzi, 1994); Maria Clelia Cardona, *La storia della villeggiatura: dall'epoca romana al Novecento* (Roma: Edizioni Abete, 1994); Marc Boyer, *Il turismo, dal Grand Tour ai viaggi organizzati* (Torino: Electa-Gallimard, 1997). We also indicate Giuseppe Rocca, *Dal prototurismo al turismo globale. Momenti, percorsi di ricerca, casi di studio* (Torino: Giappichelli, 2013) for the rich bibliography with which it is possible to explore these issues. There are numerous contributions of economic and social history dedicated to the development of tourism in the second half of the nineteenth century. Here we note some recent monographs that share many of the themes explored in the present study and are particularly valid in their methodological approach: Andrea Zanini, *Un secolo di turismo in Liguria. Dinamiche, percorsi, attori* (Milano: FrancoAngeli, 2012); the essays present in Mario Taccolini, ed., *Il turismo bresciano tra passato e futuro* (Milano: Vita e Pensiero, 2002); Andrea Leonardi, "Turismo e sviluppo in area alpina. Una lettura storico-economica delle trasformazioni intervenute tra Ottocento e Novecento," *Annale di Storia del Turismo* 6, (2007): 53–82; Idem, "Dal 'Grand Hotel' alle stazioni di sport invernali: le trasformazioni del turismo alpino italiano," in *La evolución de la industria turística en España e Italia*, eds. Carlos Barciela López, Carlos Pablo Manera Erbina, Ramón Molina de Dios, and Antonio Di Vittorio (Palma de Mallorca: Institut Balear d'Economia, 2011), 609–69; the essays present in Patrizia Battilani and Donatella Strangio, eds., *Il turismo e le città tra XVIII e XXI secolo. Italia e Spagna a confronto* (Milano: FrancoAngeli, 2007); Daniele Bardelli, *L'Italia viaggia. Il Touring club, la nazione e la modernità (1894-1927)* (Roma: Bulzoni, 2004); Idem, "Fra storia e geografia: il pellegrinaggio turistico alle origini della nazione. Il caso del Touring Club Italiano," in *L'identità nazionale. Miti e paradigmi storiografici ottocenteschi (atti del seminario Cavallino-Lecce, 30–31 ottobre 2003)*, eds. Amedeo Quondam and Gino Rizzo (Roma: Bulzoni, 2005), 167–97.

3. The collocation in the archives is as follows: Archivio storico diocesano di Pavia, *Manoscritti* VIII, 2, L. Marchelli, Viaggi—Appunti. The journals are published in part in Luciano Maffi, *Turismo dell'Ottocento. I viaggi in Italia di un prete pavese* (Milano: Cisalpino, 2015).

4. For the social, religious, and economic situation of Pavia at that time we refer to the studies of Giulio Guderzo that show how the city in the first half of the nineteenth century was isolated by a lack of infrastructures that contributed to its impoverishment: Giulio Guderzo, "1859: Pavia, Italia, Europa," *Bollettino della Società Pavese di Storia Patria* 110 (2010): 201–21; Idem, *Amore di Pavia* (Milano: Edizioni Unicopli, 2011), 34–51 and 367–73, where we read: "In Pavia, however, the railway was slow to arrive. The fortunate location of the city (almost at the confluence of two major Po rivers—the Po and Ticino—with an important bridge crossing the Ticino and served one of Italy's busiest postal roads, the Milan-Genoa) was paradoxically, for over a century (between the eighteenth and nineteenth centuries) the reason why there were difficulties and delays in the development of new communication routes." On the cultural environment of Pavia during the years of Don Marchelli's travels see: Giovanni Maria Bussedi, *Diario 1864–1869*, ed. Mirko Volpi (Milano: Cisalpino, 2013); Cesare Re-

possi, "La cultura letteraria a Pavia dalla Restaurazione alla metà del Novecento," in *Storia di Pavia*, ed. Emilio Gabba (Pavia: Banca del Monte di Lombardia, 2000), 489–537; Marina Tesoro, "Politica e amministrazione nell'Età liberale," in Gabba, *Storia di Pavia*, 85–121.

5. Only in a few cases, as will be highlighted later, did the priest consume abundant breakfasts that were, in effect, real morning meals.

6. Confirmation of this habit can be found in the famous Baedeker guidebook. Karl Baedeker, *Northern Italy, as far as Leghorn, Florence and Ancona, and the island of Corsica* (Koblenz: Baedeker; London: Williams & Norgate; Paris: Haar & Steinert, 1868), XX, which states that dinner is available in Italy at any time from noon to 8:00 pm.

7. Baedeker, *Northern Italy*, 96, 124, 184, 201, 210, 214, 273, 277, 341.

8. A list of the most common dishes served in Italian hotels is reported in Baedeker, *Northern Italy*, XXI.

9. Vito Teti, *Il colore del cibo. Geografia, mito e realtà dell'alimentazione mediterranea* (Roma: Meltemi, 2007).

10. On these topics: Maria Luisa Betri, "L'alimentazione popolare nell'Italia dell'Ottocento," in *Storia d'Italia. Annali 13. L'alimentazione*, eds. Alberto Capatti, Alberto De Bernardi, and Angelo Varni (Torino: Einaudi, 1998), 7–22; Zamagni, "L'evoluzione dei consumi"; Stefano Somogyi, "L'alimentazione nell'Italia unita," in *Storia d'Italia*, 16, (Torino: Einaudi, 1973), 839–87.

11. Zaninelli, *I consumi a* Milano, 11.

12. Zaninelli, *I consumi a* Milano, 29–40.

13. Zaninelli, *I consumi a* Milano, 40-44.

14. Alessandro Barbero, *A che ora si mangia? Approssimazioni storico-linguistiche all'orario dei pasti (secoli XVIII-XXI)* (Macerata: Quodlibet, 2017), 20. On page 85 we read: "Between the end of the eighteenth and the early nineteenth century the aristocracy in London and Paris changed the times of daily meals. Lunch, considered at the time the main meal of the day, was consumed later and later, until five, six, seven o'clock in the afternoon, while a robust breakfast was introduced, the *déjeuner à la fourchette*, at mid-morning, and the evening dinner disappeared. The new fashion was adopted in the nineteenth century by the middle classes and spread slowly even in countries such as Germany, Italy, Russia and the United States, but in the meantime the English and French aristocracy continued to shift lunch time to a later hour, to the evening."

15. Barbero, *A che ora si mangia?*, 57–59.

16. To get a better picture of the major changes affecting tourism accommodation in the second half of the nineteenth century, see: M. Mosca, *Il turismo degli affari a Milano negli anni della prima industrializzazione (1871–1914)*, in *Temi di storia economica del turismo lombardo (XIX-XX secolo)*, ed. Aldo Carera (Milano: Vita e Pensiero, 2002), 109–36; Giuliana Geronimo, "Storia e storie dell'imprenditoria alberghiera milanese," in *Storia del turismo. Le imprese*, ed. Patrizia Battilani (Milano: FrancoAngeli, 2011), 71–97.

17. A hot beverage originating in Milan, obtained by mixing coffee, cream, and chocolate.

18. On the social and cultural role of cafés, see Riccardo Di Vincenzo, *Milano al caffè. Tra Settecento e Novecento* (Milano: Hoepli, 2011).

19. Today, Via San Raffaele.

20. He also dropped off his bag at Brunetti's in 1872.

21. The Caffè della Concordia was in Strada Nuova, today via Garibaldi, between Palazzo Bianco and Palazzo Tursi. This café is mentioned in Baedeker, *Northern Italy*, 114, that mentions that it serves good ice cream and there is often musical entertainment in the evening.

22. Today Piazza Matteotti.

23. It was located in Piazza della Maddalena, inside the Torre Vegerio facing the vico del Marmo (where the *Assolibro* is currently located).

24. For a more in-depth analysis of the cost of travel, see Maffi, *Turismo dell'Ottocento*, 104–18.

25. The historiography has investigated wages and prices in the nineteenth century; reference here is made to studies relating to Don Marchelli's geographical area of origin, or to areas relatively nearby: Giuseppe Felloni, ed., "Le retribuzioni dei lavoratori edili a Genova dal 1815 al 1890," in *Archivio economico dell'unificazione italiana* 12, no. 3 (1963); Idem, ed., "Stipendi e pensioni dei pubblici impiegati negli stati sabaudi dal 1825 al 1859," *Archivio economico dell'unificazione italiana* 10, no. 2 (1960); Giuseppe Aleati, ed., "Le retribuzioni dei lavoratori edili in Milano, Pavia e nei rispettivi territori dal 1819 al 1890," *Archivio economico dell'unificazione italiana* 11, no. 1 (1961); Ugo Tucci, ed., "Stipendi e pensioni dei pubblici impiegati nel Regno Lombardo-Veneto dal 1824 al 1866," *Archivio economico dell'unificazione italiana* 10, no. 4 (1960); Aldo De Maddalena, ed., "I prezzi dei generi commestibili e dei prodotti agricoli sul mercato di Milano dal 1800 al 1890," *Archivio economico dell'unificazione italiana* 5, no. 3 (1957); Idem, *Prezzi e mercedi a Milano dal 1701 al 1860* (Milano: Banca Commerciale Italiana, 1974); Zaninelli, *I consumi a Milano*; Giovanni Vigo, *Istruzione e sviluppo economico in Italia nel secolo XIX* (Torino: ILTE, 1971). Essays dealing with these topics are also published in *Annali di Statistica* of the Ministry of Agriculture, Industry and Commerce: Paola Maria Arcari, "La variazione dei salari agricoli in Italia dalla fondazione del Regno al 1933," *Annali di Statistica* 36, (1936); Luigi Bodio, "Sulla statistica dei salari. Risultati sommari di una indagine iniziata sulla alimentazione delle classi operaie," *Annali di Statistica* 7, (1883); Pietro Rota, "Salari degli operai addetti ad alcune delle principali industrie della Lombardia negli anni 1847, 1859, 1866, 1874," *Annali di Statistica* 14, (1885). To these we add some sources contemporary to the journals that are linked to the territory of Pavia: Bernardo Arnaboldi Gazzaniga, *Monografia del circondario di Pavia. Premiata al concorso indetto dalla Giunta per la inchiesta agraria sedente in Roma* (Pavia: G. Marelli, 1880); Pietro Saglio, *Monografia agraria del circondario di Voghera* (Stradella: G. Perea, 1881); Idem, *Condizioni agricole della provincia di Pavia e mezzi per migliorarle: monografia* (Voghera: Tipografia sociale, 1879).

26. Vigo, *Istruzione e sviluppo economico*, 47–62.

27. Aleati, "Le retribuzioni dei lavoratori edili in Milano," 1–16; Felloni, "Le retribuzioni dei lavoratori edili a Genova," 16–23.

28. Idem, "Stipendi e pensioni dei pubblici impiegati negli stati sabaudi," 20–21; Tucci, "Stipendi e pensioni dei pubblici impiegati nel Regno Lombardo-Veneto," 16–21.

29. Felloni, "Stipendi e pensioni dei pubblici impiegati negli stati sabaudi," 20–21.

30. Tucci, "Stipendi e pensioni dei pubblici impiegati nel Regno Lombardo-Veneto," 16–21. The information is also taken from some essays published in *Annali di Statistica* of the Ministry of Agriculture, Industry and Commerce: Rota, "Salari degli operai," 1–36; Bodio, "Sulla statistica dei salari," 50–106.

31. Rota, "Salari degli operai," 8.

32. Information for wages in textile manufactures comes from Rota, "Salari degli operai," 9–19. These wages did not take into consideration those of the supervisors which were considerably higher.

33. The information is taken from Rota, "Salari degli operai," 19–36.

34. On the total cost of Don Marchelli's annual trips, see Maffi, *Turismo dell'Ottocento*, 117.

35. London: J. Murray, 1842.

36. Koblenz: Baedeker; London: Williams & Norgate; Paris: Haar & Steinert, 1868.

37. Either *Nuovissima guida illustrata della città di Torino e de' suoi dintorni* (Milano: Sonzogno, 1859) or a later edition.

Index

Abbots, Emma, 68
abundance, 128
Addis Ababa Café, 132–33, 136–37
Africa, 68–73, 125–26, 132–38
aging, 181n21
agriculture, 89, 93–94
agro-pastoral people, 4
Airbnb, 127
airports, 65–66, 73–76, 128, 181n7, 182n25
alcohol, 73, 154, 158, 182n24
Aldea, Eva, 130–31, 135
Aldrin, Buzz, 84
Aleati, Giuseppe, 159
Alien (film), 87–88
Alimentations contemporaines (Garabuau-Moussaoui), 9
allochronisms, 43
American food, 110
Amselle, Jean-Loup, 7–8
D'Andrea, Anthony, 127–28
Anglo-Saxons, 2
anthropology, 40, 43, 66–68, 105, 169–75
aperitifs, 101
Apollo space missions, 83–86
Arabs, 36–37, 39, 43–45, 47–48
architecture, 15, *15*
Armani, Giorgio, 115

art, 165–67
Asia, 38, 43–45, 58
    See also specific countries
astronauts. *See* National Aeronautics and
        Space Administration
attachment, 3
Australia:
    consumption in, 169;
    culture of, 125–26;
    eating in, 132–33;
    Ethiopia and, 10;
    identity in, 136–37;
    mixed race in, 133–34;
    Wondimu family in, 132–42
authentic cuisine, 119–20
Azaryahu, Maoz, 38

Barbero, Alessandro, 153–54
Barolo Boys (film), 117
Bastianich, Joe, 116–17
Batali, Mario, 116–17
Bedouin people, 10, 42–43, 169;
    Jews, 179n2;
    McDonald's for, 35–37, 39–41, 47–48,
        173
Beersheba. *See* Bedouin people
Bernus, Edmond, 1–2
Bharati, Agehananda, 120

Bianquis, Isabelle, 67
The Big Night (TV show), 116
Boiardi, Ettore, 188n12
Bordeaux. *See* France;
    Senegalese retirees
Bourland, Charles T., 88–89
Braidotti, Rosi, 129–30, 135
breakfast, 153–54, 160, *161–64*, 197n5
Brexit, 130–31
Brooklyn. *See* New York City
Buddhism, 28, 30
butter, 19, *20*
By Way of Nomadism (Braidotti), 129–30

cæcum, with butter, 19, *20*
cafés, 154, 158, 197n21
camaraderie, 102
carbohydrate drinks, 99
catering, 99
Catholics, 182n24. *See also* Marchelli
chain restaurants, 118–19, 134
Chambers, Iain, 128–29, 143
Charlier, Bernard, 3
cheese, 112–13, 153
children, 5, 35–36, 44–45. *See also* family
China, 112–13, 137, 142
chocolate, 160
Christmas, 84
circulation:
    in culture, 30–31;
    of nomadism, 119–20, 170;
    of territories, 67, 175
Classic Italian cookbook (Hazan), 115
Claudot-Hawad, Hélène, 3–5
cleanliness, 46
closed stove, *17*
clothing, 39
cocooning nomadism, 9
coffee, 154, 158
colonization, 66, 127, 181n16
commercial strategies, 175
communication, 2
communism, 13–14
concentric concept, of space, 4
conservation, 22
consumption:
    for Anglo-Saxons, 2;

in Australia, 169;
of livestock, 22;
marketing and, 61;
mobility and, 8–9
cookbooks, 115
cookies, 83–85
cooking, 8, 70
Corsica, 169, 184n1;
    environmentalism in, 186n24;
    environmental representations in, 93–94;
    GR trails in, 94, *95*, 96–97, 185n11, 186n26;
    herders in, 100–102;
    hikers in, 10, 97–100;
    marketing of, 186n29;
    mountain food in, 102–5;
    tourism in, 184n10
Corsica Regional Nature Park. *See* GR trails
Cosmopolitan (magazine), 116
creolization, 109–10
Cube, Felix von, 94
Cucina e nostalgia (Viazzi), 115
Cucina Sicilia (TV Show), 119
culinary combination, 88–89
culinary innovation, 65
culinary interference, 81–86
culinary nomadism, 125–26, 143;
    Africa and, 132–38;
    fragments of, 138–42
culture:
    in airports, 182n25;
    of Arabs, 39, 47–48;
    of Australia, 125–26;
    of chain restaurants, 118–19;
    circulation in, 30–31;
    eating and, 69;
    economics and, 60–61;
    elders in, 24;
    family and, 73–74, 138–39, 182n22;
    of fishing, 55;
    of France, 70, 117;
    globalization of, 53–54, 170–71;
    of herders, 27–28;
    of hikers, 94, 96;
    of Kenya, 104;
    in *Little Big Italy*, 114;
    of McDonald's, 42–44;

of Middle East, 35;
of migrants, 72–73;
milk tea in, 24, *25*, 26, 28;
modernity in, 173–74;
of Mongolia, 6, 13–14;
NASA and, 88–89;
New Age cultures, 127;
nomadism and, 51–59, 126–32;
nutrition and, 59;
of outer space, 82;
pop culture, 116;
preservation of, 108–9;
ritual libations in, 17–18;
of runners, 96–97, 102;
of Senegal, 181n14;
television for, 86;
of walkers, 102;
of Yakutia people, 59–60
curd, *21*
customers, 40–41, 43
customs, 1–2, 5–7

dairy, 21, 112–13, 153
Dakar, 69, 181n2, 181n6, 182n23
    See also Africa;
    Senegalese retirees
Da Mare à Mare. *See* GR trails
Deleuze, Gilles, 51–53
deterioration, 19
devotion, 72
digital nomadism, 128
dinner, 153–54, *155–57*, 160
disenchantment, 37–38, 48
dissolve, 22–23, *23*
distance, 26–27
divergent evolution, 188n7
diversity, 31, 179n16
Dolphijn, Rick, 67–68
domestic economies, 16–19, *17–19*, 32
dried food, 98
drinking, 17–18, 26, *29*, 73, 154, 158,
    182n24
Dylan, Bob, 109

eating:
    aging and, 181n21;
    anthropology and, 40, 66–67;
    in Asia, 43–44;
    in Australia, 132–33;
    Buddhism and, 30;
    cleanliness and, 46;
    conservation and, 22;
    culture and, 69;
    diversity in, 31;
    drinking and, 26;
    emotions and, 74, 109;
    ethnicity and, 61;
    exploration and, 81–82;
    fashion compared to, 115;
    in France, 9;
    funerals and, 24, 30;
    gender and, 83;
    generosity and, 70;
    gestures and, 24, *25–26*, 26–28, *29*;
    in globalization, 37–38, 116–19;
    health and, 71;
    heterotopia and, 7–10;
    history of, 2, 10, 174–75;
    homeland and, 109, 111–14;
    hospitality and, 30–32;
    hygiene and, 46–47;
    in Italy, 107–8;
    language and, 54, 56–57;
    by Marchelli, *155–57*, *161–64*;
    marketing and, 8;
    McRoyal meals, 40–41;
    of meat, 22–24, *23*, *25–26*, 26–28, *29*;
    by migrants, 75;
    mobility and, 3, 97–100, 148;
    in Mongolia, *25–26*;
    portion sizes, 71–72;
    religion and, 69–70;
    semantics of, 82, 85–86;
    by Senegalese retirees, 65–66;
    sensorial experiences from, 129–30;
    to share, 100–102;
    in Singapore, 135–36;
    society and, 1;
    soup for, *23*, *25–26*;
    space and, 8;
    standing and, 28;
    television and, 83–84;
    territory for, 8;
    by travelers, 152;

in urban centers, 18;
waste after, 96;
for Yakutia people, 54–55
ecology, 14–15, *15*
economics: culture and, 60–61;
in Dakar, 69;
of dinner, 160;
domestic economies, 16–19, *17–19*, 32;
food budgets, 75;
for Marchelli, 158–60;
of middle class, 181n20;
of Mongolia, 16–19, *17–19*;
politics and, 111–12;
religion and, 196n4;
society and, 102–3, 119–20;
of travel, 128;
of travelers, 128
elders, 24, 181n21
emotions, 74, 80, 109, 131–32
employees, 40–42, 46–47, 182n26
Empson, Rebecca, 31
energy, 99–100, 186n23
England, 131, 141–42, 197n14
environmentalism, 14, 186n24
environmental representations, 4–5, 52–53,
93–94
equality. *See* freedom;
liberation
Ethiopia, 10, 133, 139
ethnicity, 61, 71, 108, 125–34, 136–37,
141–42
ethnography, 54, 73
Europe, 69, 94, 102–3, 186n30
exploration, 81–82
exportation, 10, 58, 113–15, 142, 188n10

Fabian, Johannes, 43
Fabrikant, Michel, 94
family, 68–76, 138–39, 182n22
Farinetti, Oscar, 117
fashion, 115
fast food, 71–72
See also McDonald's
Felloni, Giuseppe, 159
fire, 17–18
fire scissors, 17
fire tools, *18*

Fischler, Claude, 26
fishing, 55–56
flags, 111–13
flexibility, 3–4
food. *See* specific topics
food budgets, 75
foodscape, 66–68
food trucks, 175
footpaths. *See* GR trails
formula food, 79–80, 86
fragments, 138–42
France:
Africa and, 68–73;
colonization by, 181n16;
culture of, 70, 117;
Dakar and, 181n2, 181n6;
eating in, 9;
England and, 197n14;
immigration in, 67, 172;
migrants in, 129–30, 181n3;
Senegal and, 182n29;
travelers in, 2.
See also Senegalese retirees
freedom, 44–48
Friends (TV show), 116–17
Fuente Ovejuna, 110
funerals, 24, 30
futurist movement, 191n64

Gabaccia, Donna, 131, 138
Garabuau-Moussaoui, Isabelle, 9
gastric pain, 72
Gebre, Yenenesh. *See* Wondimu family
Gemini (spacecraft), 80
gender, 83
generosity, 70
gentrification, 127
La geste et la parole (Leroi-Gourhan), 4
gestures, 24, *25–26*, 26–28, *29*
Glenn, John, 77
globalization:
anthropology and, 67–68;
of chain restaurants, 118–19;
of culinary nomadism, 142–43;
of culture, 53–54, 170–71;
eating in, 37–38, 116–19;
emotions from, 131–32;

history of, 38–39;
in hybridization process, 120;
ideology and, 47–48;
imaginary foods in, 10;
of Italy, 119–20;
mobility and, 175;
nomadism and, 173;
nutrition and, 58;
postmodern paradoxes from, 126, 190n48;
sedentary lifestyle and, 7;
technology and, 126–27.
See also McDonald's
goats, 178n3
Golden Arches East (Watson), 38
the grid, *16*
Grissom, Gus, 80
groceries, 99
GR routes. *See* Corsica
GR trails, 94, *95*, 96–97, 185n11, 186n26
Guattari, F. Rizhome, 51–53

d'Haene, François, 94
Handbook for Travellers in Northern Italy (Murray), 165
hard fat, 22–23, *23*
Harvey, David, 128
Hazan, Marcella, 115
health, 71–72
Helstosky, Carol, 120
Herbert, Ulrich, 77
herders:
    in Corsica, 100–102;
    culture of, 27–28;
    goats for, 178n3;
    minimalism for, 18–19;
    mobility of, 14–16, *15–16*;
    of reindeer, 58–59;
    in Siberia, 169;
    soup for, 22–23, *23*;
    storage for, 19;
    tourism for, 103
heterotopia, 7–10
hikers:
    in Corsica, 10, 97–100;
    culture of, 94, 96;
    Internet for, 100–101, 185n17;
    nomadism for, 174;

nutrition for, 185n12;
politics of, 104–5;
runners compared to, 99–100;
transportation for, 104;
ultra-trailers, 187n37
history:
    anthropology and, 169–75;
    of eating, 2, 10, 174–75;
    of globalization, 38–39;
    historiography, 158–59, 198n25;
    of humanity, 1, 7;
    of lunch, 197n14;
    of Marchelli, 147–48, *149*, 150;
    of mobility, 10;
    of NASA, 77;
    of nomadism, 59–62;
    of space-food, 78–79;
    of tourism, 166–67;
    of wages, 158–59, 198n25;
    of Yakutia people, 60–61
homeland, 3, 109, 111–14
hospitality, 14, 30–32
humanity, 1, 7–8
Humphreys, James, Jr., 80–81, 84
hunting, 57–58
hybridization process, 65–66, 109–10, 114–16, 120
hygiene, 46–47

identity:
    in Australia, 136–37;
    family and, 75–76;
    Italy and, 120;
    in nomadism, 171;
    products, 101;
    society and, 180n1;
    tourism and, 110
ideology, 8, 47–48, 57–58, 77–78
I Dream of Jeannie (TV show), 83
Illouz, Eva, 47–48
imaginary foods, 10
imaging, 125–26, 129, 138–42
immigration:
    colonization and, 66;
    Europe and, 69;
    in France, 67, 172;
    migrants, 72–73;

in New York City, 111–12;
in United States, 107–8
India, 173
ingested nomadism, 10
Internet, 100–101, 185n17
intimacy, 26–27
Israel, 10, 38–39, 41, 45–46.
     See also Bedouin people;
     McDonald's
Italy, 173;
     eating in, 107–8;
     exportation of, 113–15, 188n10;
     food traditions in, 10;
     globalization of, 119–20;
     Handbook for Travellers in Northern Italy,
          165;
     hybridization process with, 114–16;
     identity and, 120;
     marketing of, 188n12;
     nomadism and, 109–10, 116–19;
     nostalgia for, 108–9;
     Orrido di Bellano in, 166;
     Piazza San Marco in, 150;
     products in, 160;
     Sacro Monte in, 166;
     symbolism of, 111–13;
     tourism in, 10, 147–48, 196n2;
     Villa Pallavicini of Pegli in, 165–66.
     See also Marchelli
Iyer, Pico, 128
Izzo, Jean-Claude, 142–43

Japan, 173
Jews, 36–37, 40–45, 47, 179n2
Jones, Walton, L., 78
journaling. *See* Marchelli

Keats, John, 87
Kenya, 104, 133, 139
Khabarovsky, Nikolai Semyonovch, 62
knowledge, 2–3, 5–6, 170–71
Kristof, Nicholas, 38
Kubrick, Stanley, 87–88

laboratories, 79–81
ladle, *19*
language, 51, 54, 56–58, 82, 182n23

leftover food, 82–83
Leroi-Gourhan, André, 4
Lestage, Françoise, 68
libations, 17–18, *29*
liberation, 47–48
"Like a Rolling Stone" (Dylan), 109
Little Big Italy (TV show), 107–9, 114
livestock, 14, 22
Los Angeles, 117–18, 128
Lost (TV show), 114
Lovelock, James, 88
Low, Kelvin, 135–36
lunch, 197n14

Manhattan. *See* New York City
Manzoni, Alessandro, 154
Marchelli, Don Luigi:
     art for, 165–67;
     eating by, *155–57, 161–64*;
     economics for, 158–60;
     history of, 147–48, *149*, 150;
     mealtimes for, 153–54;
     travel by, 150–53
Marchesi, Gualtiero, 115, 117
Mare è Monti. *See* GR trails
marketing, 8–9, 61, 86, 175, 186n29,
     188n12
Massey, Doreen, 128, 130, 142
MasterChef (TV show), 117
master spirits, 17–18, 28, *29*
Mauss, Marcel, 5
May, Jon, 128
McCurdy, Howard, 81–82
The McDonaldization of Society (Ritzer),
     37, 44
McDonald's:
     for Bedouin people, 35–37, 39–41,
          47–48, 173;
     in Beersheba, 10;
     culture of, 42–44;
     diversity at, 179n16;
     employees at, 182n26;
     freedom and, 44–47;
     McRoyal meals, 40–41;
     in society, 37–39;
     in Spain, 74
meal preparation, 67

mealtimes, 153–54
meat, 18–19, *19*, 21, 54–55;
    in Mongolia, 22–24, *23*, *25–26*, 26–28, *29*;
    nutrition from, 56
media, 8
Mehta, Brinda, 129
merchandise, 68
metastability, 53
Mexico, 68
Miami Vice (TV show), 115
middle class, 181n20, 197n14
Middle East, 35.
    See also Bedouin people
migrants, 72–73, 75, 170–73;
    in France, 129–30, 181n3;
    in United States, 109, 116–17
milk, 153
milk tea, 21, 23–24, *25*, 26, 28, *29*
minimalism, 16–19, *17–19*, 32
Mintz, Sidney W., 22
mixed races, 125–34, 136–37, 141–42
mobility:
    attachment compared to, 3;
    circulating territories within, 67, 175;
    consumption and, 8–9;
    in domestic economies, 16–19, *17–19*, 32;
    eating and, 3, 97–100, 148;
    flexibility and, 3–4;
    globalization and, 175;
    of herders, 14–16, *15–16*;
    history of, 10;
    imaging and, 129;
    modern, 78;
    nomadism and, 169–70;
    refreshment stations, 99–100;
    relocation and, 5–6;
    roaming and, 2–3;
    sedentary lifestyle compared to, 21–22;
    society and, 2, 75;
    of space-food, 79–81, 86–88;
    in technological environments, 10, 89;
    transnational, 170–71;
    of travelers, 1
modernity, 35–36, 42–44, 53, 173–74
Mongolia, 10;
    Buddhism in, 28;
    culture of, 6, 13–14;
    eating in, *25–26*;
    economics of, 16–19, *17–19*;
    food storage in, 19, *20–21*, 21–22;
    herders in, 14–16, *15–16*;
    homeland in, 3;
    meat in, 22–24, *23*, *25–26*, 26–28, *29*;
    pastoral lifestyle in, 13, 174;
    sharing in, 30–32;
    sheep in, 178n12;
    yurts in, 5
Morley, David, 126
mountain food, 102–5
Mumford, Lewis, 88
Murray, J., 165, 167
Muslims, 36–37, 39, 73, 182n24

National Aeronautics and Space
        Administration (NASA):
    culture and, 88–89;
    formula food for, 79–80;
    history of, 77;
    nutrition for, 85;
    religion for, 84;
    science for, 79;
    Skylab mission for, 82–83, 86, 88;
    space and, 10;
    technological environments for, 78;
    Vietnam War for, 87;
    water for, 80–81.
    See also space-food
nature, 17–18, 28, *29*, 58, 102–5
Negev desert. *See* Bedouin people
Nelson, Mary K., 26
Nelson, Tony, 83
Nenet people, 5–6
Nesterov, Andrei Valeryevich, 62
Neustroeva, Vera, 62
New Age cultures, 127
New Jersey, 188n14
news, 120
Newton, John, 134
New York City, 111–12, 115–17
New Zealand, 112
Nick, John, 47–48
Nikolaev, S. I., 54
nomadism:
    By Way of Nomadism, 129–30;
    circulation of, 119–20, 170;

culture and, 51–59, 126–32;
digital nomadism, 128;
ethnography of, 73;
globalization and, 173;
for hikers, 174;
history of, 59–62;
hybridization process from, 65–66,
   109–10;
identity in, 171;
ideology of, 77–78;
Italy and, 109–10, 116–19;
mobility and, 169–70;
nomadic foodways, 67;
reindeer and, 58–59;
rhizomes in, 52–59, 61;
territory and, 169;
for Yakutia people, 61–62.
   See also culinary nomadism;
   specific topics
non-places, 181n7
nostalgia, 108–9, 113–15, 125–26
Nove (television channel), 107
Noyes, John, 127, 129
Nuer people, 3
nutrition:
   culture and, 59;
   emotions and, 80;
   globalization and, 58;
   for hikers, 185n12;
   from meat, 56;
   for NASA, 85;
   resources and, 54, 61;
   for runners, 186n23;
   for Sakha people, 55–56;
   from snacking, 97;
   in soup, 24;
   for Yakutia people, 56–57, 60

oil, 153
Olive Garden restaurant, 118–19
Orrido di Bellano, 166
outer space, 82, 170.
   See also National Aeronautics and Space
      Administration;
   space-food
ownership, 35

packaging, 8–9, 89
Padan, Omri, 47
Pan Am (airline), 84
Panella, Francesco, 107–8
Un Papillon dans la Cité (Pineau), 129–30
pasta, 109–10, 114–16
pastoral lifestyle, 4, 13–14, *15*, 93, 174
Pavia. *See* Marchelli
PDO. *See* Protected Designation of Origin
performance, 71
Petrini, Carlo, 115
Piazza San Marco, 150
picnics, 97
Pineau, Gisele, 129–30
pizza, 114–15, 118–19
politics:
   Brexit, 130–31;
   economics and, 111–12;
   for employees, 42;
   of futurist movement, 191n64;
   of hikers, 104–5;
   Slow Food movement, 115, 117–18;
   for women, 44–45
pop culture, 116
porridge, 57
portion sizes, 71–72
postmodern paradoxes, 102–5, 126, 190n48
Potts, Rolf, 127
Poulain, Jean-Pierre, 8
preparation, 98–99
preservation, 7, 74–75, 93–94, 108–9
products, 101–2, 160
Protected Designation of Origin (PDO),
   113
psychiatric wards, 86–87

Ram, Uri, 39
Rapp, Rita, 83–85
refreshment stations, 99–100
refrigerators, 70
refugees, 133
reindeer, 58–59
religion, 69–73, 84, 147–48, 174, 182n24,
   196n4.
   See also Marchelli
relocation, 5–6, 14–15, *15*

resources, 7, 54, 61
rhizomes, 52–59, 61
risotto, 114–16
rituals, 17–18, 57
Ritzer, George, 36–37, 44
roaming, 2–3
Rocca, Giuseppe, 166–67
Rota, Pietro, 160
runners, 96–100, 102, 185n19, 186n20, 186n23, 187n37
Russia. *See* Yakutia people

Sacro Monte, 166
Sakha people, 54–56, 58.
    See also Yakutia people
salads, 98
salamat (porridge), 57
Sardinia, 159
Schirra, Walter, 80
science, 53, 79, 99–100, 186n23, 188n7;
    for leftover food, 82–83;
    of taste, 113–14
science fiction, 87–88
Scott, James C., 77
sedentary lifestyle, 3, 7, 21–22
semantics, 86–88
semantics, of eating, 82, 85–86
Senderens, Alain, 115
Senegal, 73, 171–72, 181n14, 182n29
Senegalese retirees, 10, 69–76;
    eating by, 65–66;
    foodscape and, 66–68
sensorial experiences, 129–30
Sentier de la Transhumance. *See* GR trails
Sex and the City (TV show), 116
Shalhoub, Tony, 116
sharing, 30–32, 100–102
sheep, 178n12
sherping, *15*
Siberia, 5, 169, 171–72
Silent Running (film), 87–88
Silverton, Nancy, 116–17
Singapore, 135–37
Skylab mission, 82–83, 86, 88
Sleptsova, Antonina, 62
Slow food movement, 115, 117–18
snacking, 97
Sobal, Jeffery, 26

sobo, 55–56
soccou, 182n28
society, 1–3, 37–39, 68, 75, 102–3, 119–20, 180n1
socioanthropology, 105
"Song of the Road" (Whitman), 127
soup, 22–24, *23*, *25–26*, 151
space, 4–10, 27, 47–48, 52–53, 74, 172–74.
    See also mobility
space-food, 77–80, 87;
    as culinary combination, 88–89;
    culinary interference and, 81–86
spaghetti, 109–10, 132–38
Spain, 74
speed, 42–44
stability, 52–53
stereotypes, 8, 41–44, 47
Stern, Mario Rigoni, 113
storage, 19, *20–21*, 21–22, 70, 98–99, 181n15
stoves, 16–17, 28
stroganina, 55
subversions, 138–42
sugar, 8
superstitions, 30–31
superstores, 181n15
symbolism, 111–13

Tang, 86
taste, 109–10, 113–14
technology, 96–99, 185n15;
    globalization and, 126–27;
    technological environments, 10, 77–81, 89
television, 83–84, 86, 107–9, 114–17, 119–20
tents, 4–5
Testart, Alain, 19
A Thousand Plateaus (Deleuze/Guattari), 51–52
Thrift, Nigel, 128
tools, 14, 17–19, *18–19*, 57, 70, 178n5
tourism:
    art and, 165–66;
    authentic cuisine and, 119–20;
    in Corsica, 184n10;
    Europe and, 94, 186n30;

for herders, 103;
history of, 166–67;
identity and, 110;
in Italy, 10, 147–48, 196n2;
products for, 101–2;
religion and, 147–48, 174;
technology for, 96
Toynbee, Polly, 37–38
traditions, 57–58
trails. *See* GR trails
transnational mobility, 170–71
transportation, 128;
culinary innovation from, 65;
dried food for, 98;
for hikers, 104;
minimalism in, 16–19, *17–19*;
space and, 74;
of water, 98–99
travel, 128, 150–53
travelers, 1–2, 151–52;
breakfast for, *161–64*;
Handbook for Travellers in Northern Italy
(Murray), 165.
See also tourism;
transportation
Treadwell, J. P., 84
Troisgros, Pierre, 115
Tropiano, Joseph, 116
Trump, Donald, 131
Tuareg people, 3–5
Tucci, Stanley, 116
2001: Space Odyssey (Kubrick), 87–88

Uber, 126–27
Ultra Trail di Corte, 100
ultra-trailers, 187n37
United States:
American food, 110;
England and, 131;
immigration in, 107–8;
Israel and, 38–39, 41;
Los Angeles, 117–18;
Mexico and, 68;
migrants in, 109, 116–17;
New Jersey, 188n14;
New York City, 111–12, 115–17;
psychiatric wards in, 86–87;

sugar in, 8.
See also Italy
urban centers, 18

Vagabonding (Potts), 127
Verdier, Yvonne, 24
Versace, Gianni, 115
Viazzi, Alfredo, 115
Vietnam War, 87
Villa Pallavicini of Pegli, 165–66
Virilio, Paul, 126

wages, 158–59, 198n25
walkers, 102.
See also hikers
waste, 96
water, 185nn14–15;
for NASA, 80–81;
for stoves, 28;
transportation of, 98–99
Watson, James, 38
Webber, Max, 37, 48
Whitman, Walt, 127
Williot, Jean-Pierre, 67
women, 44–47
Women's Day (magazine), 116
Wondimu family, 132–42

Yakutia people:
culture of, 59–60;
eating for, 54–55;
ethnography of, 54;
food collecting for, 56;
history of, 60–61;
language for, 51;
nomadism for, 61–62;
nutrition for, 56–57, 60
Young, John, 80
yurts:
architecture of, 15, *15*;
curd and, *21*;
on the grid, *16*;
in Mongolia, 5;
stoves in, 16–17;
tools and, 14

Zaninelli, Sergio, 152–53

About the Editors and Contributors

Nir Avieli is a cultural anthropologist and the president of the Israeli Anthropological Association. He is an associate professor at the Department of Sociology and Anthropology at Ben Gurion University, Israel. Nir has been conducting ethnographic fieldwork in the central Vietnamese town of Hoi An since 1998. His book, *Rice Talks: Food and Community in a Vietnamese Town* is a culinary ethnography of Hoi An. His book, *Food and Power in Israel* is based on multisited ethnography carried out in Israel since the late 1990s. Nir convened the international conference on Food, Power and Meaning in the Middle East and Mediterranean at Ben Gurion University in 2010, and has edited two special issues for the *Food, Culture and Society* and *Hagar* journals. In 2015, he edited a special issue on "Everyday Life in Contemporary Israel" for the journal *Ethnologie Française*. He is currently conducting an ethnographic study entitled "Food for the Body and Soul" that is about the food, identity, and cosmology of the African Hebrew Israelite community.

Isabelle Bianquis is professor of anthropology at the University of Tours. Her research team is Citeres (UMR 7324). Her fields of specialization are sociocultural anthropology, food studies, alcohol, political rituals, traditions, and transformations. Ethnographic areas of specialization are Mongolia, Russia, and France. She studies the social and ritual life of the nomads of Mongolia and currently heads a research program on food mutations of the northern peoples in collaboration with the North-Eastern Federal University of Yakutsk (Russia).

Izabella Borisova is a professor of the North-Eastern Federal University (Yakutsk, Yakutia, Russian Federation). Her research interests include urban food cultures as forms of communication, stereotypes, and intercultural communication in the multinational society.

Giovanni Ceccarelli is associate professor of economic history at the University of Parma. A graduate in medieval history, he has a PhD in economic history from Milan's Bocconni University. He was awarded a post-doctoral grant from the University of Padua in 2003. His research interests focus on early modern commerce and finance, late medieval economic thought, and food and retail history, with a specific interest in typical products and food marketing in the nineteenth century. His recent publications include *Il gioco e il peccato. Economia e rischio nel Tardo Medioevo*, il Mulino, 2003, and *Un mercato del rischio. Assicurare e farsi assicurare nella Firenze rinascimentale*, Marsilio, 2012. He is a founder of the Food Lab Food History Research Center at the University of Parma, a visiting researcher at the Centre d'Études des Mondes Moderne et Contemporaine at Bordeaux-Montaigne University, a member of the *TERESMA Produits des terroirs, espaces et marchés, hier et aujourd'hui* (2016–2020) research project team, which is funded by the Nouvelle Aquitaine regional council, and editor of *Typicality in history: tradition, innovation, and terroir / La typicité dans l'histoire. Tradition, innovation et terroir*.

Chantal Crenn is an assistant professor at Bordeaux Montaigne University and a CNRS researcher in the "Les Afriques dans le monde (Africas in the World)" team at the Bordeaux's Institut de Sciences Politiques. Her research interests include migrations, ethnicities, and the anthropology of food. She is the co-author of "Migration, Food Practices, and Social Telations: When Continuity Is Not Reproduction and Discontinuity Is Not Rupture," *Anthropology of Food* [Online], December 7, 2010. Her recent publications include articles that investigate the links between migration, agriculture, ethnicities, and poverty in rural areas.

Alwin Cubasch is a researcher in the history of medicine at the Department of History and European Ethnology, University of Innsbruck. He studies the interconnections of food, science, and medicine during the twentieth century. Focusing on NASA's food experiments during the early days of space flight, he researches how science, industry, and military interests shaped those experiments. He has co-authored one article on the history of technology of the twentieth century and one on the safety of Roman merchant ships. He is also interested in environmental history and its links to culinary systems and technologies of food.

Jean Duruz is an adjunct senior research fellow at the Hawke Research Institute of the University of South Australia. She has published in food/cultural studies/cultural geography journals and multiauthor works, such as *The Globalisation of Asian Cuisines* (ed. James Farrer). Recently, she has written with Gaik Cheng Khoo *Eating Together: Food, Space and Identity in Malaysia and Singapore*.

Luciano Maffi has a PhD in modern and contemporary history. He teaches economic history at the Cattolica del Sacro Cuore University of Milan and collaborates with the University of Pavia. His work concerns economic and social history, with particular attention to the primary sector and food production in early modern and modern history. His studies also include the history of tourism, especially in relation to the demographic trends and infrastructure and economic changes of the nineteenth and twentieth centuries. He is the author of *Turismo dell'ottocento. I viaggi in Italia di un prete pavese*, Cisalpino editore universitario, Milano, 2015.

Stefano Magagnoli is associate professor in economic history at the University of Parma. A graduate in contemporary history, he was a scholarship holder at Turin's Luigi Einaudi Foundation, and in 1996 was awarded a PhD in contemporary history from the University of Turin. His research interests focus on the contribution of institutions to local development and food history, particularly on the subject of typicality. His recent publications include "The Invention of Typicality: Parmigiano-Reggiano Cheese between Tradition and Industry," in the *China-USA Business Review*, 11, 2015; *Les produits typiques: une construction urbaine? Réputation et terroir à partir d'une perspective italienne*, in C. Marache and P. Meyzie (ed.); and *Les produits de terroir. L'empreinte de la ville*. He is a founder of the Food Lab Food History Research Center at the University of Parma, a visiting researcher at the Centre d'Études des Mondes Moderne et Contemporaine at Bordeaux-Montaigne University, a member of the *TERESMA Produits des terroirs, espaces et marchés, hier et aujourd'hui* (2016–2020) research project team, which is funded by the Nouvelle Aquitaine regional council, and editor of *Typicality in history: tradition, innovation, and terroir / La typicité dans l'histoire. Tradition, innovation et terroir*.

Philippe Pesteil is an anthropologist and professor at the University of Brest. He studies issues related to regional identity, its modes of expression, and territorial changes in relation to social changes and diet. His work also deals with the issue of stereotypes and marvelous footprints (*empreintes merveilleuses*).

Sandrine Ruhlmann is a researcher in anthropology at the CNRS (UMR 8173 China, Korea, Japan). She studies Mongolian food practices and the changes that affect food patterns. She is also interested in the food compromises that the Mongolian people have made under the domination of the Soviet communist system in Mongolia (the historic Outer Mongolia) and the Chinese communist system in Inner Mongolia. Her research includes animal disease management in the two Mongolias and the role of sentinel that has recently been assigned to herders. She has published many articles on her various areas of interest in French and international journals as well as in multiauthor works. She has also written a book on the connection between the concept of happiness and the sharing of food in Mongolia: *L'appel du bonheur. Le partage alimentaire mongol* (*The Call of Happiness: Mongolian Food Sharing*).

Antonina Vinokurova is a professor of the North-Eastern Federal University (Yakutsk, Yakutia, Russian Federation). She is conducting research on the problem of the nutrition of the Evens and the transformational processes of the traditional heritage and their impact on the language.

Jean-Pierre Williot is professor in economic and social history at Sorbonne University. He is author or co-author of twenty books about various topics (history of gas industry, history of railways, food history). He has experience with oral history, with 150 interviews on different subjects on the contemporary history of France. A member of research center UMR 8138 SIRICE in Paris, his main research interests are the history of consumption and innovation. He is co-director of a collection for Peter Lang Publishing Group: "European Food Issues."